MERGED
METHODS

CW00566962

Sara Miller McCune founded SAGE Publishing in 1965 to support the dissemination of usable knowledge and educate a global community. SAGE publishes more than 1000 journals and over 800 new books each year, spanning a wide range of subject areas. Our growing selection of library products includes archives, data, case studies and video. SAGE remains majority owned by our founder and after her lifetime will become owned by a charitable trust that secures the company's continued independence.

Los Angeles | London | New Delhi | Singapore | Washington DC | Melbourne

MERGED METHODS

A Rationale for Full Integration

Giampietro Gobo
Nigel G. Fielding
Gevisa La Rocca
Wander van der Vaart

Los Angeles | London | New Delhi
Singapore | Washington DC | Melbourne

Los Angeles | London | New Delhi
Singapore | Washington DC | Melbourne

SAGE Publications Ltd
1 Oliver's Yard
55 City Road
London EC1Y 1SP

SAGE Publications Inc.
2455 Teller Road
Thousand Oaks, California 91320

SAGE Publications India Pvt Ltd
B 1/I 1 Mohan Cooperative Industrial Area
Mathura Road
New Delhi 110 044

SAGE Publications Asia-Pacific Pte Ltd
3 Church Street
#10-04 Samsung Hub
Singapore 049483

Editor: Jai Seaman
Assistant editor: Charlotte Bush
Production editor: Victoria Nicholas
Marketing manager: Ben Griffin-Sherwood
Cover design: Shaun Mercier
Typeset by: KnowledgeWorks Global Ltd.
Printed in the UK

© Giampietro Gobo, Nigel G. Fielding, Gevisa La Rocca and Wander van der Vaart 2022

Apart from any fair dealing for the purposes of research, private study, or criticism or review, as permitted under the Copyright, Designs and Patents Act, 1988, this publication may not be reproduced, stored or transmitted in any form, or by any means, without the prior permission in writing of the publisher, or in the case of reprographic reproduction, in accordance with the terms of licences issued by the Copyright Licensing Agency. Enquiries concerning reproduction outside those terms should be sent to the publisher.

Library of Congress Control Number: 2021935628

British Library Cataloguing in Publication data

A catalogue record for this book is available from the British Library

ISBN 978-1-5297-1774-7
ISBN 978-1-5297-1773-0 (pbk)

At SAGE we take sustainability seriously. Most of our products are printed in the UK using responsibly sourced papers and boards. When we print overseas we ensure sustainable papers are used as measured by the PREPS grading system. We undertake an annual audit to monitor our sustainability.

CONTENTS

ABOUT THE AUTHORS

Nigel Fielding, BA (Sussex), MA (Kent), PhD (LSE), is Emeritus Professor of Sociology at the University of Surrey, a Fellow of the Academy of Social Sciences and a member of the Community of Experts of the European Science Foundation, and served on the Mixed Methods Research Association's presidential task force on the future of Mixed Methods. His interests in research methodology include Mixed Methods, socio-spatial methods, qualitative software, interview methods, field observation and digitally mediated fieldwork. Nigel has authored/edited 27 books, many in research methodology, including the *Handbook of Online Research Methods* (with Grant Blank and Ray Lee, Sage, 2018, second edition).

Giampietro Gobo, Professor of Methodology of Social Research and Sociology of Science at the University of Milan (Italy), was one of the founders of the 'Qualitative Methods' Research Network of the European Sociological Association. His interests are concerned with the scientific controversies on health issues and workplace studies. He is currently undertaking projects on immunization and COVID-19 policies, and ethnographic experiments in the area of cooperation in small teamwork. His books include *Doing Ethnography* (Sage, 2008), *Qualitative Research Practice* (co-edited with C. Seale, J. F. Gubrium and D. Silverman, Sage, 2004), *Constructing Survey Data: An Interactional Approach* (with S. Mauceri, Sage, 2014).

Gevisa La Rocca, Associate Professor of Sociology of Communication at the Kore University of Enna (Italy), is a member of the Scientific Council of the Processes and Cultural Institutions Group of the Italian Association of Sociology. She has a background in sociology, communication, quantitative and qualitative research methods. Her research interests cover communication research, hashtags studies, textual data analysis and risk studies. On these topics, she has written several articles for national and international journals (*Sage Open, Revue Internationale de Sociologie, Barataria, Revista Castellano-Manchega de Ciencias Sociales*) and co-edited the book *Technological and Digital Risk: Research Issues* (with J. Martìnez-Torvisco, Peter Lang, 2020).

Wander van der Vaart is Associate Professor of Social Research Methodology at the University of Humanistic Studies, Utrecht (The Netherlands) and serves as a Vice-President for Finance of RC33, the Research Committee on Logic and Methodology of the International Sociological Association. He has a background in quantitative and qualitative research methods, political science and psychology. His interests are in flexible surveys and study designs for hard-to-study populations and phenomena. His publications appeared in methods-oriented journals (e.g., *Field Methods, Journal of Official Statistics, Quality and Quantity, International Journal of Public Opinion Research*) and substantive journals (e.g., *Journal of Aging and Environment, Applied Cognitive Psychology*).

INTRODUCTION

SETTING THE SCENE OF MERGED METHODS

While to contemporary eyes the history of social research methodology appears to have been marked by the contrast between qualitative and quantitative methods, this contrast has preoccupied methodological debates only since the 1950s. Indeed, for almost a century, this distinction was not present in social research (see Chapter 1). In fact, unburdened by this dichotomy, the French engineer, sociologist and economist Frédéric Le Play during the 1840s, the Norwegian theologian and sociologist Eilert Sundt in the 1850s, the British sociologists Charles Booth, Beatrice Webb (who also contributed to economics) and Seebohm B. Rowntree from 1889 onwards, the German sociologist and economist Max Weber between 1891 and 1912, the American sociologists Robert Staughton Lynd and Helen Merrell Lynd in 1924–25, the Austrian mathematician, statistician and social psychologist Paul F. Lazarsfeld, the social psychologist Marie Jahoda, and lawyer and statistician Hans Zeisel at the beginning of the 1930s, all jointly used different methods and 'blended qualitative and quantitative data as they studied their communities' (Johnson et al., 2007, p. 113). Only later were the methods they used pigeonholed into a binary classification that eventually came to be regarded as constituting distinct 'paradigms'.[1]

Merged Methods (which, as we will see, integrate qualitative and quantitative methods in a single method) seek to recover the spirit typical of the founders of the social sciences, and make them take a further step in the direction of an ever-greater integration between methods. The practice of jointly using qualitative and quantitative methods re-emerged in the late 1970s with the advent of **Mixed Methods**, defined as those 'designs ... that include at least one quantitative method (designed to collect numbers) and one qualitative method (designed to collect words), where neither type of method is inherently linked to any particular inquiry paradigm' (Greene et al., 1989, p. 256); or, more briefly, 'the combination of at least one qualitative and at least one quantitative component in a single research project' (Bergman, 2008, p. 1); or, again, 'using both qualitative and quantitative approaches or methods in a single study or a program of inquiry' (Tashakkori & Creswell, 2007, p. 4).[2] Mixed methods maintained continuity with the foundational research practice of the 1840s through to the 1930s, but during the foundational period mixing methods was not seen as a specific methodological approach whereas now (in what we could call the 'Second Wave') a central feature of Mixed Methods is its claim to be a distinct approach. So much so that some authors have talked about an 'independent *methodology*' (Tashakkori & Teddlie, 1998), a 'third paradigm' (Morgan, 2007 – with the potential to open a new era in the field of behavioural and social sciences), a 'separate methodological orientation with its own worldview, vocabulary, and techniques' (Tashakkori & Teddlie, 2003a: x), a 'third methodological way' (Karasz & Singelis, 2009) and an approach with its own philosophical assumptions as well as methods of inquiry (Creswell & Plano Clark, 2007).

Some limits of Mixed Methods

Mixed Methods certainly represented a fruitful attempt to overcome the boundaries and divisions that arose, starting from the 1940s, from the contrast between a positivist

---

[1] We note that, in this case, the use of the term 'paradigm' appears quite improper. In fact, Thomas Kuhn, proponent of the paradigm concept, believed that the social sciences were not strictly scientific disciplines because a multitude of different and sometimes irreconcilable methods, concepts, theories, and research questions coexisted in them. These disciplines had not yet achieved the status of 'normal science'. That happens when the majority of the community of scientists adhere to the same paradigm, that is, they agree on the same basic principles and share the same interests, practices, tools etc. Achieving this (paradigmatic) consensus is the criterion that elevates a discipline to the rank of *mature* science.

[2] These are only three (authoritative) definitions among the many that can be found in the literature. Johnson et al. (2007, p. 113) compare 19, propounded by leaders in the field.

and an interpretivist vision of research. Mixed Methods thus has the undoubted merit of having reduced the distance between qualitative and quantitative methods. It has also enhanced the transparency of research design, making the steps involved in the research process more accountable, and brought greater awareness of the central importance of having an explicit data integration strategy when combining findings from the methods in combination.

However, despite these great merits, the attempt as a whole appears to us not completely successful for a number of reasons.

First of all, this second life (or renaissance) of Mixed Methods, strongly influenced by the quantitative tradition,[3] remains entangled in positivist assumptions. This quantitative imprinting is apparent in several aspects:

- *the ambiguity of the term 'qualitative'*. From the 1990s onwards, the term 'qualitative' has been stretched and expanded, with a consequent dilution of its original meaning into a multitude of concepts to such an extent that it now encompasses almost everything – even approaches considered positivistic in the 1950s (see Chapter 2). While this semantic extension made it possible to legitimize Mixed Methods in the eyes of qualitative researchers (initially suspicious of them), in the process the term 'qualitative' has been devalued and its expansive and indiscriminating use muddies the qualitative–quantitative debate. Today, 'qualitative' assumes a mere featureless identity, recalling Hegel's famous statement: 'the night in which all cows are black';

- *the uncritical use of the measurement approach*. In Mixed Method research papers and theoretical essays, especially those related to research design (see Chapter 3), the terms 'measures' and 'measurement' (and their positivistic imprinting and use) are treated as unproblematic. There is no trace of the important epistemological and methodological debate on the problematic nature of measurement in the social sciences, which received much attention between the 1960s and 1970s (see Torgerson, 1958; Cicourel, 1964; Marradi, 1981; Hammersley, 2010). Hence, very different operations, such as **measuring**, **counting**, **scaling** and **classifying**, are continually confused, producing questionable research findings, as well as methodological weakness;

- *a* **naïve pragmatism**. Many Mixed Methods researchers consider the conflict between qualitative and quantitative methods as belonging to the past and think that it has no effect on current research. It has been stated that 'one

---

[3] In fact, the major impetus to propose Mixed Methods came from the universities of Michigan (Ann Arbor) and Nebraska-Lincoln, centres of excellence in quantitative methods.

paradigm (like pragmatism) serves as an adequate foundation for concurrent or parallel types of designs, while paradigms may shift during a sequential design in which one starts from a postpostivist perspective … and then moves to a constructivist (qualitative) worldview' (Creswell, 2009, p. 102). Hence, the pragmatic approach does away with all the 'metaphysical concerns …related to the nature of reality and truth' (Morgan, 2007, p. 49), because they are too abstract and 'tell us little about more substantive decisions such as what to study and how to do so' (2007, p. 53); in addition, they deliver too few insights for translating such metaphysical issues into practical guidance for how to make decisions about actual research. Therefore, they produce a 'belief system [which] remains disconnected from practical decisions about the actual conduct of research' (2007, p. 64). To this end, a '**bricolage methodology**' is invoked (Krontoft et al., 2018; Sharp, 2019; Yardley, 2014, 2019). However, theorizations based on pragmatic philosophy (specifically the 'American pragmatic school') are not always adequate to resolve the practical problems that research poses and that we encounter in the field;

- a *'bricolage methodology'*. In fact, at the truly practical level (i.e., being really pragmatic), we find that the metaphysical concerns are not so much … metaphysical. For example, in their empirical inquiries, will pragmatic researchers use a classic (and positivistic) questionnaire with forced choices and closed-ended answers (selected by the interviewees), which are the negation of any interactional perspective? Will they use those conventional fixed formats, knowing they are responsible for many response errors and biases such as social desirability effects, the yea-saying and response set phenomena, the influence of the response alternatives on respondents' formation of their answers, the misunderstanding of response alternatives by interviewees, the multiple meanings of ambiguous response alternatives, and the invented opinions (or lies) phenomenon (see Chapter 6)? Hence, the pragmatist approach can harbour methodological and epistemological weaknesses precisely at the level of research practices.

Secondly, as previously mentioned, Mixed Methods have been presented as an independent *methodology* (Tashakkori & Teddlie, 1998), a 'separate methodological orientation' (Tashakkori & Teddlie, 2003a, p. x), an approach with its own philosophical assumptions as well as methods of inquiry (Creswell & Plano Clark, 2007), a 'third major research approach or *research paradigm*, along with qualitative research and quantitative research (Johnson et al., 2007, p. 112), a 'third paradigm' (Morgan, 2007), a 'third methodological way' (Karasz and Singelis, 2009).

If so, it has apparently never taken off because it has not yet been entirely emancipated (epistemologically, methodologically and technically) from a binary understanding of the two approaches that it wants to mix. To really be a third approach, it should have three features: an epistemology, a methodology and a suite of methods alternative to the two previous 'paradigms' (qualitative and quantitative). Mixed Methods may, from time to time, draw techniques from the toolbox of one or the other but it has yet to propose a comprehensive new and independent approach. In fact, many Mixed Methods researchers use in a traditional (and often positivistic) way terms such as 'hypothesis', 'indicator', 'variable', 'measurement', 'sampling', 'generalization' and so on. Much still needs to be done to achieve a 'conceptual' integration and an independent vision, as the few praiseworthy attempts to challenge the received view testify (such as Hammersley, 1987 on 'validity' and 'reliability', Hammersley, 2008 on '**triangulation**', Hammersley, 2010 on 'measurement', Maxwell, 2012 on 'causality'). For instance, on issues of sampling and generalization (see Chapter 3) the Mixed Methods literature is heavily entangled in traditional quantitative and qualitative positions, without questioning that constellation of terms and concepts or confronting the contrast between quantitative and qualitative positions on these matters.

The 'Merged Methods' stance

As we demonstrate in Part Two of this book, Merged Methods fully integrate qualitative and quantitative approaches *in a single instrument*, blending the advantages of both *in a single technique*. With the benefit of increasing the consistency among methods that often (by their nature and history) have inconsistencies, this simplifies data construction and data analysis, makes research findings more grounded and valid, and lowers research costs. Hence, Merged Methods research is conducted with one method only (instead of two or more, as in Mixed Methods or multimethods research).

Merged Methods are an attempt (albeit seminal, under construction, still unstructured, bearing promise but also unknowns) to build an approach that epistemologically, methodologically and technically constitutes a genuine third way compared to the quantitative and qualitative paths. The attempt is in continuity with the direction pointed to by Mixed Methods (therefore totally sympathetic with them), but with a more coherent and consistent methodological apparatus, and which endorses Maxwell's (2010, p. 478) attitude: 'I believe that the main *value* of mixed method research, as Greene (2007), argued, is in creating a dialogue between different ways of seeing, interpreting, and knowing, not simply in combining different methods and types of data.' However, Merged Methods try to pursue this path with greater systematicity and scope than has been done so far. In other words, while in Mixed Methods research qualitative and quantitative methods and techniques remain clearly visible by remaining separate, in Merged Methods research they are no longer separated and visible because they are features of a whole that is hybrid, integrated and completely distinct. Using a culinary analogy, Mixed Methods look more like a fruit salad (where the pieces of the different fruits are clearly visible, separate, distinctive, and autonomous, hence we can still recognize the different fruits/methods); while Merged Methods are like a smoothie, where the differences disappear and any single fruit/method is no longer traceable. Alternatively, changing metaphor, the former looks more like a music collection, while the latter are a medley or rhapsody. The 'merged' approach aims for a *fusion* (music metaphor), a *creole* (linguistic metaphor), a *hybrid* (technology metaphor) or a *merger* (business and corporation metaphor) between methods. Borrowing Solanke's (2009) analogy, when hydrogen and oxygen meet they create air and not oxydrogen; tin and copper create bronze and not tiper. Intersectionality therefore creates a new composite subject, a synergy, a true hybrid. Hence, the merged option yields a new tool, a new technique, a new product, a unique method, satisfying the 'equal status' or 'pure mixed' called for by Johnson, Onwuegbuzie and Turner (2007, p. 123).

Overcoming some weaknesses of Mixed Methods

If, after decades of Mixed Method research, experience and debate, the integration pursued by the 'mixed' strategy remains elusive (see Bryman, 2007; O'Cathain et al., 2007; Hesse-Biber, 2015), perhaps it means that this strategy pursues a very difficult mission. In fact, the traditional way of pursuing integration seems quite problematic from several points of view, as Hammersley and Atkinson (1983, p. 199), Blaikie (1991), Flick (1992), Silverman (1993, pp. 156–158; 2000, p. 99), Mason (1996, p. 27), Howe (2004), Denzin and Lincoln (2005), all leading scholars external to the Mixed Methods community, have pointed out.

Merged Methods could represent a valid path to a full integration, built on its own (merged) epistemology (see Chapter 2), its own (merged) methodology (see Chapter 3) and its own suite of (merged) methods (see Chapter 4 and Part Two of the book). Even if, at the moment, only a few Merged Methods are fully developed and satisfy these requirements, the methodological literature of the last 50 years offers many theoretical insights that can help in constructing a complete **merged epistemology** (integrating the needs of measurement with the awareness that data are a co-construction), a merged methodology (where the language of variables can be fully integrated with the indexicality of research topics and situations) and merged techniques (single instruments condensing the advantages of qualitative and quantitative methods).

Merged Methods and techniques:
the 2for1 offer

At this point one might ask: where is the food? That is, where is the substantial difference between Mixed Methods and Merged Methods? Part Two of the book is devoted to presenting research methods and techniques that can be classified as merged. There are at least a dozen (see Table 0.1): some recent (*Multimodal Content Analysis, Videography,* **Intervey**, *Mystery Shopping, Text and Data Mining*), others with a long history (*Delphi Method, Card Sorting, Q-Methodology,* **Symlog** and *Calendar Method*); some are merged

Table 0.1 Merged methods and techniques

Name	Type of merge	Kind of merge
Collecting and analysing opinions and attitudes		
Delphi Method	Survey + open-ended questions + group interview	QT + QT/QL + QL
Multimodal Content Analysis	Content Analysis + multimodal discourse analysis + multidimensional scaling	QT + QL+ QT
Calendar Method	Survey + discursive interview	QT + QL
Intervey	Survey + discursive interview	QT + QL
Card Sorting	Open card sort + close card sort + focus group + cluster analysis	QL + QT + QL + QT
Q-Methodology	'Think-out-loud' narrative or a discussion + card sort + factor analysis	QL + QL + QT
Text and Data Mining	NLP + text analysis + computational linguistics + topic models	QT + QL + QL/QT + QT
Collecting and analysing behaviours		
Mystery Shopping	Ethnography + grid analysis + scaling	QL + QT/QL + QT
Videography	Video analysis + ethnography + talk analysis	QL + QL + QL
Symlog	Non-participant ethnography + fixed observational grid + factor analysis	QL + QT + QT

NLP, natural language processing; QL, qualitative; QT, quantitative.

also in epistemology and methodology (*Intervey*, *Calendar Method*, *Mystery Shopping*, *Videography*, *Multimodal Content Analysis*, *Text and Data Mining*), others are merged only from a technical point of view, because they are still affected by the positivist background in which they originated but could still more fully evolve. Nevertheless they are all true hybrids, fully integrated methods.

Two for the price of one

As mentioned in the third column of Table 0.1, Merged Methods usually embody and fuse two (but sometimes three or four) methods or techniques. For instance, survey and discursive interview can merge in the 'Intervey' and the 'Calendar Method' (Chapter 6); ethnography and scaling can be fused in 'Mystery Shopping'; group interview and survey can be unified in the 'Delphi Method', and so on. While several Merged Methods already exist, the methodological imagination (Smith, 1975) can undoubtedly invent others. Part Two of the book presents and describes selected Merged Methods, as follows.

The *Delphi Method* (Chapter 5) is a systematic, interactive forecasting method which relies on a panel of experts. It merges in one method the three main features of three traditional methods usually practised separately, one quantitative and two qualitative: respectively, **closed-ended** questions in questionnaires (Survey Method), **open-ended questions** (discursive or in-depth interview method) and group discussions (focus group methods). Consensual agreement between a panel of experts is pursued through repeated iterations (two or more rounds), now usually by email, of anonymized opinions and of proposed compromise statements from the group moderator. The first round is based on open-ended questions (like a written in-depth interview), while the last round is conducted with closed-ended questions (similar to a questionnaire). The researcher practises active listening in considering the opinions expressed by the experts and by re-modulating the content of the questionnaire in subsequent rounds. The rounds' results are the outcome of the interpretations provided by the experts. Researchers consider them cumulatively, distinguishing the orientation of the majority and minority, asking the reasons for the agreement and disagreement with them, eliminating some items for the following rounds. Through repeated rounds, agreement is reached between panel participants, who are the holders of expert knowledge and information useful for forecasts.

The *Calendar Method* (Chapter 6) merges survey and discursive interviews. Because retrospective reports in survey interviews (and questionnaires) are subject to many types of recall error, concerns about this problem have led to the development of so-called 'calendar' or 'time diary line methods', designed to help respondents gain better access to long-term memory by providing a graphical time frame in which life history information can be represented. Calendar methods are based on 'conversational' or 'flexible' interviewing, an alternative style of survey interviewing that allows deviations from the norms of standardized interviewing. Under **conversational interviewing** procedures, interviewers are allowed to ask respondents if they did not understand a question and provide unscripted feedback to clarify the meaning of questions as necessary. Calendar interviewing adds further flexibility by navigating back and forward through the participant's life history domains, making the interview a cooperative effort between interviewers and participants. Proponents of flexible interviewing techniques argue that standardized procedures may reduce the accuracy of survey responses because standardization precludes conversational interactions that may be required for respondents to understand some questions.

The *Intervey* (Chapter 6) is a new technique/method for collecting survey data through CATI (computer-assisted telephone interviewing). It merges (the advantages of) the discursive or in-depth interview and the survey interview. It is based on the idea of a 'conversational survey' (contrasting standardization and overt fixed response alternatives) and revitalizes sociologists Rensis Likert's practice and Johan Galtung's interview method: the interviewer poses closed-ended questions as if they were open-ended questions and – after a short conversation – classifies the respondent's answer in one of several predetermined categories. The neologism 'Intervey' puts together two characteristics: 'int' indicates the conversational component drawn from the (qualitative) in-depth interview; 'vey' transfers this dialogic component into the (quantitative) survey. However, it might be that in the future (taking into account Solanke's criticism above) its name will simply be 'conversational survey'.

Q-Methodology (Chapter 7) merges 'think-out-loud' narrative or discussion, Card Sorting and **factor analysis**. It is used in psychology and social sciences to study people's 'subjectivity'– that is, their viewpoint. Q-Methodology was developed in the 1930s by the British psychologist and physicist William Stephenson. It has been used both in clinical settings for assessing a patient's progress over time (intra-rate comparison), as well as in research settings to examine how people think about a topic (inter-rate comparisons).

Q-Methodology aims at exploring the subjective narration of phenomena from the point of view of the participants and asks them to attribute a meaning by giving a score or expressing a scale of agreement/disagreement to statements or images, which are shown above the cards. *Card Sorting* merges open card sort, close card sort, focus group and cluster analysis. It is applied in user experience design in which a person tests a group of subject experts or users to generate a dendrogram (category tree) or 'folksonomy'. Card Sorting uses a relatively low-tech approach: the person conducting the test (usability analyst, user experience designer, etc.) first identifies key concepts and writes them on index cards or Post-It notes; then, the test participants, individually or as a group, arrange the cards to represent how they see the structure and relationships of the information. Groups can be organized as collaborative groups (focus groups) or as repeated individual sorts. It is the participant who establishes the number of elements to use and then assigns them a position in the ranking of the Symmetrical Q-grid. When the participants have finished positioning their cards on the grid and there are no more empty cells in the grid, the participants' Q-sorts are obtained – the ranking of the cards in the grid is called a Q-sort and there are as many Q-sorts as there are participants.

Multimodal Content Analysis (Chapter 8) is a Merged Method for working with the polysemic communications of social media. It merges Content Analysis and **multimodal** discourse analysis. Content Analysis features in the attention placed on the content of communication, such as text decomposition, the creation of categories and the reconstruction of frames. The essence of Content Analysis is an enumerative strategy based on listing, counting and categorizing the individual words in a text. It begins by counting the frequency of each unique word within the text, on the assumption that frequency reflects a word's salience to the topic. Content Analysis is mostly applied to (already) existing texts like newspaper articles, political speeches, blogs and other online postings. The content analyst's interest in word frequencies challenges the importance given to context in qualitative data analysis. In several breaking areas of technique and method around text analysis a large part is played by the affordances of the online environment and born-digital research technologies. These breaking areas include **Sentiment Analysis**, the application of topic models to the analysis of text, and Multimodal Content Analysis.

Multimodal Content Analysis merges Content Analysis with the multimodal discourse analysis features in the study of speech/text in combination with other resources, such as images, **emojis**, links, symbols and videos, aiming to produce accounts of meaning that can be visualized in three-dimensional space using **Multidimensional Scaling (MDS)**.

Text and Data Mining (Chapter 9) is a young interdisciplinary field, borrowing techniques from the general field of Data Mining and combining methodologies from various other areas to transform the knowledge contained in a dataset from tacit to explicit. Text Mining follows a chain of operations: text refining (TR), Natural Language Processing (**NLP**), Information Retrieval (IR), Information Extraction (IE), computational linguistics, clustering, categorization (CT), topic tracking, concept linkage and machine learning (ML). With the growth of computer systems for the analysis of textual data and with the growing interest in **Big Data**, Text Mining has also increased its appeal in the social sciences. Nowadays there are many applications and packages developed for analysis. Underpinning these is the statistics of textual data, from which Text Mining takes its techniques (e.g., tokenization, stemming, lemmatization, term extraction, n-grams, disambiguation, tagging and so on). Texts are interrogated through queries and, subsequently, the data are synthesized and visualized by using vector model, probabilistic model, latent semantic indexing model, clustering and text categorization. A closely associated technique that also works with texts and words is *Sentiment Analysis*, which is one of the principal Big Data Text Mining applications currently in use (Emotional Text Mining).

Symlog (Chapter 10), an acronym for SYstem for the Multiple Level Observation of Groups, was initially developed by the American social psychologist Robert F. Bales, for (1) observing social interactions in classes (in a non-participant way behind a one-way mirror), (2) collecting behaviours through a fixed observational grid and (3) analysing data by factor analysis. In addition to being a method, or better, a set of methods for the measurement of interactive behaviour, Symlog is an integrated theory of personality and group dynamics. Symlog takes effective account of the fact that every act of behaviour takes place in a larger context, an interactive field of influences. The approach assumes that one needs to understand the larger context – personal, interpersonal, group and situation – in order to understand patterns of behaviour and to influence them successfully. One purpose for the in-depth studies was to better understand effective leadership, group dynamics and superior team performance. The results of the investigation include: a comprehensive theory of social interaction; a highly refined measurement system; and a set of precise tools for analysing and improving effectiveness for people who live and work in groups of all sizes.

In its workflow, Symlog uses several techniques: non-participant ethnography, questionnaires, factor analysis. The results of Symlog analyses can also be combined with a group sociogram.

Part Two of the book outlines each method by providing an introduction, a definition, a brief history (of the method); sketching the 'knowing and know-how': what, when, where and why (i.e., data collection, data organization and data analysis); and explicating the merging point, to show where the merge occurs, and the advantages and disadvantages.

There are other Merged Methods that are not covered in this book for space reasons, but which are widespread in social and market research.

Mystery Shopping is a technique born in the 1930s and used by market research companies and organizations that wish to evaluate sales and service, job performance, regulatory compliance, or to gather specific information about a market or competitors, including products and services. In sales, service and job performance fields, Mystery Shopping involves making purchases with one's identity disguised or concealed. The researcher has in mind a checklist and, with some degree of flexibility, requests an action by the sales personnel (e.g., to show the latest release of a particular mobile phone); if the sales personnel avoids the request, the researcher has a range of 4–5 probes in order to obtain a response. The interaction continues (usually 10–15 minutes) until the items in the checklist are fully explored. Hence, the researcher is a kind of performer. At the end of the performance, the researcher compiles a short grid, consisting of both closed-ended (and scaled) questions, and open-ended questions, in which s/he must justify the answers assigned to the closed-ended and scaled questions. Mystery Shopping is a merge of focused covert ethnography, checklist/grid analysis and scaling. It is simultaneously a positivist and a reflexive technique: positivist because it does not attend to the actors' (i.e., sale assistant) 'point of view' and their meanings; reflexive because the open-ended questions require the researchers to think about their judgements, to give details (thick description) about their assessments and to explain their evaluations. This process enlarges researchers' understanding and improves the reliability of the technique.

In social sciences, *Videography* (Knoblauch and Tuma, 2011; Knoblauch and Schnettler, 2012) refers to a specific interpretive method for collecting and analysing 'natural' video recordings. It merges *ethnography*, for collecting video-data, *talk analysis* (conversational or discursive) of interactional sequences and *visual methods*. In addition, video analysis requires a systematic account of the subjectivity, both of the actors analysed as well as of the analysts. This video analysis methodology is improved by reflecting on researchers' own practice of analysing video in data sessions (i.e., the 'video analysis of video analysis'). *Videography* is particularly widespread in workplace studies.

The performativity of methods

What is often missing or undervalued in proposals for integrating quantitative and qualitative aspects of methods, is the **performativity of the method** itself (see Chapter 3), its capacity for constructing data. In other terms, research methods are not just (neutral, interchangeable and easily mixable) tools, but have an inner force (as per language in Austin's speech act theory; Austin, 1962). There is a performativity effect of each method, which has (according to the actor-network theory by Michel Callon, Bruno Latour and John Law – see Law, 1986) an agency. Each method incorporates a specific epistemology, a defined methodological worldview. It embodies a distinct capacity for (partially) constructing data. Hence, it highly corresponds (to the researcher, the participants, the research setting, the organizational and institutional constraints and opportunities) in how it constructs the data and represents the social world. This is why the findings of one method of investigation often conflict with those of another, and data collected by survey interviews, discursive interviews, focus groups, ethnographies and so on, are often different, seldom overlapping (see Bazeley, 2016; Graffigna & Gambetti, 2015). Whilst this conflict might be considered an enrichment, in the sense that it yields additional insights useful to the researcher, it may be problematic when a study is required to provide precise answers, especially in the field of applied research and management research. Hence, there is a strong link (though not deterministic, of course) between the type of datum collected and the type of method (see Chapter 4): what you get with a certain method, you do not catch with another one (see Becker & Geer, 1957, for a comparison between participant observation and conversational interview). For this reason integration can be reached only at the level of *specific methods* (by carefully considering and balancing their nature, diversity, limits and potential), not simply because the design mixes qualitative and quantitative.

Conclusion

The merged epistemology and methodology aims to give voice to those critical instances (towards the qualitative, quantitative and merged approaches) that have been neglected or left unheard. Such criticisms can reorient and re-establish empirical research, starting from the key concepts (recalled in Chapter 3) of the methodology of social research.

Obviously, Merged Methods do not have behind them the tradition, practice and reflection (in some cases centuries-old tradition, if we think of the First Wave; in others 40 years, if we think of the Second Wave) of Mixed Methods (discussed in Chapter 1). Therefore, they cannot be required to solve all the problems that other approaches suffer. However, a process has begun and many perplexities, weaknesses and gaps of Merged Methods can be improved and overcome with the contribution of those who believe in them.

Although the result of a cooperative effort, Chapter 1 has been principally written by Nigel Fielding, Chapters 2 and 3 by Giampietro Gobo, Chapter 4 by Wander van der Vaart, Chapter 5 by Gevisa La Rocca, Chapter 6 by Wander van der Vaart and Giampietro Gobo, Chapter 7 by Gevisa La Rocca, Chapter 8 by Nigel Fielding and Gevisa La Rocca, Chapter 9 by Gevisa La Rocca and Nigel Fielding, Chapter 10 by Gevisa La Rocca. The Introduction and Conclusion have been co-authored.

PART ONE

EPISTEMOLOGY AND METHODOLOGY

1

MERGED METHODS: DEVELOPMENT AND EMERGENCE OF A NEW APPROACH

The history of social research methods tells us that (i) Mixed Methods are not a novelty that emerged in the 1990s; (ii) the 'First Wave' of Mixed Methods studies prior to the 1990s majored on creative methodological combinations whereas the contemporary 'Second Wave' tends toward increasing standardization and methodological closure; (iii) engaging with the concept of 'Merged Methods' is a means to advance key debates in the current state of Mixed Methods development. Amongst these debates are the vexed question of data integration; the cautious response to new research technologies and data sources; and the overarching balance between systematization and creativity, which sometimes differentiates form from substance. Accordingly, this chapter summarizes key debates in Second Wave (contemporary) Mixed Methods and their differences from the First Wave (the predecessors), pursuing a concern that the spirit of the

First Wave has been diminished by the dynamic created by the Second Wave. Merged Methods – both established kinds and new kinds presented in this book – carry forward the spirit of the First Wave, and this chapter profiles contemporary Mixed Methods to establish points of connection, synergies and benefits to that field from engaging with Merged Methods.

Where we are starting from

As elsewhere in human endeavour, there are fashions in social research methods, and like fashions in clothing, those in methods are cyclical. A method, tool or technique will dominate for a time, then fade from view, then be re-discovered. Presently, Mixed Methods are in fashion. Their use is not confined to a niche but is found across social science *disciplines*. Moreover, Mixed Methods research designs increasingly feature in empirical research across a range of substantive *topics* (Ivankova & Kawamura, 2010). Mixed Methods are also well received by research funding organizations and the policy community that commissions and consumes applied social research (Fielding, 2021). The social research equivalent of the catwalk is the conference, and Mixed Methods has its own conference series, plus an international professional association, two dedicated journals and a voluminous literature.

The problem with things that are in vogue is that increasing ubiquity can create orthodoxy. A few years ago it would have been demeaning if one appeared in public with holes and tears in one's denims. Then celebrities and an increasing legion of 'influencers' decided this was not a sign of poverty but an interesting look, and soon pre-torn jeans were on sale. In some settings it became difficult to find any younger person wearing an intact pair of denims. Somewhere along the way, the disruptiveness of the poverty 'look' became standard-issue casual wear. Not only did it lose the power to shock, illustrating the ephemerality of fashion, it also meant that people were wearing clothes that were dysfunctional when it rained. Just so, a few years ago Mixed Methods were seen as 'difficult', or as an uneasy compromise between quantitative and qualitative, or as dangerously positivist, betraying an outdated science-of-society outlook. Now they are in vogue, and we worry about the signs of increasing standardization. Standardization sometimes means that an approach is used whether or not it is appropriate to the research question at issue. It also means that boundaries start to be set, with some methodological practices being sanctioned and others excluded. Methodological closure is applied. Creativity suffers.

Methodological closure is not just contrary to the reality of Mixed Methods practice but a breach of what Mixed Methods research can and should be – 'not ... a fixed entity but instead one that is flexible and fluid' (Hesse-Biber, 2010a, p. 415). The benefits that can be gained are frustrated by building boundaries around Mixed Methods principles and procedures. In particular, insistence that the default Mixed Methods design is QUAN + QUAL (typically a sample population SURVEY combined with semi-structured INTERVIEWS) tends toward a positivist assumption that social reality is an objective observable rather than a social construction (Hesse-Biber, 2010b), whereas sophisticates would argue that it is both. Some detect ulterior motives behind the elevation of the quantitative element in applied Mixed Methods research; for instance, the fact that the use of hypotheses and likely nature of the findings of quantitative methods are more readily predicted enables the powerful to satisfy themselves whether funding a given project may lead to embarrassing or controversial outcomes (Maxwell, 2010). What is undeniable is that standardization risks the rendering of the canon to a set of legitimated approaches that are captured in textbooks and thus shape fields.

Mixed Methods as a resurgence
The First Wave

We have referred to Mixed Methods as a potential 'orthodoxy' but it sometimes also resembles a bandwagon. The noise around Mixed Methods is, nevertheless, somewhat curious. Methods have been mixed for many decades, and what is sometimes treated as a radical new discovery actually has long roots. Mixing methods has been practised since the beginnings of social research, initially in Europe with Pierre La Play (France), Eilert Sundt (Norway), Benjamin Rowntree (UK), Max Weber (Germany) and Paul Lazarsfeld (Austria), and, somewhat later, in the United States with the Chicago School and the Columbia School (see Gobo and Mauceri, 2014, pp. 7ff), often by eminent figures usually associated with the quantitative tradition. Moreover, its fundamental epistemological premises inform disciplines across the social sciences. So we should really talk about the vogue as a re-discovery. The psychologist Donald Campbell championed Mixed Methods 'triangulation' in the late 1950s but Lazarsfeld, Jahoda and Zeisl's landmark analysis of the relationship between long-term unemployment and mental illness mixed a large range of data sources and methods in a case study of the Austrian village of Marienthal that was first published in 1933 (see Fryer, 1992). 'Marienthal' employed creative methodological combinations unfettered by preconceived roles for quantitative and qualitative components, and even recognized that each had shadings of the other (see Gobo and Mauceri, 2014, p. 10).

In contrast, Plano Clark's (2010) study of Mixed Methods practice in US federal-funded research found a pattern of mixing that appeared to confirm the subordination of the qualitative partner into an exploratory and descriptive role while the quantitative element assessed constructs and variables, driving the analysis. This echoes the US textbooks one of us (Fielding) studied in the 1960s. Indeed, in some ways there was more radicalism and creative innovation in Campbell and Fiske (1959) than is easily found in the contemporary mainstream, and it is worth recalling that in his later work the supposed 'experimentalist' Campbell became an advocate of qualitative methods.

The triangulation metaphor itself has long roots (Webb et al., 1966). Denzin (1970) developed Webb et al.'s approach, suggesting that using multiple data sources, methods, investigators and theories gave greater reliability and validity. Denzin also argued that there was no logical reason that triangulation could not be achieved using solely qualitative methods (see also Flick, 2011) while Hammersley (2008) observes that triangulation can involve comparing sources of data (e.g., several observers of the same event) rather than combining methods. Jick (1979) offered a continuum from simple to holistic triangulation designs, arguing that qualitative methods particularly produce holistic understandings. In elaborating the idea that different methods compensate each other's weaknesses, Jick acknowledged that triangulation requires researchers who understand the weaknesses of methods they do not themselves customarily use. Pursuing the 'delicate exercise to decide whether or not results have converged', Jick (1979, p. 607) emphasizes that it ultimately depends on judgement rather than weightings and formal tests. He also presents qualitative components as vital in handling surprising/ discrepant results, because they are in more direct encounter with the phenomenon than are quantitative tools.

Implicit in these early contributions is the importance of anticipating and weighing up what each method brings to the mix. Zelditch (1962) recognized that it was crucial to consider what kinds of methods and information best suit given research questions. Using criteria of 'informational adequacy' (accuracy and completeness) and 'efficiency' (cost per added item of information), Zelditch suggested certain combinations of methods and types of information for certain research questions (see Table 1.1).

Efficiency pertains when we consider cases where several methods could yield adequate information, such as in studying the political structure: we know the United States is led by 'presidents', and to identify the incumbent we do not need to sample the population but can ask one well-informed member. A survey with a probability sample would answer the 'president question' but would be inefficient. Likewise, combining interviews with Survey Methods is more efficient than full-scale ethnography (Verd, 2013). Choice of method depends on comparing the strengths and weaknesses of different methods (see Chapter 3).

The idea that one uses different tools for different jobs is common sense, and few would dismiss Zelditch's criteria. But his approach maintains a separation of quantitative

Table 1.1 Methods of obtaining research information

Information types	Enumerations and samples	Observation	Interviews
Frequency distributions	Optimal	Inadequate, inefficient	Usually inadequate, if adequate it is efficient
Incidents, histories	Inadequate, inefficient	Optimal	Adequate with precautions, efficient
Norms & statuses	Adequate but inefficient	Adequate but inefficient	Optimal because most efficient

(*Source:* Zelditch, 1962)

from qualitative methods by pursuing appropriate but separate use. However, where all three types of information – frequency distributions, incidents and histories, norms and statuses – are required to solve an analytical problem, then all three techniques are called for. The exact method to address each of the three must be specified to the research question, and then we must consider how the data from them can be integrated.

The triangulation heuristic put emphasis on the compensation-for-weakness idea. Sieber (1973) cites his project on suburban schools in which fieldwork identified an issue that not only became the focus of the study but dictated the design of the survey component. He identified several contributions that qualitative methods can make to a quantitative research design. Exploratory interviews help survey design by providing information about the receptivity and frames of reference of potential respondents. This can improve response rates, focus the questionnaire, and accommodate unanticipated population features, like willingness to provide extended responses (Langenwalter, 1967). Rapport from fieldwork can balance the impersonal nature of surveys. Field data can assist interpretation of statistical relationships and provide case studies to give life to them. Hesse-Biber (2010b) adds testing representativeness/generalizability on subgroups, locating target populations or defining them for in-depth study; demonstrating reliability and validity by strategic sampling; addressing inconsistent results; and deepening understanding of the research question.

Likewise, survey data can enhance fieldwork. Statistical profiles can guide field site selection, identifying major divisions like social class and identifying unrepresentative cases for subgroup analysis. **Survey facesheets** save time in interviews by collecting standardized socio-demographics. Survey data can correct bias from focusing fieldwork on respondents who are articulate and/or familiar from access negotiations. It can also solve puzzles in field data. In Sieber's (1973) suburban school study, teachers in one district voted less often in bond issue elections, which local government used to get public approval for school improvements. Fieldwork suggested bureaucracy had alien-ated teachers in that district. But survey data showed that a much larger proportion of teachers in the district lived outside it; since only those living in the district could vote in the bond elections this explained the difference, saving Sieber reporting a false interpretation.

To gain these advantages we must work out in advance the rationale for choice of methods and their expected contribution. When assessing the merits of the First Wave, prominent amongst these are the idea that the research question comes first, that it dic-tates the research design, and that the 'right' combination does not involve choosing off-the-shelf solutions but creative thinking informed by a keen grasp of the strengths and weaknesses of a range of methods (see Chapter 3).

The Second Wave

Latterly, Mixed Methods has presented as a distinct research approach rather than an unfettered creative response to a research question. Unsurprisingly, having established a distinct methodological domain, proponents have set about institutionalizing their practices. In the course of this Second Wave, periods of development and consolida-tion are apparent. Campbell and Fiske's major contribution was followed by quietude, because quantitative methods were in the ascendant. Interest in Mixed Methods revived in the 1970s. The social science publisher Sage found its early niche around short introductions to specific methods ('greenbacks' for statistical techniques, 'blue-backs' for qualitative methods) and the series included a title on Mixed Methods (Field-ing & Fielding, 1986), indicatively, in the *blueback* series. In the first decade of the 21st century prominent figures in the Mixed Methods community turned their attention to producing textbooks that consolidated certain understandings of Mixed Methods principles and techniques. The first editions of major works like Tashakkori and Ted-dlie's handbook (2003a, with a second edition in 2010) and Creswell's contribution on designing and conducting Mixed Methods studies (2011a), appeared. Calling such contributions 'textbooks' is no slur, because they provided a sophisticated rendering of practicalities and procedures.

Nevertheless, the 'era of the textbook' relies heavily on the quantitative/qualitative distinction, with recipe-like measured doses of quantitative and qualitative sustaining rather than subverting the binary distinction. Yet methodologists increasingly question the distinction. Bergman (2008) deems it the 'straw man' of research. Bazeley (2018a) observed that despite elaborating numerous paired characteristics along which quali-tative and quantitative differ, there are examples of most such characteristics where a given study displays the hallmark characteristic of the supposedly contrasting method. We should remember that the turn toward pragmatism, widely remarked as typifying the contemporary methods environment, was a turn away from the rigid association of methods with philosophical paradigms, a position prevailing in the 1980s and 1990s and an obstacle to starting with the research question and considering what methods would best address it.

During that transition, proponents of Mixed Methods worked hard to show that legitimate mixing was possible, producing and promulgating guidelines in what, in Bazeley's (2018b, p. 335) analysis, was a counter-productive effort to rebut the epistemological critique, counter-productive because it 'institutionalized' the supposedly impermeable distinction between quantitative and qualitative (Hammersley, 2018, p. 258). That counter-productive position is represented by the criterion that to be published in the *Journal of Mixed Methods Research* studies must include at least one definable quantitative method and one definable qualitative method. We might, for instance, consider the survey questionnaire. While it includes binary or multiple choice or scalar items from which respondents choose, it will usually also include Open Ended Questions, which may be analysed as text or rendered into a number. Thus, the workhorse quantitative method involves both text and judgement, i.e., qualitative characteristics (Bazeley, 2018a). Bazeley deems the survey a hybrid method, citing Jick's (1979, p. 609) formula for resolving mismatch between findings from different sources by employing qualitative analysis, that being 'the glue that cements the interpretation of multimethod results'.

Unsurprisingly, the idea that the quantitative/qualitative distinction is overdrawn, or even meaningless – 'the indistinguishability thesis' (Morgan, 2018) – has been hotly debated. Sandelowski's (2014) prominent statement of the thesis presents quantitative/qualitative as a false dichotomy that leads Mixed Methods astray by asserting that good research must combine both, and by underplaying the within-method options available. Even so, Sandelowski (2014, p. 6) does *not* claim that the two approaches are indistinguishable. Morgan's (2018) critique of the thesis is that despite there being no accepted list of necessary and sufficient conditions constituting quantitative and qualitative, and their boundary being fuzzy, a tangible binary exists in their associated features. Each shares 'family resemblances' distinguishing it from the other.

Hammersley (2018) finds Morgan's position itself overly absolute. 'One can believe that the differences between quantitative and qualitative research are often overstated and may do more harm than good, without assuming that "it is not actually possible to distinguish" between quantitative and qualitative methods' (Hammersley, 2018, pp. 256–257). Since his own studies often involve overlap between the two methods, because each has a heterogeneous range of techniques and procedures, Hammersley

(2018, p. 257) concludes that 'we would be better off not using the global quantitative/ qualitative distinction' (see also Bazeley, 2018a; Mason, 2006). Illustrating the move toward full description of a research design as opposed to adopting a standard design, Mason et al. (2019) provide a case study of the full integration of quantitative and qualitative methods at all stages of a project. Researching child welfare, they provide detailed accounts of how confirmatory, expansionary and discordant data were handled while accommodating the particularities of the quantitative or qualitative component from which they originated.

We earlier noted the role that pragmatism has played in neutralizing epistemological barriers to mixing. Poth (2018) applies **complexity science** and **relational systems analysis** to the practical problems presented by researching complex dynamic relationships. The starting point is to understand the research intervention as a multidimensional social system in its own right. In these circumstances researchers are regularly required to innovate to capture 'the behaviour of a research system whereby its components (such as research participants, researchers, their environments) interact in multiple, nonlinear ways without direction' (2018, p. 3). Six adaptive practices are recommended to support innovations in Mixed Methods. They are: researcher responsiveness (to emergent developments such as on-the-fly changes made to an intervention as it is being implemented); mixing purposes when framing research problems (such as including indicators or measures that capture political dimensions of a policy even when the main focus is how the policy works on the ground); system considerations when defining interrelated Mixed Method research contexts (i.e., the interaction between methods and measures, such as reactivity effects from interviews on survey response from the same sample); design creations for agile Mixed Methods procedures (being willing to modify instruments to capture features of the object of study whose importance is only recognized after the research has been designed); capacity decisions (recognizing where to draw the line in terms of what the available resources can reasonably be expected to provide); quality indicators when integrating findings (being clear about the marks of robustness particular to each method in the mix and how they relate to each other). Poth's approach is (gently) at odds with the textbook approach. She argues that treating the Mixed Methods process as 'organic' leads to an understanding of the process as 'more creative, evolving and emergent than it is sometimes portrayed' (2018, p. 26). Since no social phenomenon stands still, research designs need to adapt *in vivo,* and respect for those involved in the phenomenon compels researchers to adjust to this and capture change. These are not just sound principles for responding to complexity and dynamic systems of relationships but, we will argue, hallmarks of Merged Methods.

State of the debate in Mixed Methods

The centrality of data integration

The route by which the Mixed Methods community recognized that data integration was at the core of the Mixed Methods heuristic was indirect. In Creswell's (2009) systematic, staged procedures for designing and executing a Mixed Methods study, integration features, but the emphasis is on *when* to integrate, not *how* to integrate. There is an implicit assumption that integration is a distinct procedure, performed at a particular point, not something intrinsic to all the stages. Integration is essential to Merged Methods, since such methods rely on all components.

Prominent accounts of integration often rest at an abstract level ('bring together', 'merging', 'connecting'; Creswell and Plano Clark, 2007) that cannot match the transparent rationale and assumptions in, say, conventions for assigning a given weighting to each variable in a statistical relationship. Uprichard and Dawney (2019) observe that standard discussions of integration assume that a good 'fit' arises from alignment – each data source pursuing the same point, measure, indicator or processual stage. However, the 'cuts' that methods take through a phenomenon do not necessarily cohere. A 'diffraction' metaphor considers how data produced through different methods can splinter and/or interrupt the phenomenon. Simple 'fit' is not a matter of homogeneity or convergence.

There are four logically possible outcomes of mixing methods: convergence between findings (classic triangulation for convergent validation); contradiction between the findings; findings that relate to different aspects of the issue but are complementary; and findings that have nothing to do with each other. Convergent validation or 'triangulation' assumes that if the same findings emerge from different methods validity is enhanced so long as you avoid combining methods that suffer similar threats to validity. Despite calls for its abolition (Morgan, 2019), triangulation remains important, especially in policy-related research. However, a more recent approach mixes methods for 'analytic density' (Fielding, 2009, 2012). This works from the condition where findings relate to different aspects of the issue but are complementary, and the condition where there are contradictions.

The analytic density approach seeks a holistic understanding and is always ready to consider new information by adding a new method. This is in tension with the triangulation approach. Convergent validation implies a single 'right' answer, whereas the analytic density approach is drawn to adding new dimensions, including those arising from contradictory findings. Such contradictions would have the researcher pursuing triangulation running back to the design and data collection stage to see if something has gone 'wrong'. In the analytic density approach contradictions are accepted as signs of an incomplete understanding, requiring revision of the analysis and/or applying further methods.

Thus, mixing does not necessarily put findings into a position where fit can be explored. Applying Barad's (2007, p. 36) diffraction metaphor, Uprichard and Dawney (2019, p. 23) ask 'what if one method captures the "ear of the elephant" and another captures the "tail of a mouse"? What if Mixed Methods, very successfully, capture *multiple* aspects of multiple parts that are entangled together instead of revealing some (singular) "thing"?'. Different 'cuts' of the phenomenon produced by the different methods make some aspects visible, masking others. An example might be a study of diabetes that mixes quantitative clinical aetiology, a symptomology of onset and identification data, and patient accounts of their symptoms. The clinical list of symptoms is long but individual patients have their own unique set. A diffractive account that accepts this disparity rather than seeing it as contradictory acknowledges the multiple pathways into and through being diabetic. Disparity of individual accounts from clinical symptomology, and between individual accounts, results from the ontology of the data and of the object, just as diffraction in physics involves change in wave direction as obstructions occur, including the force from other waves. Uprichard and Dawney (2019) do not repudiate integration but argue for a wider analytic repertoire than simple 'fit'.

The ground for Merged Methods is prefigured by other contributions from Mixed Methods, including the recognition of methodologies that don't neatly fit into an either/or quantitative/qualitative binary – Q-Methodology, social network analysis, **fuzzy logic** qualitative comparative analysis, and Geographic Information Systems (Bazeley, 2010, p. 433; see also Bazeley, 2018b on 'inherently mixed, hybrid methods', which adds repertory grid scale development techniques). Another hybrid is **agent-based modelling** (ABM), whose computer simulations benefit from combination with qualitative methods when modelling its output of putative social mechanisms (Saetra, 2016). ABM involves qualitative reasoning when scripting interactions that change the simulated actors and interpreting what interactions led to which changes (Gobo, 2008a).

There is also a Mixed Methods thread about 'converting' data by 'quantitizing' qualitative data (Tashakkori & Teddlie, 1998; see Bazeley, 2018a, pp. 179–235, re data transformation). Its mirror is less discussed. Examples of qualitizing data with a quantitative origin include using quantitative sources to build life histories (Elliott, 2005) and using cluster analysis to generate comparative narrative profiles. Following Heise (1969), work by the mathematical sociologist Peter Abell (2009) uses comparative narrative profiles derived from ethnographic fieldwork to create '**di-graphs**' for quantitative analysis, an approach Blossfeld and Rohwer (1995) elaborated as a means of producing causal analyses from qualitative data.

Full-scale integration via combination and conversion can be iterative or can generate blended data (Bazeley, 2006). While these approaches are logically possible, they are seldom done. This is the nub of our reservations about conversion as an integration strategy. While having an affinity for Merged Methods principles, in practical terms conversion is not only demanding, it requires data in a format that is rarely elicited by qualitative fieldwork – simple binaries (e.g., absence/presence of a characteristic of interest). In practice, integration mostly occurs when final conclusions are drawn (Bryman, 2006). Integration at the data analysis stage accounted for only seven of 232 Mixed Methods studies in Bryman's survey. This may reflect the difficulty of full integration and/or the fact that integration obstructs convergent validation, which requires independence of methods (Caracelli & Greene, 1993). As Bazeley (2006, p. 65) observes, integration 'requires a breadth of skills that has not commonly been available in a single researcher'.

New technologies

Bazeley (1999) moved towards Merged Methods in proposing 'fusion' of qualitative and quantitative methods, using them interdependently in an integrated design, and, following Fielding and Lee (1991), argues that qualitative software has facilitated this by including gateways for import/export of quantitative data to/from statistics packages, and by providing tools to produce matrices from cross-tabulated, coded data, enabling **quantitative techniques** like correspondence analysis (Bazeley, 2002). A glimpse of the merged approach appears in Bazeley's (1999) comment that creating dichotomous codes (e.g., presence/absence) can feed into the truth tables of qualitative comparative analysis (QCA) (Ragin, 1995). QCA has the equal reliance on built-in quantitative and qualitative components that features in Merged Methods, and seeks the convergence of **interpretative** and **structural dimensions** that Merged Methods pursues.

A number of commentaries consider the role of qualitative software in Mixed Methods (Silver & Lewins, 2014). Team research, often involving collaborations between dispersed researchers, has spurred adoption of qualitative software in Mixed Methods studies. However, it is mostly used as a digital filing cabinet rather than for its analytical affordances, in contrast to citizen research (Hardey & Burrows, 2008). Citizens who do not identify as professional researchers increasingly conduct research using digital/online resources and an eclectic approach to mixing findings from them (Fielding, 2014). Like citizen research, '**Indigenous Research**' by non-traditional research communities broadens who does social research, why it is done and what it legitimately involves (Tuhiwai Smith, 1999; Liamputtong, 2010; Chilisa, 2011; Gobo, 2011b; Ryen & Gobo 2011).

Citizen research and Indigenous Research also challenge accepted epistemological and ontological constraints. Crowd-sourcing data, information 'mash-ups', and basic Sentiment Analysis are used. These new computational techniques using semi- and fully automated strategies to bring datasets together offer lessons for the central issue of data integration. Contemporary CAQDAS provides tools for semi-automation of *code-based analysis* (Franzosi et al., 2013). Digital tools for *Content Analysis* enable new approaches to mixed datasets (Hogenraad et al., 2003; Popping & Roberts, 2009), including full automation (Grimmer & Stewart, 2013) and Text Mining (Lee et al., 2010). A Noah's Ark approach – one quantitative method, one qualitative method – diverts engagement with technologies that are themselves increasingly hard to classify as either quantitative or qualitative, or indeed as either 'technology' or 'method'.

One branch of social science has heavily invested, though. The new human geography declares itself inherently mixed, combining not only social and physical geography but quantitative and qualitative. Methods that integrate Geographic Information Systems with CAQDAS (Cisneros-Puebla & Fielding, 2009; Jung, 2009; Jung & Elwood, 2010) bring together the spatial and the social. The new geography is a committed practice that places research resources in the service of communities (Craig et al., 2002), exemplified by applications of GIS in urban planning (Knigge & Cope, 2006) and community safety (Fielding & Fielding, 2013). Grounded in Mixed Methods, the new human geography also promises new Merged Methods strategies and techniques.

Systematization and creativity: form and substance

Whatever our perspective, we benefit from remembering the roots of Mixed Methods in the work of Donald Campbell (Campbell & Fiske, 1959). Campbell's role is acknowledged by key Second Wave figures but they draw their inspiration largely from one aspect of Campbell's contribution, that of bringing the practice of the social experiment into social science. That strand reflects Campbell's stance on experimental designs at a stage of his intellectual career when he accorded qualitative methods a relatively minor role in mixing methods. Yet the later Campbell came to regard qualitative methods as essential to convergent validation, and to achieving 'analytic density' (Fielding, 2009), although he did not use that term. This shift followed experience of applied projects in which small-scale qualitative research reached the same or, sometimes, deeper and more accurate, conclusions as the survey element in the research design, and did so more quickly and cheaply. '[I]n borrowing the quantitative emphasis from physical sciences by way of philosophy of science, quantitative-experimental social science has made the mistake of assuming that quantitative methods replaced qualitative knowing.

Instead, valid quantification depends on qualitative monitoring of the experimental and measurement setting' (Campbell, 1987, pp. 423–424). Campbell saw the qualitative element 'using ... everyday modes of knowing, observing, gossiping, and asking' as so important that he believed applied projects should employ an ethnographer to guarantee their 'quantitative applied scientific validity'. While the Second Wave valorizes the work of the early Campbell, that of the Multitrait Multimethod Matrix' (MTMM), equally compelling insights can be drawn from Campbell the mature thinker, whose understanding of how evidence is constructed for application was open and inclusive, pursuing rigour through creative combination.

The approach we value in Mixed Methods is its encouragement to think – systematically – outside the standard design box, finding provocative and stimulating answers to the research question. The Mixed Methods field is marked by diversity but it is increasingly a 'bounded diversity'. To us, the important thing about Mixed Methods is its stimulus to imaginative research design solutions. We worry that this increasingly encounters approaches that suggest there is one right 'mix' to address a given question. The authors of 'Marienthal' did not set rules for mixing methods. Yet advocating creativity does not mean anything goes. Where methodology provides a validated procedure we should use it. But we *are* saying that more than one thing goes – there is more than one useful way to mix, and genuinely integrate, methods. Indeed, it is precisely the ontology of the data in combination with the research question that requires creativity if valid outcomes are to be gained. Validated procedures are only and always validated to a certain sub-population in a specific context, and adopting a validated procedure does not guarantee validity for every study.

It is over 50 years since Lyman and Scott (1970) published their critique of treating social research data, especially interview data, as if its meaning were available on the surface and its face validity was unquestionable. That was soon followed by Deutscher's (1973) definitive account of why, and how, 'what we say' is not 'what we do'. Yet instead of pursuing a more sophisticated treatment of our data we too often blithely continue as if rapport was enough to elicit reliable, valid data, and analysis could safely proceed immediately to coding, producing 'analyses' whose evidential authority can be secured by the occasional interview extract, an artefact of the 'stubbornly persistent Romantic impulse' reflecting 'the elevation of the experiential as authentic' (Atkinson and Silverman, 1997, p. 305). The critique was profound, the impact modest.

While foundational figures like Max Weber used Mixed Methods – statistical tables (of, e.g., religious adherence) and experiential data (e.g., sermons) informed his work on the origins of capitalism – he nevertheless agonized over the drawbacks of every method he used (Lazarsfeld & Oberschall, 1965). Prominent was his concern that behaviour is mostly conducted with little consciousness of its subjective meaning (Silverman, 2017,

p. 148). Social actors may often be no more authoritative about the actions they author than those who receive or observe their actions. Merged Methods do not primarily measure attitudes but gauge actions. Where attitudes are considered it is as a foil against which to compare actual behaviour. This is consistent with Charmaz's (2014) approach to coding field data, where coding is not by topic/theme but by actions. Coding in gerunds like 'getting' or 'preferring' shows talk as an action rather than a literal description of reality. Merged Methods respect the original meaning of the triangulation metaphor taken from navigation. Taking bearings on two landmarks locates one's position as a matter of the angle between the two fixed points and the distance between them, one's position being at the point of the triangle created by the lines. In navigation, the second point does not 'verify' or 'validate' the first but is the necessary complement to it. In methodology, the validity of the first point (or datum) is not known and one seeks it by reference to the second (Erzberger and Kelle, 2003). In Merged Methods, each component is the necessary complement of the other. The difference is one between checking an answer and producing an answer (Hammersley, 2008, p. 24). Classic Mixed Methods triangulation is directed to the former, while Merged Methods is directed to the latter.

Surfing the Third Wave: enter Merged Methods

The status of qualitative methods remains a thorny issue in Mixed Methods. Critics of qualitative research often look askance at Mixed Methods, seeing it as a Trojan Horse to sneak qualitative methods into the research design (Bazeley, 2015a). Scepticism from quantitative-oriented researchers has been reinforced by the experimentalist outlook of the 'Evidence-Based Policy' movement, despite the susceptibility of random control trials to 'spin', with over half of behavioural science RCT articles exaggerating their findings' importance or downplaying findings casting doubt on those highlighted (Jellison et al., 2019). Merged Methods does not have this problem, because methods like Gobo's 'Intervey' or **RAND**'s Delphi Method simply do not work without their qualitative component.

All of this said, there is a *creative* tension between Mixed and Merged Methods. Merged Methods have an affinity for most core characteristics of Mixed Methods research identified by Tashakkori and Teddlie (2010), including paradigm pluralism; an iterative approach; focus on the research question in determining methods to be used; tendency toward balance and compromise; affinity for visual representations (e.g., infographics). Moreover, 'most, but not all, leading Mixed Methods researchers … agree that the terms qualitative and quantitative are not necessarily polar opposites but define boundaries on a multidimensional continuum' (Bazeley, 2015a, p. 29). Bazeley (2015a) reports a comparative analysis of research design in empirical studies published in two established management journals. Considerable interpretation was required to classify these as quantitative, qualitative or mixed, and where quantitative and qualitative components were both present there was interactive 'moving back and forth' during analysis.

As Bazeley (2015b, p. 311) observes, 'despite attempts to classify them, Mixed Methods studies are infinitely variable in their design'. The distance from that position to hybrid methods with both quantitative and qualitative features is not far. If there is a need for much interpretation to classify a study as mixed perhaps it is not so necessary to police the borders around Mixed Methods, one of which is with Merged Methods. By their nature, Merged Methods are particularly hard to classify, especially given the case of the management studies Bazeley (2015a, 2015b) reviewed, where a number of studies included considerable qualitative work but were nevertheless presented by their authors as purely quantitative.

Essential principles of Merged Methods

The Merged Methods concept rests on straightforward foundations, but the other side of the coin is that each forms an essential principle and all must be present for a research design to register as Merged Methods (see Box 1.1).

Box 1.1 The principles emphasized by Mixed Methods research

- The importance of combining 'interpretative' and 'structural' approaches in approach/data collection;
- Keeping both sides in (some) balance as tailored to the complexity of the empirical issue that is being studied, which is, in particular, 'essential' in case the core of the issue at hand is a kind of dependency between 'interpretative experience' and more 'structural' external influences;
- This involves paying attention to how study designs and data collection methods otherwise might be 'over-steering' the data (due to either too much openness or too much selection/direction); on the very practical side this ultimately includes attention to topics like interview style, question wording and so on.

Note that the heuristic does not revolve around a binary quantitative–qualitative distinction. Rather, it revolves around the distinction between interpretative and structural approaches to data collection and to understanding social phenomena. This alternative binary is not simply a replacement of terminology. It is perfectly possible to use a quantitative method to prosecute an interpretative approach, just as it is possible to use a qualitative method to capture aspects of structure. The heuristic is concerned to identify methods that represent within themselves both interpretative and structural dimensions of social phenomena and capture how they interact.

Combining quantitative and qualitative data in a complementary or comparative way tends to make one method take precedence over the other (Bazeley, 1999). Despite Caracelli and Greene (1997) differentiating 'component designs' from 'integrated designs', which include 'nested designs' and 'holistic designs' as well as iterative designs, it is the less exacting forms of complementary combination that often predominate. Dominance and subordination feature less sharply in Merged Methods because each component is integral. In Chapter 2 we explore how Merged Methods principles address and build from current debates in Mixed Methods.

2

MERGED EPISTEMOLOGY: ASSUMPTIONS, EXPERIENCE, KNOWLEDGE

The Second Wave of Mixed Methods research (see Chapter 1) arose as a counterreaction to claims of incompatibility between quantitative and qualitative methods (Howe, 1988; Brannen, 1992; Teddlie & Tashakkori, 2010). Later, Morgan (2007) gave to Mixed

Methods research the status of a 'third paradigm', alternative to the quantitative and qualitative paradigms, with the potential to open a new era in the field of behavioural and social sciences. He followed the position put forward by Tashakkori and Teddlie (1998), who saw Mixed Methods as an (independent) *methodology*. Later they reinforced this emphasis, stating 'mixed methods research has evolved to the point where it is a separate methodological orientation with its own worldview, vocabulary, and techniques' (Tashakkori & Teddlie, 2003a, p. x).

However, these challenging aspirations did not always deliver what was promised, and an imbalance favouring a quantitative methods mindset still prevails. That is, the Mixed Methods landscape still suffers from a quantitative imprinting and the quantitative post-positivist epistemology is still dominant. While this epistemology (see Chapter 1), based on the ideas of Karl Popper (1935), Ian Hacking (1983) and Nancy Cartwright (1989), is 'softer' than simple positivism (because it accepts qualitative input), it generally retains the idea of objective truth and still adheres to conventional hard-line criteria of robustness, which means it can never grant equal status to qualitative input.

In addition, Mixed Methods discourse is much less innovative than its claim to be a new paradigm suggests. In fact, its vocabulary includes few new terms and, overall, retains old concepts. For example, the apparently new research designs, like 'convergent (parallel) design', 'explanatory sequential design', 'exploratory (sequential) design', 'embedded design' etc., were already used (without naming) in the First Wave of Mixed Methods by Le Play, Weber, Lazarsfeld. Moreover, there is little sign of new techniques having been invented by Mixed Methods researchers; indeed, novel recent data integration techniques (well presented in Bazeley, 2018a), such as CAQDAS or network analysis, were already devised and developed outside the Mixed Methods community.

In order to truly be a 'third paradigm', Mixed Methods should increase its effort to integrate the quantitative and the qualitative paradigms into a new, distinctive and really mixed paradigm: retaining and mixing the valuable contributions of both and emancipating itself from being a simple juxtaposition of different methods.

The need for an epistemological integration

The contemporary quantitative approach grew up in the first decades of the 1900s as a descendant of positivism and behaviourism, and (later) of neo-positivism. Its main methods are the survey, the test (IQ test, attitudinal tests, etc.) and the experiment. The qualitative approach (or interpretativism, to use just one of many labels in use) arose as a counterreaction to neo-positivism in the 1950s (although its antecedents can be found in the Chicago School of the 1920s). Its main methods are the discursive interview, the focus group (formally, 'group discussions') and ethnography.

There are many differences between the two approaches (also *inside* each approach, because their practitioners have created different 'schools' and sensibilities within each approach) on the nature of reality, truth, knowledge, objectivity and values. However, the most striking (and often unnoticed) difference is the measurement issue: the quantitative approach aims to measure social phenomena (behaviours, attitudes, opinions), while the qualitative approach rejects measurement, considering it a task not within the reach of social science and presenting a spurious precision (Cicourel, 1964).

Although some measurements, various counting practices and a lot of implicitly numerical reasoning such as *many, often, typically, sometimes* and so on (see Becker, 1970 and Chapter 3), are present in qualitative research, measurement has never been the main aim of the qualitative approach, which prioritizes collecting and interpreting participants' narratives and/or observing interaction intensively.

Most Mixed Methods researchers consider the conflict between paradigms as belonging to the past and, under the aegis of a rather naïve pragmatism, think that it has no effect on current research. Thus they mix, for example, surveys (which they continue to use in a behaviourist mode) and the discursive interview, which is used as a simple tool and within a post-positivistic attitude. This way of mixing methods without taking into account their nature and intrinsic limits is one of the causes (albeit not the only one) of the inconsistency of much Mixed Methods research (see Chapter 3).

In order to mix methods properly, it is first necessary to mix the epistemologies that produced them. That seems, at first glance, an impossible feat: how is it possible to mix such conflicting epistemologies, which historically have been the source of such heated conflicts (Blaikie, 1991)? The way forward is seeing which aspects of these two epistemologies are compatible, integrable and borrowable, discarding those which are not, while being aware that some apparent incompatibilities are born from linguistic and conceptual misunderstandings. Hence, our first task is merging *some* terminologies, codes and mindsets from the two approaches.

A common Mixed Methods language and an agreed conceptual background are the premise for reuniting methods and approaches currently considered distinct and irreconcilable. The desired full integration of Mixed Methods research could be achieved if different approaches can find a home in a single, revisited and updated, framework.

The quantitative imprinting in Mixed Methods

The Second Wave of Mixed Method research (see Chapter 1) has its roots in an initial opening by some quantitative researchers towards the (eventually irresistible) rise of qualitative methods. Open-minded sociologists, psychologists and methodologists (Vidich & Shapiro, 1955; Campbell & Fiske, 1959; Diesing, 1971; Sieber, 1973; Cronbach, 1975; Smith, 1975), their assistants (Webb et al., 1966) and young graduates (Jick, 1979), all with a quantitative background and training, proposed the concept of 'triangulation' (then seen as the core of Mixed Methods). Although, at that time, qualitative research was in danger of fast becoming extinct, since it could not match the formal procedures and validity claims of quantitative methods (see Glaser & Strauss, 1967, whose *grounded theory* was a response to this threat), the move by these open-minded quantitative researchers was prescient, because, from the 1980s, the blooming of several 'turns' (cognitive, linguistic, pragmatic, interpretative, interactional, narrative, postmodern and so on) soon began to undermine the traditional survey. Consequently, quantitative methods would increasingly look epistemologically outdated and methodologically inadequate. For this reason triangulation (and now Mixed Methods) was a providential lifesaver for quantitative methodologists; a way to recognize the limits of the quantitative approach and avoid the risk of becoming methodologically marginal and losing their intellectual power.[1]

It is no coincidence that a major impetus towards the use of Mixed Methods came from the universities of Michigan (Ann Arbor) and Nebraska-Lincoln, centres of excellence in quantitative methods. As a matter of fact, initially Mixed Methods were not proposed by qualitative researchers, who did not feel the need nor the urgency. Rather, some of them expressed worries about how Mixed Methods researchers treated qualitative methods (Howe, 2004; Denzin & Lincoln, 2005; Morse, 2005; Giddings, 2006). At most, qualitative methodologists proposed mixing amongst only qualitative techniques. Accordingly, severe appraisals such as that of Giddings (2006) emerged – 'the thinking in mixed-methods research rarely reflects a constructionist or subjectivist view of the world. The majority of studies use the analytic and prescriptive style of positivism, albeit with a postpositivist flavor [p. 200] … The "thinking" of positivism continues in the "thinking" of Mixed Methods, [with] its postpositivist pragmatic underpinnings' (p. 202; see also Smythe, 2005, p. 257).

---

[1]   Although without paradigm wars, also in natural sciences (astronomy, geology, medicine, epidemiology, ethology with the exception of the *new archeology*) qualitative methods were sometimes introduced to supply the limits of quantitative ones (see Maxwell, 2016).

The original sin in the qualitative–quantitative debate: the multiple meanings of 'qualitative'

The quantitative imprinting of Mixed Methods is traceable in the qualitative–quantitative debate, particularly in the meanings assigned to the term 'qualitative'. Exactly when the term 'qualitative' entered the methodological literature is elusive. When the Chicago School was in fashion (a century ago) the term was not on the lips of its affiliates. They referred to 'Field Methods' (even though survey researchers also referred to 'fieldwork' and 'fielding a survey'). The qualitative–quantitative divide was not strong in the first 50 years of sociology as a named discipline. Also lacking was the belief that direct exposure to the field was essential to understanding social phenomena – most Chicago School scholars had their fieldwork done by graduate students or even people without any academic training at all, and some important qualitative studies were based completely on case notes written by third parties (e.g., social workers) for purposes other than sociological research.

Up to the early 1940s discussions of sociological methodology were marked by a controversy between 'humanistic' and 'scientific approaches' (Platt, 1996: 11). After World War II developmental work on qualitative methods almost vanished. The dominant themes became survey research, experimentation and measurement. A significant revival of methodological work on qualitative issues followed articles published in the 1950s. But from sociology's origin through the 1960s the label 'qualitative' was little used, if at all, and 'quantitative methods' was a term confined to advanced, specialist techniques. The debate was over specific methods, without assignment to paradigms – in the 1940s it was the use of documentary sources (especially personal documents), in the 1950s it was participant observation and the practicalities of interviewing. The strengths and weaknesses of specific methods and data sources were debated without invoking a quantitative/qualitative divide (Platt 1996: 12–18).

As Platt shows, the emergence of 'qualitative' as a methodological category was muddied by the odd trajectory of 'case study method'. Before World War II the divide was between the 'social survey' and 'case study method'. The techniques associated with the latter originated in social work, which overlapped with sociology until the 1940s. Surveys were thought to be unable to access 'meanings', which were the forte of the case study. The association between meaning and the case study weakened as the techniques of case study stagnated while Survey Methods developed apace. Belated attempts to make case study method more 'objective' led to more emphasis on cases as representing 'types' and thus a convergence with survey classifications, while surveys grew more sophisticated in their means of pursuing attitudes and values. By the 1950s case study methods had vanished and the need for a residuum term (i.e. 'qualitative') to describe non-survey methods was not felt, because Survey Methods had become dominant. The residuum was not represented by the term 'qualitative' but by 'participant observation', which replaced 'case study' in the textbooks of the 1950s and 1960s. As courses and programmes in sociology became more widespread 'Field Methods' became the descriptor for non-survey methods, occupying the 'specialist' category to which 'quantitative methods' had once been assigned. With Glaser and Strauss (1967) the groundwork for a labelled approach emerged via their acknowledgement that quantitative methods had gained dominance via their claimed association with scientific method.

Thus it was probably the 1960s that witnessed the emergence of this simultaneously misleading/fortunate/ruinous term, although we do not find references to 'qualitative sociology' in flagship journals like *American Journal of Sociology* and *Social Forces* before the 1970s. Misleading, because, through its ambiguity it became an abused buzzword, 'a "catch-all" for non-positivist inquiry' (Giddings, 2006, p. 199); fortunate, because it became (and remains) a fashionable term. Ruinous, because it contributed to the 'paradigm wars' and obstructed a more subtle and sharper exploration of the diverse epistemological and methodological problems of doing research. For this reason, many scholars have pointed out the questionable use of qualitative and quantitative descriptors (and its false dichotomy), stating that this binary distinction does not hold in practice and encourages an unacceptable polarization that minimizes the diversity in methods (Giddings, 2006; Vogt, 2008; Sandelowski et al., 2009; Sandelowski, 2014; Hammersley, 2018). The essential problem in identifying an origin point for 'qualitative' as a descriptor is the lack of consensus over the definition of qualitative methods (Aspers and Corte, 2019).

Facts as theory-driven material–symbolic phenomena

When talking about his dog, Alfred Schutz said, 'I look at him as my friend and companion Rover [...] without a special motive, not induced to look at Rover as a mammal, an animal, an object of the outer world, although I know that he is all this too' (1953, p. 8). Hence:

> strictly speaking, there are no such things as facts, pure and simple [...] They are, therefore, always interpreted facts [...] This does not mean that, in daily life or in science, we are unable to grasp the reality of the world. It just means

that we grasp merely certain aspects of it, namely those which are relevant to us either for carrying on our business of living or from the point of view of a body of accepted rules of procedure of thinking called the method of science. (Schutz, 1953, p. 5)

In other words, our mindset assembles social reality (see Box 2.1).

Box 2.1 Facts as theory-driven: the case of the economic value of a job

The New Economics Foundation (NEF) is a group of 50 economists, known for having brought into the G7 and G8 agenda issues such as international debt. According to its proposal to connect salaries to the contribution to well-being that a job brings to the community, the NEF has calculated the economic value of six different jobs: three very well paid and three very poorly. In its conclusions, NEF puts bankers at the bottom of the ranking, because they stifle companies and damage the global economy. This view results from NEF's new approach to assessing the value of work, going beyond the view about how a profession is evaluated economically and checking how a profession contributes to the welfare of the whole society. NEF's key point is that there should be a direct correspondence between how much people are paid and the value that their work generates for society, and this underlies its method of calculating social value and appropriate financial compensation. According to these foundational principles, the NEF quantifies social, environmental and economic impact and contribution of the work done by different professions, finding that low pay jobs are the most useful to society. For example, comparing dustmen with tax advisors, for the NEF the former contribute to the safety of the environment, while the latter harm societies because they do their best to help clients pay less tax (see https://neweconomics.org/2009/12/a-bit-rich).

This example, among many that could be shown, highlights how facts are always material–symbolic constructions. Because reality, according to Windelband (1894), Weber (1922), Rickert (1926), Rorty (1979), and more recently according to systemic theories, has no intrinsic meaning but reduces to disorder, chaos, turbulence, nebulousness and opacity without precise boundaries, researchers are like the group of blind men in the Hindu tale who have never come across an elephant before and who learn and conceptualize what the elephant is like by touching it. Each blind man feels a different part of its body, but only one part, such as the side or the tusk (Figure 2.1). They then describe the elephant based on their partial experience, and their descriptions are in complete disagreement on what an elephant is. They come to suspect that the other

Figure 2.1 The elephant metaphor.

(*Source*: Illustrator unknown. From Charles Maurice Stebbins and Mary H. Coolidge, *Golden Treasury Readers: Primer*. New York: American Book Co. (p. 89); https://commons.wikimedia.org/wiki/Category: Blind_men_and_an_elephant#/media/File:Blind_men_and_elephant3.jpg)

persons are dishonest and come to blows. The moral is that humans have a tendency to project their partial experiences as the whole truth.

Is the 'pragmatic' approach/paradigm a valuable alternative?

The 'pragmatic' approach/paradigm has been proposed 'as a philosophical programme for social research, regardless of whether that research uses qualitative, quantitative or mixed methods' (Morgan, 2014, p. 1045). It has been presented as a third way between positivism/realism/post-positivism and constructivism/interpretativism/critical theory (Maxcy, 2003; Johnson & Onwuegbuzie, 2004; Morgan, 2007, 2014; Biesta, 2010; Tashakkori & Teddlie, 2010; Pearce, 2012; Hall, 2013).

This third way is inspired by the tradition of American pragmatic philosophy and is based on 'concepts such as "lines of action" (from William James and George Herbert Mead) and "warranted assertions" (from John Dewey), along with a general emphasis on "workability" (from both James and Dewey)' (Morgan, 2007, p. 66). In its intentions, this approach does away with all the 'metaphysical concerns ... related to the nature of reality and truth' (2007, p. 49), because they are too abstract and 'tell us little about more substantive decisions such as what to study and how to do so' (2007, p. 53); in addition, they deliver too few insights for translating such metaphysical issues into practical guidance for how to make decisions about actual research. Hence, they produce a 'belief system [that] remains disconnected from practical decisions about the actual conduct of research' (2007, p. 64).

The three pragmatic concepts above should theoretically allow Mixed Methods researchers to approach (on a practical level) researchers from different paradigms, in order to build shared meanings and joint actions based on common communication and reciprocal persuasion, focusing on methodology and research questions rather than metaphysical assumptions; because 'methods are not automatically "appropriate." Instead, it is we ourselves who make the choices about what is important and what is appropriate, and those choices inevitably involve aspects of our personal history, social background, and cultural assumptions' (Morgan, 2007, pp. 67, 71).

Much of the pragmatic position is wise and fully acceptable. However, when we move to the really practical side (i.e., really being pragmatists), we realize that the metaphysical concerns are not so much ... metaphysical. For example, in their actual inquiries, should pragmatic researchers use a classic (and positivistic) questionnaire with forced choices and closed-ended answers, which are the negation of any interactional perspective? Should they use those conventional fixed formats that are responsible for many response errors and biases such as social desirability effects, the yea-saying and response set phenomena, the influence of the response alternatives on the formation of the answer, the misunderstanding of the response alternatives by the interviewees, the multiple word meanings of response alternatives, the invented opinions (or lies) phenomenon (see Chapter 6)? Hence, the pragmatist approach shows its methodological and epistemological weakness precisely on the level of research practices. This weakness is traceable in statements like: 'one paradigm (like pragmatism) serves as an adequate foundation for concurrent or parallel types of designs, while paradigms may shift during a sequential design in which one starts from a postpostivist perspective ... and then moves to a constructivist (qualitative) worldview (Creswell & Plano Clark, 2007)' (Creswell, 2009, p. 102). Rightly, this way to envision the linking of paradigms and methods is not appreciated by qualitative researchers (e.g., Denzin & Lincoln, 2005), who have taken the stance that the panoply of different kinds of method cannot fit with every paradigm.

The pitfalls of a pragmatic approach are also revealed when Morgan (2007, pp. 70–73) affirms that Mixed Methods research is characterized by abduction (while qualitative researchers would proceed by induction and quantitative ones by deduction), intersubjectivity (while the former would be focused on the study of subjective processes and the latter on objective ones) and transferability (while qualitative researchers remain anchored to context and quantitative researchers to generalizability). Characterizing Mixed Methods research as abduction forgets that abduction is a human cognitive process, therefore applied (unconsciously) both by qualitative and quantitative researchers; that intersubjectivity is continuously studied by both qualitative (symbolic interactionist and ethnomethodological) and quantitative researchers.[2]

Although the pragmatic approach is presented as a paradigm for dissolving differences and neutralizing epistemological barriers (Onwuegbuzie & Leech 2005; see Chapter 1), in practice, by not problematizing and reforming current research methods, it ends up reproducing the realist paradigm in disguise.

The great misunderstanding

Instead of highlighting the differences and diversities in methods (useful in epistemologically understanding which methods can be combined and which not), a consistent part of the 1990s Mixed Methods movement promoted a vision where the differences and diversities were levelled, stating that the quantitative–ualitative distinction was overdrawn, or even meaningless (see Chapter 1). The mantra has been: there is quality in quantity, and quantity in quality; they are the two sides of the same phenomenon; they are complementary, like yin and yang. This has been named the 'indistinguishability thesis' by Morgan (2018), who rightly rejects this position.

On the other hand, however, it is also true that there is no accepted list of necessary and sufficient conditions constituting the quantitative and qualitative, their boundary thus being fuzzy.

However, this debate does not wholly capture the deeper core nature of the problem, as the following ethnographic note (collected in a doctor's office) illustrates:

> In the waiting room, there are 8 people. Most are elderly and only 2 are young. The length of the visits varies: from few minutes to half an hour. Interviewed after the visit, nearly all were very pleased with the conversation with the doctor. Only one confided to be very disappointed, regarding the way she had been treated.

---

[2] Lazarsfeld (1958), for example, was the inventor of the *sociometric* survey, which links the individuals being studied to their friends, relatives, neighbours, co-workers and the social network generally. Because individuals' behaviour and attitudes must be related to the social contexts in which they live and work, reflecting Lazarsfeld's theoretical awareness of the socially situated nature of human actions. Finally, an important part of (for example) sociological theory (see Gouldner, Dalton, Becker, Goffman, Garfinkel, Cicourel) is based on research conducted on a few cases or even on haphazard or convenience samples (see Gobo, 2008b).

In this description, the researcher 'counts' (8 people), 'measures' (around 30 minutes), 'classifies' (elderly and young patients) and 'scales' (very pleased, very disappointed). This note shows that 'measuring', 'counting', 'scaling' and 'classifying' social instances and sequences are just different-but-complementary ways of collecting, assembling and analysing data, even in qualitative research (see Becker, 1970).

The misunderstanding was to use this shared truth about the lack of rigid distinction between qualitative and quantitative to radically level the (enduring) multiple and ineradicable differences between quantitative and qualitative methods. The misunderstanding appealed especially to quantitative or post-positivistic researchers. Thus, from the 1990s onwards the term 'qualitative' has been stretched and expanded, with a consequent dilution of its original meaning into a multitude of concepts to such an extent that it encompasses almost everything. In Mixed Methods literature, 'qualitative' is now synonymous with 'interpretation', **'classification'**, 'theory and judgements' (Gorard, 2010), 'texts' (Fakis et al., 2014), 'understanding of the world', 'exploration', 'comparison', bibliographic research', 'review of the literature', 'maps and visual formats', 'definition of the research topic and levels of the analysis', 'archival research to identify variables'. In addition, the 'case study' is considered qualitative, though it has nothing to do with a specific method, being, by definition, an intensive study of a more or less bounded entity. In fact, a *survey* conducted in a specific college would entirely legitimately be a 'case study'.

The misunderstanding continues: long ago statisticians invented the 'qualitative variable' (dichotomous, dummy or categorical variables useful for regression and factor analysis). For them a qualitative activity is also 'interpreting statistical results', or the 'interpretation of rotated factors or identification and naming of multivariate clusters and dimensions'. What, in the past, was quantitative now has become qualitative. Even 'words', for Greene, Caracelli and Graham (1989, p. 256), are qualitative, in contrast with numbers.

Surprisingly, ordinary features of commonsense reasoning (making inferences, deduction and abduction) and everyday life activities (observing, watching, describing, listening to, talking, asking questions and so on) have been framed as qualitative. For example, Maxwell (2016, p. 14) talks about 'qualitative and quantitative thinking', 'qualitative and quantitative concepts'. He affirms, 'astronomy, since the time of the Greeks, has used both observational description and quantitative measurement' (2016, p. 14). However, classifying 'observation' as qualitative is misleading because, following this argument, laboratory experiments (which are based on observations) become Mixed Methods research. Consequently, everything is Mixed Methods research, which assumes a mere featureless identity, recalling Hegel's famous statement: 'the night, in which all cows are black'. However, there must be a difference between fieldwork and a vacation, ethnographers and tourists, though both observe, describe and ask questions of natives. In the same way, labelling induction and subjectivity as qualitative, and deduction and objectivity as quantitative, as Morgan (2007, p. 71, table 2) does, reverts to an obsolete and unhelpful distinction.

Removing the bug

Stretching the term 'qualitative' has left unsolved many hoary epistemological and methodological problems. As Smythe (2005) and Giddings (2006) have argued, traditional positivist pre-assumptions are still reproduced and active in most of Mixed Methods research, flirting with the ambiguity (and extended semantics) of the term 'qualitative'.

From this perspective it is misguided to continue to use the expression 'qualitative' methods. The term 'qualitative' transmits a genetic bug which continues to produce negative effects. Some suggest it would be better to abandon quantitative and qualitative descriptors in favour of other expressions, like 'multiple methods' research (Stange et al., 2006; Morse & Niehaus, 2009). On closer inspection, in social research what 'really' exist are very different research practices: the discursive interview, the focus group, the ethnography, the document analysis etc. (see Table 3.2 for a more subtle and procedures-based classification). They are so diverse that they cannot be grouped under the term 'qualitative'. Abandoning this misleading term will help to remove the genetic bug.

Reset and start over

We can summarize the above reasoning in three general arguments:

1. The traditional distinction between qualitative and quantitative research is false; in fact, we have measurement, counts, scale and classification procedures in many and different methods. In addition, as Hammersley (2018) noted, features of these two paradigms may overlap because each embraces a heterogeneous range of techniques and procedures. For this reason it would be wise to abandon the general quantitative–qualitative distinction in favour of more specific research descriptors (Bazeley, 2018a; Hammersley, 2018; Mason, 2006) and method-specific distinctions.

2. However, criticizing the polarization as crude and misleading does not lead (*pace* the view of many Mixed Methods researchers) to the conclusion that there are no differences or incompatibilities amongst the assumptions underlying different methods. Although not always so limpid and clear, in many cases the differences remain and hinder integration or mixing.
3. These residual differences do not relate to traditional distinctions between qualitative and quantitative but sharper and deeper distinctions (Sandelowski, 2014; Hammersley, 2018), embodied in different research styles, data collection practices and reasoning with the data.

Let's consider three examples to move us beyond abstractions. First, a conversation analyst has very little in common with those who do thematic analysis of discursive interviews (Silverman, 2017). Their research practices are diverse and irreconcilable. Yet both would be classified, in Mixed Methods literature, as qualitative researchers.

Second, Qualitative Comparative Analysis (QCA) is a data analysis technique, originally developed by Charles Ragin (1987, 2000), for determining which logical conclusions a data set supports. The analysis begins with listing and counting all the combinations of variables observed in the data set, followed by applying the rules of logical inference (or Boolean algebra) and truth tables to determine which descriptive inferences or implications the data supports. In this technique, social actors' intentions, meanings, motives, accounts, beliefs (the basics of any qualitative research) are narrowly considered. An ethnographer would be uncomfortable with this technique. Yet both would be classified, in Mixed Methods literature, as qualitative.

Third, Robert F. Bales (a US social psychologist specialized in small group interpersonal interaction) developed the Symlog (SYstematic Multilevel Observation of Groups) method of group observation. This method, employed in different settings (see Bales, 1950), is based on nonparticipant observation, structured by a repertory grid. The information collected is organized in a matrix, for a subsequent factor analysis. Bales' aim was measurement. In fact, his approach was strongly criticized by interactionists, discourse analysts, and conversation analysts (see, e.g., Psathas, 1995). Yet both would be classified, in Mixed Methods literature, as qualitative approaches.

These examples (among many others) show that it is necessary to reset the proposal of a (naïve) compatibility between qualitative and quantitative, and supersede the term 'qualitative'. Then, it is fundamental to start over at the level of each specific method, looking at its intrinsic nature, limits and potentials, rather than pursuing simplistic and naïve combinations of methods and techniques that replicate an unhelpful dichotomy that leads to a sort of 'epistemological bricolage'.

Method as a (specific) data builder

What is often missing or undervalued, in proposals about integrating quantitative and (so-called) qualitative aspects of methods, is the performativity of the method itself (see Chapter 3), its capacity for constructing data. That is, methods have an inner force (as with language in Austin's speech act theory): the data they produce to account for the social world are strongly inflected by the researcher, the participants, the research setting, the organizational and institutional constraints and opportunities (Gobo, 2016). This is why data collected by survey interviews, discursive interviews, focus groups, ethnographies and so on, are often different, seldom overlap and often conflict (Graffigna & Gambetti, 2015). There is a strong (but non-deterministic) link between the type of datum collected and the type of method: what a certain method captures another does not (see Becker and Geer's (1957) comparison between participant observation and conversational interviews). For this reason, integration can be reached only at the level of *specific methods* (carefully considering and balancing their diversity), not at the (general) qualitative–quantitative level.

Structures and actions/interpretative and structural

'Social research that focuses on people, organisations, institutions, culture and society often requires information on the (aggregated) individual level and the level of meso or macro contexts that surround and influence individuals' (Coleman, 1986; Fulop et al., 2009; Harkness et al., 2010). An example is the impact of societal conceptualizations of growing old on meaning in life as experienced by older people (Fung, 2013). Societal conceptualizations also affect social policy and institutions like provisions for elder care. In ontological terms this means that a main focus of such research will be on interaction between these different levels. It is not only about picturing, for example (aggregated), individual experiences on the one hand and organizational factors on the other, with scrutiny of how both levels interact only coming during data analysis. Interaction between different levels is also practised in data collection (Nico & Van der Vaart, 2012).

This underlines the importance of putting the problem statement and research question upfront rather than the method. When researchers state that their choice of methods was pragmatic and dictated by the research question the tone is sometimes apologetic, with 'pragmatic' acquiring a negative connotation (Mertens, 2003). However, in Merged Methods the decision is not so much pragmatic as ontological, reflecting the requirement for data that represents the interaction between individual action and social structure. When a 65-year-old person retires, sells their spacious house and moves to a retirement home because they feel this fits the cultural image of how an 'older person' should live, we learn much from their interpretation of that cultural image, but also from understanding the wider trends apparent when assigning cases to standardized life events like 'retirement' (Nico and Van der Vaart, 2012; Fung, 2013).

Merged Methods aim to grasp the interpretative and structural components of social phenomena through one instrument or procedure, tailoring the balance between both components to the complexity of the empirical issue. This has practical consequences for a study design and though this may look 'pragmatic' it results from the essential core interdependency between 'interpretative experience' and 'structural influences'. Tailor-made Merged Methods require creativity and thoroughness to build valid procedures (Campbell & Fiske, 1959). At the same time, because the instrument or procedure needs to be elaborated to fit the phenomenon, it is vulnerable to bias (Tourangeau et al., 2000; Harkness et al., 2010). 'Tailor-made' study designs and data collection methods risk 'over-steering' the data, through excessive flexibility or excessive selection and direction. Avoiding these risks requires ample attention to classical data collection issues like interview style, question wording and so on (e.g., Schuman & Presser, 2000; Sudman et al., 2010). Data quality controls are a *lingua franca* between Mixed and Merged Methods.

Interpretative study elements also profit from the Survey Methods literature on steering and unintended bias (e.g., Maynard et al., 2002; Harkness et al., 2010). Valuing rich and authentic data does not excuse systematic attention to potential sources of bias in study design or methods. More research on the impact of study design and data collection procedures on the quality of qualitative study outcomes would be welcome (Moerman, 2010, p. 7). Likewise, social survey studies can learn from interpretative methods to gather more, and more diverse, meaning from questionnaire and scalar data (Holstein & Gubrium, 1995; Kvale, 2006; Hammersley, 2008). Merged Methods seek to benefit from the assets of both interpretative and structural approaches, while minimizing the weaknesses of each.

Two (complementary) ways to integration: mixed and merged

There are (at least) two ways to integration:

1. mixed (amalgamated or blended); and
2. merged.

In the mixed option, methods remain separate, distinctive and autonomous. Like a fruit salad, where you can still see and recognize the different fruits (methods). However, in the merged option, the integration is full, like a smoothie, where the differences disappear and the single fruit (method) is no longer traceable. The merged option yields a new tool, a new technique, a new product, a unique method, really reaching the 'equal status' or 'pure mixed' desired by Johnson, Onwuegbuzie and Turner (2007, p. 123).

The 'merged' choice aims at a *fusion* (music metaphor), a *creole* (linguistic metaphor), a *hybrid* (technology metaphor) or a *merger* (business and corporation metaphor) between methods. For example survey and discursive interviews can merge in the 'Intervey' and in 'Event History Calendar' techniques (Chapter 6); ethnography and scaling can be fused in the 'mystery shopper' instrument; group interviews and surveys can be unified in the 'Delphi Method' (Chapter 5). Many other Merged Methods exist in the literature (see Part Two). Doubtless, the methodological imagination (Smith, 1975) could invent many other new methods and techniques.

Why 'merged' methods can overcome some of the weaknesses of 'mixed' methods

If (after decades of Mixed Method research, experimentation and debate) the integration pursued by the 'mixed' strategy is still elusive, perhaps it indicates that this approach represents a very difficult mission. In fact, this (traditional) way of pursuing integration seems quite problematic, as leading scholars from outside the Mixed Methods community, such as Hammersley and Atkinson (1983, p. 199), Blaikie (1991), Flick (1992), Silverman (1993, pp 156-158, 2000, p. 99), Mason (1996), Howe (2004), Denzin and Lincoln (2005) have pointed out from various points of view.

Hence, it remains uncertain whether Mixed Methods really keeps its promise to 'provide a better understanding of a research problem than either qualitative or quantitative research alone' (Creswell, 2011b, p. 270). As Tashakkori and Teddlie (2003b) themselves admit, the added value of Mixed Methods seems to be more a dogma than an empirically proven statement. John Madge's old reflection about methodology seems also to fit Mixed Methods research quite well: 'it must be admitted that there can be something rather stultifying in concentrating on methods of investigation, so that there is almost a negative correlation between the rigor of methods and the importance of results' (1962, p. 147). Later, Berger (2002) criticized sociology for falling foul of 'methodological fetishism'.

Bryman (2007), too, was uncertain about Mixed Methods research. In his Content Analysis of 232 Mixed Methods research social science articles (published between 1994 and 2003), he showed that the rationales that are given for employing a Mixed Methods research approach and the ways it is used in practice do not always correspond. In addition, only in 10 articles out of 232 (4.3%) was there a clear indication that qualitative and quantitative methods had each been deployed to answer to specific and different research questions.

In addition, O'Cathain, Murphy and Nicholl (2007), after examining 81 studies, note that:

> only 21% mentioned any integration of their findings; 28% were found to integrate findings somewhat. What the overall analysis showed was, in fact, that integration of qualitative with quantitative findings was not a common occurrence, especially at the publication stage. In addition, it was difficult to discern exactly how two different methods – qualitative and quantitative – were used overall, leading the researchers to conclude that there was a lack of reflexivity with regard to just how the use of two different methods added synergy to the research project. (Quoted in Hesse-Biber, 2015, p. 779)

After decades, the difficulties about integration remain unresolved. Should we continue to insist on (traditional) integration or might it be better to recognize its flaws and limited contribution, and attempt another approach, pursuing a different idea of integration? Because a Merged Method has the potential to be more consistent and better integrated, posing fewer problems both in terms of data collection and analysis, we think that in many studies there would be added value in merging *selected* methods rather than simply mixing them.

The challenges with which data integration presents Mixed Methods include how to incorporate findings from earlier cycles of data collection into the next cycle of data collection in sequential research designs. Research designs with multiple phases also present challenges of time, cost and maintaining stakeholder relationships, all things for which Merged Methods offer solutions. According to the Mixed Methods Research Association's task force on the future of Mixed Methods, other issues include: 'How can researchers integrate quantitative and qualitative thinking at all levels of the research study, that is, at the philosophical and theoretical levels, for data collection and analysis, and for reporting and use? How can the Mixed Methods community provide a supportive environment for creative thinking and the emergence of new methodological combinations?' (Mertens et al., 2016). Respectfully, we believe that Merged Methods not only address quantitative–qualitative integration but offer new methodological combinations that exactly represent the creative solutions the task force called for.

Steps towards 'merged epistemology'

A genuine third approach (i.e., a network of assumptions, beliefs and practices that guide a specific research community in selecting research questions and methods) can arise by merging the main or essential principles of the two epistemologies traditionally linked to qualitative and quantitative approaches. From the former these are *phenomenology* (Alfred Schutz), *interactionism* (Herbert Blumer), *constructivism* (Bruno Latour), *enactivism* (Francisco Varela, Karl Weick) and their followers; from the latter, recent forms of soft realism/objectualism such as *transcendental or critical realism* (Roy Bhaskar), *moderate realism* (Willard Van Orman Quine and D. M. Armstrong), *agential realism* (Karen Barad), *dialectical realism* (Ian Hacking), *internal realism* (Hilary Putnam). These two sets of worldviews are distinct from their respective cognates: relativism and realism/positivism.

This third approach epistemology merges (only) the main principles of the quantitative and qualitative approaches, such that they are treated as reciprocally compatible and integrable in a unique epistemological stance. The main/essential principles are:

- social reality is not a simply out-there entity, but a circular and reflexive material–symbolic construction made by people, technologies and contexts/environments, in a continuous feedback of feedbacks;
- the social environment is not an external fixed entity, but is selectively and continuously created through people's capacities to interact with the world;
- researchers produce only findings, not a complete picture (of the phenomenon or reality), because the observer's perspective is always partial;
- reality is meaningful only if we consider it in conjunction with people's sense-making, through which they impose order on the chaotic flow of information and experiences that come from the environment;
- organizations are not external and static entities characterized by 'objective' properties, but are entities constantly built and reconstructed by organizational actors who construct (enact) their environments, by creating cognitive maps, and producing meaning, reinventing (objectifying) organizations;
- the environment of an organization does not exist independently of the organization and is constantly being built and rebuilt by those who collect information, make decisions, and act;
- cognition is not the representation of a pre-given world by a pre-given mind, but is rather the enactment of a world and a mind on the basis of a unique, individual history of the variety of actions that a human being in the world performs;
- cognition is situated and embodied;

- meanings are not simply in people's heads but arise in the context of behaviour and data collection practices;
- the interaction has a socio-linguistic and 'situated' character;
- a pragmatic theory of truth is adopted, i.e., a theory in which truth is what it is epistemically right to believe;
- the aim of any inquiry involves taking the actors' point of view, while incorporating contextual and structural influences and analysing processes (and outcomes) instead of structures, avoiding the determinism of predicting behaviour from socio-demographic features like class, gender, race and so on.

Consequently, from a strictly methodological perspective, Merged Method researchers orient their inquiries by pursuing and applying the following practical criteria:

- data (opinions, attitudes and behaviours) are co-constructed (with research participants and methods) rather than being fixed and pre-existing entities located in people's minds or actions that researchers simply collect;
- therefore, data are always relational and interactional outcomes;
- methods predetermine the way the world is assembled;
- it is better to abandon the concept of validity (truth-value) when working with data such as attitudes and opinions, in favour of the concept of fidelity (see Chapter 3);
- the researcher's orientation is not to find an out-there truth but to create the best (social and relational) conditions for gathering information;
- all social actors under study are participants (not objects or subjects);
- the main aim is to guarantee participants' free expression; for this reason the classical questionnaire offering only fixed-choice response alternatives to respondents is inadequate (see Chapter 6);
- researchers' active listening should be pursued; hence, standardization of the interviewer's behaviour must be avoided (see Chapter 6);
- results/findings are interpretations, which should be transparent, i.e., showing how they were derived, the assumptions that were made and their limits.

Conclusion

The proposal for a single epistemology may resemble the neo-positivist idea of the unification of all sciences under a single methodology. However, neo-positivists attempted to make the social sciences conform to the physical and natural sciences by importing their methods (mainly experimental observation and statistical analysis). Instead, the Merged Methods proposal is confined to bringing together only the social sciences, basing them on an interactionist and constructivist perspective expressed in research designs that construct a common methodological framework.

3

MERGED METHODOLOGY: A RATIONALE FOR MERGED METHODS

In order to bridge the two different philosophical approaches or paradigms (represented by the shorthand of 'quantitative' or 'qualitative') and construct a real third approach (an 'independent methodology', just as it was in the intentions, not fully accomplished, of Tashakkori and Teddlie, 1998), after having constructed a common *epistemological* background, the next step involves the construction of a common *methodological* framework.

To do this it is certainly important (as already stated by several authors) to overcome the conventional binary classification of qualitative and quantitative methods. However, this overcoming must take place in a complete, organic and systematic way; and should not stop simply at the joint use of those methods within the same research.

In other words, it is also necessary to overcome the languages, concepts and mental models of the two approaches. To use an example from gender studies, the complexity and articulation of gender identity cannot be understood if the dichotomy between male and female remains the point of reference. In the same way, a 'third approach' can be constituted if also the methodological (and not only epistemological) foundations of the quantitative and qualitative approaches are questioned and replaced by a different methodological language, constructed by melting and fusing the previous two; retaining what is good in them and eliminating the rest.

This merging could take place by revitalizing (attributing new and different meanings) conventional terms and embedding them in a unique methodology. Because, as the pragmatist philosopher John Dewey (1938) pointed out, the logic of social-scientific research is unique and always follows the same criteria of scientific validation and the same general procedural steps: formulation of the problem, conceptualization, construction of the empirical base, and analysis and interpretation of the data.

Hence, it is possible to reconcile the quantitative and qualitative divide by developing a single framework; not, however, from a neo-positivist point of view, but from a phenomenological and constructivist one. On the one hand, by suggesting a new classification of social research methods, where this old dichotomy disappears. On the other, envisioning a conceptual constellation, where old terms (such as 'hypothesis', 'indicator', 'variable', 'measurement', 'operationalization', 'sampling', 'generalization' etc.) can acquire new meanings (as frequently happens in the history of ideas) compatible with a merged epistemology. These alternative meanings are not entirely new, as they can be detected in some of the most influential and authoritative voices associated with 'qualitative' methods (e.g., Anselm Strauss, Barney Glaser, Aaron V. Cicourel) and 'quantitative' (e.g., Paul F. Lazarsfeld, Rensis Likert, Johan Galtung, Alberto Marradi).

Too little has been done so far, within Mixed Methods, to achieve this 'conceptual' integration. With the exception of praiseworthy attempts (Hammersley, 1987 on 'validity' and 'reliability', Hammersley, 2008 on 'triangulation', Hammersley, 2010 on 'measurement', Maxwell, 2012 on 'causality'), most Mixed Methods scholars have accepted the received view, without questioning its constellation of terms and concepts. Hence, in most of the Mixed Methods literature, we continue to use terms and implement concepts (such as 'sampling', 'measurement', 'triangulation', 'validation' etc.) in a positivist way.

Revitalizing old terms by attributing new meanings

In Mixed Methods literature, it is common to find an intensive use of the terms just mentioned, which qualitative researchers consider as old-fashioned concepts and remnants of positivistic approaches. There is some truth in that. However, it is possible to divert (instead of abandoning) these terms from both the positivist ideology and the prejudices of qualitative researchers, changing their customary meanings, presenting them in a new framework, showing their 'natural' pervasiveness in any form of social research.

According to Maxwell's spirit: 'the main *value* of mixed method research ... is in creating a dialogue between different ways of seeing, interpreting, and knowing, not simply in combining different methods and types of data' (2010, p. 478).

'Topics', not research 'objects'

A first step in moving away from a positivistic mentality and embracing a moderate constructivism[1] is to use the term research 'topic' (i.e., concepts) rather than the conventional 'object', because the world is populated more with concepts than objects. For example, if we do research on family studies, we will recognize that a family is a much less palpable object than is commonly believed. When researchers try to define theoretically what constitutes a family (in order to later select a sample of families to interview), they realize that their own beliefs have a tremendous effect on its definition: is a group of monks or of students living under the same roof a family? Is a gay couple a family? Must there be a couple for a family to exist or can separated or divorced people (with children) also be defined as families? In the past, 'family' meant the union between two people of opposite sex (i.e., a heterosexual couple) formalized by a marriage ceremony. Today the *concept* of family is very different (and also contested) and extends to include many other types of relationship. As can be seen, the 'family' is more a matter of discourse rather than an object in the world (Holstein & Gubrium, 1999); hence, the social and political construction of the object 'family' is an important factor in how it is commonly understood and, even, how it is operationalized by researchers.

So, what we call (materialistically) 'objects' are, in fact, concepts, topics, or discourse accomplishments shaped by researchers' negotiations and theoretical assumptions which, in their turn, are a mixture of commonsense and scientific knowledge. Rejecting both 'objectualism' and 'idealism', social phenomena are primarily ideas, which *become* objects through research practices; but their inner nature is conceptual and discursive.

---

[1] Fielding (2009) made a similar argument about 'moderate postmodernism', which in certain respects can be reconciled with 'triangulation', moving towards a position less concerned with convergent validation and more concerned to create greater analytic density and conceptual richness.

'Attributes' (of a concept), not 'properties' or 'characteristics'

It follows that the concepts are composed of attributes, not properties or characteristics. Let's consider the example shown in Box 3.1, from the history of biology.

Box 3.1 Why mammals are called mammals

In the tenth edition of *System Naturae* (1758), the Swedish botanist Linnaeus introduced the term Mammalia (which means 'with the breast') to indicate the species (that, after him, we know as mammals) previously known, following Aristotle, as 'quadrupeds'. In naming this species as 'mammals', Linnaeus considered only one (the breasts) of the few properties common among mammals, that one which fully fits the females of that species only.

The historian of biology Schiebinger (1993) proposed five possible equivalent and alternative terms that Linnaeus could have chosen (but he did not): Pilosa (who have hair) or Aurecaviga (who have ear pits), or Lactentia (breastfeeding) or Sugentia (who suck), or Vivipora ('rearing of young'). However, Linnaeus' choice was embedded in the process of cultural eroticization of the female breast, which right in those years came to its fulfilment, with visible accomplishments in the history of clothing.

In addition, Linnaeus was also politically engaged in a socio-cultural battle (in which he had just been involved) against the increasing habit of women of the upper classes to give their babies to nurses for breastfeeding (1993, p. 66). He believed that 'mercenary' breastfeeding was a social catastrophe, while breastfeeding was a natural law. This battle hid Linnaeus' more general dislike for the female emancipation, although he was probably not aware of the political belief embodied in his classification.

This historical example, among the hundreds we could exhibit, demonstrates that the features of a concept are *attributes*, that is subjective ascriptions rather than objectively discovered characteristics or 'properties' (as argued also by Glaser and Strauss, 1967, pp. 23, 36–39, 55–58, 106–109, 193, 248–249), terms that fit with an ontological epistemology. These features are not (independent) components of a (supposed 'out there') thing or object that a researcher has only to register. They are 'cognitive instruments', which always result from a discretionary operation performed by the researcher. Hence, the term *attribute* more clearly conveys the idea that researchers work with *concepts* and *attributes* as constructively constituted features of them.

Operationalization: what is it and why do we need it?

'Operationalization' is another term rejected by qualitative researchers because it is a vestigial holdover from logical positivism. They are right on this. However, by doing so, the risk is 'to throw the baby out with the bathwater'. Looking strictly at the semantics of these (considered) positivist terms, it is possible to regain/attribute to them a different (more constructivist) meaning related to the formal properties of human reasoning. It is also important to notice a distinction between 'operationalization' (which has a more circumscribed, set meaning, one that aims to insulate it from changes arising from the contingencies of data collection) and 'operational' (practical).

The research work of social scientists consists mainly in making sense of observed events through classifying them from their point of view (hence, it is a construction). For example, on observing the way that nursing staff at many rest homes keep the elderly residents in bed for as long as possible, a social scientist may ask why they do so.

This behaviour may be a 'sign of status' (Glaser & Strauss, 1967, pp. 23, 83–85, 210) or a *clue* to:

(a) the nursing staff's concern for the well-being of the elderly residents;
(b) the existence of practices designed to achieve greater social control;
(c) an organizational response to a shortage of staff.

The relation between the event and the three different concepts (explanations, therefore causes) takes the form of a *relationship of indication*, where the event is *evidence* for the presence of a particular concept. This logic is not a prerogative of scientific reasoning; rather, it is a formal property of commonsense reasoning. In other words, when social actors (researchers included) interpret behaviour, they constantly – often unawares – connect together concepts and attributes, indicators and variables. Interpretation is nothing other than the rapid, tacit and recurrent activation of relationships of indication.

Operational practices

Operational practices consist of the set of conventions that guide the researcher's interpretative activity. They are called *operational* (in order to distinguish them from the *lexical* ones usually found in dictionaries) because it tells researchers what to do: that is to say, it has a practical intent. Hence, through these conventions, the status of each case on the attribute X is determined, assigned to one of the categories established (coding), and recorded so that it can be analysed using the techniques that researchers intend to employ. Many of these conventions are customs, which guide the knowledge-gathering process. Among these customs are the procedures used to gain access to the field, the devices (guarantees, informal contracts) employed to overcome actors' potential diffidence, the way in which information and notes are collected, and the procedures followed in order to check the truthfulness of the replies delivered by participants.

Operational practice helps researchers to discipline the observation, the information-gathering and the attributes that they deem to be connected to the topic studied, within a relationship of indication. In other words, operational practice adds rigor to data collection.

The expression 'operational definition of a concept' comes from the quantitative approach. However, in qualitative approaches one can also find a parallel (amended) conceptual framework. Particularly Glaser and Strauss talked extensively about relating dimensions, concepts, categories and properties (1967, pp. 23, 36–39, 55–58, 106–109, 193, 248–249). Although they and Denzin (1969) recommended that the operational definition of the concept be developed only *after* the research has begun (when the researcher has obtained an initial understanding of the phenomenon and 'the situated meaning of concepts is discovered' [1969, p. 925]), there is nothing to stop the researcher from developing it *before* the research starts, if they already have specific hypotheses to check. Indeed, they should be explicit about any preconceptions.

Operational practice represents a cognitive activity that is unique to science and which distinguishes it from other knowledge-gathering endeavours. Other cognitive activities found in science (such as formulating hypotheses, sampling, generalizing, drawing comparisons, making forecasts, checking the veracity of statements, etc.) are also present in commonsense reasoning. However, operationalization is not so present (or, at least, is very rare). It enables us to 'problematize the observation' (Cicourel, 1964, p. 128), *de-naturalize* the social world that we are investigating, in contrast to the behaviour of the member who observes it as natural, obvious, taken-for-granted, normal; what Schutz called the 'epoché of the natural attitude'.

Rescue the variable!

Qualitative researchers have also been much opposed to the use of variables, believing that research should not be impeded by such restraints. However, indicators and variables could have a refreshed meaning. In fact, variables are also part of common-sense reasoning as (previously seen for) indicators; variables, too, are constantly present in our discourses and thoughts. Consider the following verbal exchange between Amanda and two friends, eating a cake in the cafeteria:

Amanda: How's the cake?
Bernie: So so.
Carl: For me it's quite good.

What difference is there between this evaluation and a Likert-like 4 points scale (*very good/fairly good/fairly bad/very bad*) commonly used in questionnaires? None. Hence, there is space for a refreshed meaning of 'variable', alternative to the positivist mindset.

Glaser and Strauss (1967, pp. 205–210, 211–220, 245–249) deal at length with variables in a new and a non-positivist way. In addition, Strauss and Corbin, when talking about their researches on chronic diseases, write: 'One can conceptualize this dimension as pertaining to the property of **degree of intensity**. Pain can vary along a continuum of degree from very bad (severe) to not so bad (mild) ... Is it continuous, intermittent, or temporary?' (1990, p. 205, bold in the original). Previously, in their book, on representing properties and dimensions graphically, they ended up with the schema depicted in Table 3.1, which closely recalls the Lazarsfeldian framework (to which even Glaser and Strauss [1967, p. 23, note 3 and pp. 190–1933] explicitly refer).

It is within this mindset that one can comprehend (without misinterpreting) Blumer's criticism of 'variable analysis'. He did not criticize the use of variables in itself, but rather its standardized usage. Indeed, he mentioned three kinds of 'generic variables' useful for social research and stated: 'obviously the study of human groups calls for a wide range of variables' (1956, p. 683). In contrast, his criticism related to the automatic use of the same operational definition for any research: 'each of these variables, even though a class term, has substance only in a given historical context. The variables do not stand directly for items of abstract human group life' (p. 684).

The conventional distinction between thinking of the world in terms of variables and correlations, and (at the opposite) in terms of events and processes, holds neither in theory nor in practice. It is *just* a matter of ideological and identity contrapositions.

Indeed, if we analyse the work of ethnographers without too many ideological prejudices, we find that they use indicators (Glaser & Strauss, 1967, p. 23, ch. III and IV, p. 210) and variables to distinguish among statuses on attributes. The point is shown by Geertz's famous analysis of Balinese cockfighting (see Box 3.2).

Table 3.1 The link between category, properties and dimensional range

Category	Properties	Dimensional range (applied to each incident)	
Watching	Frequency	Often	----------------------------- Never
	Extent	More	----------------------------- Less
	Intensity	High	----------------------------- Low
	Duration	Long	----------------------------- Short

Source: Strauss and Corbin, 1990, pp. 72 and 101–102

Box 3.2   Indicators and variables in Balinese cockfights

Clifford Geertz studied the clandestine bets wagered on cockfights in Bali. He watched a total of 57 cockfights and constructed the meaning of the practice, the logic of betting and other details. He then classified the clandestine bets (using a dichotomous variable) as 'deep' and 'shallow'. In the former, usually 'the amounts of money are great [as opposed to smaller amounts of money wagered in shallow games], much more is at stake than material gain: namely, esteem, honor, dignity, respect – in a word ... status. It is at stake symbolically, for (a few cases of ruined addict gamblers aside) no one's status is actually altered by the outcome of a cockfight' (1972, p. 433).

How could a deep game be distinguished from a shallow one? How could the observer know that one type of situation rather than the other was in progress? What was it that differentiated between the two types of game? Geertz lists 17 'facts' (p. 473) – that we can straightforwardly call indicators – for the presence of a deep game. The first of these indicators was 'kin loyalty': 'A man virtually never bets against a cock owned by a member of his own kingroup. Usually he will feel obliged to bet for it, the more so the closer the kin tie and the deeper the fight. If he is certain in his mind that it will not win, he may just not bet at all, particularly if it is only a second cousin's bird or if the fight is a shallow one. But as a rule he will feel he must support it and, in deep games, nearly always does' (1972, p. 437).

By the way, first cousin or second cousin, and so on, are just statuses on the variable 'kingroup'! Had he so wished, Geertz could also have constructed a grid showing the frequency of each of the 17 indicators. For example, he could have associated the indicator 'kin loyalty' with the variable 'betting against a kinsman's cock', and then added the following alternative responses: 'never', 'sometimes', 'often'. A systematic observation might have shown that (for instance) there was kin loyalty in 95% of cases, or in only 72%. The latter finding would have made a major difference to assessment of the level of the community's compliance with the kin loyalty convention – which at first sight had seemed unwavering.

This is not new. As Maxwell writes:

> Becker (1970), Erickson (2007), Hammersley (1992), and Miles and Huberman (1984) have supported the inclusion of numerical data in qualitative research practices and reports" (2010, p. 476). Becker (1970) argues "qualitative researchers frequently make quantitative claims in verbal form, using terms such as *many, often, typically, sometimes* and so on. He argued that numbers have the value of making such claims more precise and coined the term *quasi statistics* for simple counts of things to support terms such as *some, usually* and *most* (Maxwell 2010, p. 476).
>
> Becker (1970) states that all analysis is implicitly numerical. Sandelowski, Voils and Knafl (2009) made a similar point about 'quantitizing' qualitative data, stating that this is done in qualitative research 'to facilitate pattern recognition or otherwise to extract meaning from qualitative data, account for all data, document analytic moves, and verify interpretations' (p. 210, quoted in Maxwell, 2010, p. 476).

In summary, the operational practice transforms the indicators (relative to the attributes of a concept) into variables. A variable is, therefore, the outcome of the operational definition – its terminal; the device with which the researcher collects information or analyses their ethnographic notes. Indicators and variables are, therefore, two sides of the same coin: the indicator is situated at the conceptual level, while the variable pertains to the practical one. Just like a coin has a national symbol on one side (such as the head of a historical figure) and a number on the other side, denoting its relative value. Variables serve to detect differences and communicate them. The main difference from qualitative research is (recalling Blumer) the standardized use of these devices.[2] Unlike survey and experimental researchers, qualitative researchers do not reify, objectify or standardize their devices, using them always in the same way in all their research. Instead, qualitative researchers construct their devices situationally, finding *ad hoc* remedies for each research problem.

---

[2] Of course, the variable sometimes could impose some restraints with respect to the category/indicator. The latter could have boundary overlap (between two or more categories). Usually, a variable doesn't act like that because if there is a boundary the thing on the other side of it is a variable that is equally self-contained (discrete). However, this issue should be addressed from time to time, practically, depending on the type of category. This is the case we are faced with in *fuzzy sets*, whose elements have degrees of membership.

Inventing hypotheses

Another common misconception about qualitative research is that it approaches a research topic without any hypotheses and, instead, tries to understand and describe phenomena better (Agar, 1986, p. 12).

Apart from the fact that, as Silverman ironically points out, 'qualitative research would look a little odd, after a history of over 100 years, if it had no hypotheses to test!' (2000, p. 8), making hypotheses and understanding/describing are not in conflict but complementary, because they are grounded in the same logical reasoning that we routinely use, often unconsciously.

Moving on to a more formal level, from a *methodological point of view*, a hypothesis is an assertion – conjectural in nature – about the relationships between certain attributes in a research topic. *From an operational point of view*, a hypothesis is an assertion about the relationships between two or more variables that produces an observable expected outcome.

Glaser and Strauss (1967, pp. 83, 194ff, 230, 241), Schatzman and Strauss (1973, pp. 12–13, 53, 57, 76), Strauss and Corbin (1990, pp. 107, 108, 111–113, 148, 253) argue that hypotheses are indispensable for research; though these should be formulated and tested only *after* the ethnographic notes have been collected (inductive hypotheses) so that the researcher goes into the field without preconceived ideas, on the basis of a 'blank canvas' (i.e., the researcher should enter the field with no preconceptions about the topic they were researching). However, this principle is impossible to achieve because no social phenomenon worthy of investigation comes without the researcher having some ideas about it. The important thing is that preconceptions are treated as falsifiable, just like the analysis that will come later, once data are gathered.

Unlike Hymes (1978), Silverman (1993, p. 44) and Yin (1984, pp. 29–35) maintain that ethnographers can perfectly well conduct a hypothesis-oriented ethnography, provided that they already have a good level of knowledge about the culture that they are studying.

Whether hypotheses are more or less specified and formalized also depends on the amount of knowledge that the researcher possesses. Based on our level of confidence in our expectations we may design *working* or *guiding* hypotheses.

Drawing models

Models are graphical representations of hypotheses, as we can see in some charts produced by textual analysis software.

A hypothesis may be descriptive, when it states the existence of a relationship between two attributes or variables without specifying its direction; or it may be directional and explanatory, suggesting a causal relationship (e.g., A → B). For example, Strauss, Schatzman, Buchner, Ehrlich and Sabshin (1964) conducted an empirical study on the rules and informal agreements present in various psychiatric hospitals. They then constructed a causal model in which the differences among the rules applied at the hospitals were explained by the existence of different patient care practices. However, these practices were, in their turn, conditioned by the professional models learned at different schools by the hospital staff and which reflected different psychiatric ideologies. Other models can be found in Glaser and Strauss (1967) illustrating the 'social loss' phenomenon, or in Strauss and Corbin (1990, p. 222) about the relationship among body, biography and trajectory.

Maxwell has persuasively shown, unlike many qualitative researchers who believe that causation is an inappropriate concept in qualitative research, that thinking in terms of causality (besides being part of everyday reasoning) is highly compatible with qualitative research; the latter, due to its capacity to focus actions and meanings, could enlighten us about causal *processes* much better than conventional quantitative research. In addition, he points out: 'if you want to work against injustice and oppression, you need to understand the *causes* of the particular forms of injustice and oppression you are dealing with, and how to counteract and overcome these causes' (2012, p. 658).

The relationship between variables may take various forms: a simple association or correlation, a symmetric relation, or an asymmetric relation such as causation. We must be careful, in the social sciences, with regard to making claims about causation. Causal relations require, in fact, more than the evidence of correlations because, at the very least, the researcher must be able to identify the cause and the effect, where the cause precedes the effect in time, and must be able to exclude the intervention of other factors ('counterfactuals'). It is evident that it is very hard to have enough information to satisfy both these requirements simultaneously. Also because, far from determinism and mechanistic visions about the straight line relationship between cause and effect, in an over-time perspective an effect can retroact on the cause in an inter-dependence relationship. For instance, a bad effect can lead to an adjustment in the cause so as to avoid it having a bad effect the next time; as the case of a strict imprisonment policy for minor acts of delinquency that makes prisoners more committed criminals can lead to relaxing the policy of strict imprisonment by replacing imprisonment with rehabilitation programmes. As well as in Labov's model of reading failures, some effects can feed back on some causes (Figure 3.1).

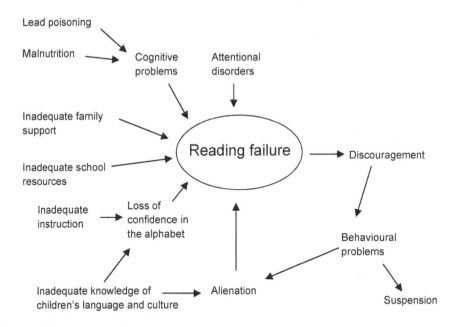

Figure 3.1 Some causes of reading failure.
(*Source*: Labov, 2006)

Of course, we know (and have done so for a long time) that reality is more complex than a model can depict. In the 1930s, Alfred H. S. Korzybski stated this principle in a frequently abused quote: 'a map is not the territory' (1933, p. 58). Later, Solomon W. Golomb, referring to mathematical modelling, put it nicely: confusing a model with reality would be like going to a restaurant and eating the menu.

However, notwithstanding the greater complexity of reality, we should not abandon modelling because it makes the complexity more understandable. The simplest theories are usually the ones most successful in communicating such complexity.

Spurious associations

Spurious associations are widely neglected in qualitative research methodology. However, they are very common in both commonsense reasoning and social theory; consequently, many research findings are trapped by them, affected by ecological fallacy (Robinson, 1950; Cicourel, 1996): we could believe that A -> B, but this is an illusion because both A and B are influenced by C, an intervening variable (or 'intervening condition' in Strauss and Corbin, 1990, pp. 86, 102–104, 151–152), which we have not considered, as the following example shows.

Box 3.3 Case study: Closed-circuit television (CCTV) and crime

The methodologist Ray Pawson and the criminologist Nick Tilley describe the following case. Closed-circuit television (CCTV) is installed in a car park and a decrease in car thefts is noted. At first sight, politicians and decision-makers could believe that there is a cause/effect relation between a given action and the subsequent social change, that the introduction of CCTV (A) has produced the decrease in thefts (B). However, it is unlikely that television cameras in themselves possess this magical power: 'there is nothing about CCTV in car parks which intrinsically inhibits car crime' (1997, p. 78). Hence, the reduction in car theft could have little to do with CCTV. Instead, the concomitance of specific conditions is necessary for them to be really effective:

1. There should be someone (a police officer, security guard, etc.) who observes the images transmitted by the CCTV cameras in real time and is able to intervene immediately. Otherwise a thief wearing a balaclava or a hood concealing his face can act undisturbed, without the risk of being identified.
2. The CCTV cameras should be linked to a police station situated in the immediate vicinity so that the police can intervene immediately.
3. There should be no obstacles (pillars, guard rails, etc.) blocking the camera sightlines and behind which the thief is able to act unobserved: but this only happens in the case of open-air car parks.
4. The car park should be well lit; otherwise, the camera images will not be sharply defined and thieves will be more difficult to identify.
5. Car thieves from other towns (even a considerable distance away) may be unconcerned about the presence of CCTV. Their faces are often not in the local police force's files (which contain photographs of local criminals), so that there is little risk of their being recognized. In fact, this type of criminal is different from a terrorist or serial killer, whose photographs are displayed in all police stations.

If these conditions (and many others – see Pawson and Tilley,1997, pp. 78ff) are not in place, CCTV in itself may be ineffectual. Instead, the decline in car crime may (also) have been due to many factors. For instance, the presence of CCTV cameras may have:

- induced car owners to lock their vehicles: their carelessness might be recorded on film, and some insurance companies do not reimburse careless policy holders;
- increased traffic in the car park, thus increasing social control: if it becomes widely known that CCTV has been installed in a car park, so that people consider it more secure, there may be more users, and therefore greater social control. Thieves will consequently be deterred.

The deception of spurious association is often lying in wait, and it is not always easy to avoid. However, if the reasoning is extended to include spurious associations, the research becomes more complex and difficult, but also more interesting and counter-intuitive because it makes our explanations much less ingenuous, our theories more refined and social research more credible.

Measurement: a rare achievement in social sciences

In Mixed Method literature the terms 'measures' and 'measurement' (and their positivistic imprinting and use) are still largely diffuse. Both in research papers and theoretical essays (e.g., Howe, 1988), especially those related to research designs (Wheeldon, 2010; Creswell & Plano Clark, 2011, ch. 3; Luyt, 2012; Daigneault & Jacob, 2014; Sedoglavichet al., 2015; Urban et al., 2015; Howell Smith et al., 2020). This is also a consequence of the 'bricolage methodology', embedded in the pragmatist approach (see Chapter 2) so dominant in Mixed Methods, which claims to measure anything. So much so that many researchers speak without reservation of 'ordinal measurement', and even of 'nominal measurement'.

However, as Hammersley points out, 'adopting a pragmatic approach does not mean treating whatever we find we *can* do as *good enough*, as if what is possible determines what is necessary' (2010, p. 414). Consequently, this (subtle positivistic) approach confuses measurement with counting, using numbers with measurements, and the term 'measurement' is used to indicate extremely different processes (Marradi, 1981). Hence, 'bricolage methodology' neglects other important epistemological, methodological and technical problems related to measurement.

In social sciences the term 'measurement' has undergone a progressive 'semantic stretching of the original meaning coming from physical sciences, where we speak of classifying, counting, ordering, and not only, obsessively, of measuring' (Marradi, 1981, p. 597). In fact, it is only in the social sciences that we speak of *ordinal* and *nominal* measurement.

At the origin of the semantic dilution of the term 'measurement', there is certainly the (positivist) aspiration of social sciences to a 'scientific' status, similar to that of physical and natural sciences; without questioning the effective applicability of this concept in the social sciences.

In the physical sciences, the concept of 'measurement' is quite clear:

it is the process by which the magnitude of a property X (owned by an object A) is compared with the magnitude of the same property owned by the instrument-unit, chosen conventionally to measure the property X (unit of measure). The instrument is the unit of a numerical scale and the measurement converts a certain property into numeric symbols (multiples of that unit). E.g., if object A has 10 times more of the X property than the unit of measurement does, then A has '10 units'. (Marradi, 1981, p. 597)

Measuring means establishing, by comparison, how many times the unit of measurement is contained in the quantity to be measured.

Objects

From a measurement perspective, in the world there exist two kinds of 'objects' (although it is more epistemologically adequate to refer to 'concepts'). These objects possess two different properties (or attributes): *continuous vs discrete.*

Continuous is a property that has an infinite number of statuses (on the property itself), subtly different from each other; hence, there is no outright 'jump' between one status and another, and differences between them are difficult to discern. For instance, the object 'income' belongs to this category: if one person earns £1,264 and another £1,265, there is no obvious 'jump' between the two statuses; these two different numbers are adjacent along a continuum, as a straight line. Time, space, height, age, income, authoritarianism etc. are objects, which belong to this species. In addition, these numbers are 'real' because further divisible into smaller quantities (e.g., £1,264.13).

In contrast, a discrete property has a finite number of distinct statuses (on the property itself): education, vote, religion, gender, publications, children etc. fall in this category. In fact, there is no dot or comma with which to divide them. Hence, a key problem here concerns whether the object-properties to be measured have the character that is demanded by metric measurement in other words, whether they have a quantitative structure.

On this point, it can be noted that mathematical measurements and social sciences differ irreconcilably. In fact, for mathematics, if the discrete properties are cardinal (e.g., the number of pears in a box) you can calculate the average, which can be a rational number (i.e., with decimals). This makes sense, because pears can be divided, a half pear or a quarter eaten, and exist in reality. However, from a mathematical perspective, you can also fractionate traffic accidents, smartphones and computers per capita, beds in a hospital, dead persons, children, infected persons etc.– objects that do not exist in reality. However, we often read in scientific reports that, for instance, the Rt (the basic reproduction number of an infection) has fallen in the last two weeks from 1.72 to 1.4.

Or that, in most OECD countries, the total fertility rate sits at somewhere between 1.4 and 1.9 children per woman, because in a mathematical perspective the fertility rate is a metric cardinal number, since it is the ratio between two discrete cardinals (number of children and number of women in fertility age). It is a 'real' number, with infinite possible values between 0 and infinite. All this is flawless from a mathematical point of view, but inappropriate from a sociological one.

In other words, in mathematics we compute means where in sociology we can calculate (*stricto sensu*) medians and modes only. Hence, mathematical measurement applied to the social sciences is somewhat misleading.

Conditions

According to Marradi (1981, 1985), there are two mandatory requirements to being able to measure: the presence of an object possessing a continuous property (therefore, objects holding discrete properties are not measurable) and the existence of a unit of measure (a convention). For example, time has a continuous property, a standard unit of measure for it (i.e., the second) and an instrument for measuring time (the chronometer). The same for space: the simplest measure of space is the length, whose unit of measurement is the metre, and uses the tape-measure as instrument.

Measuring versus counting

There follows from this an important distinction (often forgotten by social scientists) between measuring and counting, because these two socio-cognitive processes use two different units for calculation: respectively, a unit of measure and a unit of account (Marradi, 1985, 231–232).

However, while the latter is (somehow) 'natural' (because to enumerate children a researcher does not need special training or a particular instrument), measuring is not natural but 'conventional': in order to measure the researcher needs an operational convention and a special instrument. The practical implication is that time, space, height, age, income etc. could be measurable; but number of children, educational qualification, hospital beds, religion, gender etc. cannot be measurable, only countable (Marradi, 1981, p. 608; 1985, p. 233).

This distinction is only quirky in appearance, because treating objects with discrete properties as if they had continuous properties leads to neglect of the social dimensions of the phenomena. In other words, to possess £4 is like having two times £2. However, to have 4 children is not like having two times 2 children, because in the latter social conditions are essential: did the family have children close or distant in age? These are two different situations, which have an impact on the family management, financial resources, job conciliation policies and so on. Hence, from a socio-psychological perspective, the *number* of children has its *cardinal property only apparently* and when society (the context) enters in the mathematics and statistics will be always too late.

Further restriction to measurability: cooperation

To have an object with a continuous property is a necessary-but-not-sufficient condition for measuring it. Another (last) feature is necessary: an object (having continuous properties) is measurable if its statuses can be recorded without its (active) cooperation. For example, to measure the 'waiting time' in a hospital emergency room, the researcher does not need the cooperation of any of the participants. Only in this way can we guarantee intersubjectivity (of the measurement outcome) among researchers. This is what happens in physics and natural sciences, where the researchers do not need the cooperation of subatomic particles or biological cells.

In contrast, to register the status of other objects with continuous properties (such as opinions, attitudes, beliefs) the active collaboration of the sample is necessary: researchers have to ask questions, talk with the participants, and obtain consent. Hence, opinions, attitudes, beliefs are not measurable.

The lack of the unit of measure in social sciences

Most of the properties pertaining to social sciences, such as psychological ones expressed in opinions, attitudes or values (authoritarianism, social cohesion), have often been conceived as continuous like the measurable continuous properties. However, unlike the latter, there is no unit of measurement for the former. For this reason, Cicourel (1964, pp. 18–22) stressed that it is very difficult to talk of measurements in the social sciences because their concepts, unlike those of the physical sciences, do not have corresponding definitions (lexical and operational) on which there is general consensus in the scientific community. Whilst a tape-measure, a pair of scales or a chronometer are (consensually considered) necessary for the operational definition of 'quantity of motion', there are no equally (consensually accepted) instruments with which to obtain operational definitions of concepts like 'democracy', 'rationalization', 'authority' or 'political participation'.

'Social' measurement and its scales

For measuring opinions, attitudes and behaviours, social and political scientists do not have the resource of the chronometer (for time) or the meter (for space). However, they need an instrument, which is the scale. It was invented by Likert (1932), and subsequently systematized by Stevens (1946) describing four scales: *nominal, ordinal, interval* and *ratio*. In doing this, Stevens crafted a new definition of 'measurement', introducing a 'nominal level of measurement' distinguished from ranking, and from two forms of metric measurement (interval and ratio scales). In this way, he made up for the absence of a unit of measurement (and therefore the epistemological impossibility of measuring) through 'scaling techniques'.

However, Stevens' error has been precisely to include in the term 'measurement' significantly different operations, creating a semantic stretching of the term. In particular, Stevens, on the one hand did not distinguish between continuous and discrete properties (therefore the difference between the unit of account and the unit of measurement), and on the other, invented two monsters or Frankenstein-measures: the nominal and ordinal scales. In fact, using the concept of 'nominal scale', he also expanded the term 'measurement' to the activity of assigning objects to classes; that is, he confused the measurement with the classification. But a classification is the opposite of a measurement (Sartori, 1970, p. 1040). As Torgerson points out, 'numeric labels can be used to name classes ... and this commonly happens. However, the fact that the number 8105 is assigned to a book in a library does not mean that the librarian measured the book ... Otherwise, the classification, and even the naming of individual cases, becomes a form of measurement' (1958, p. 9).

Even using the expression 'ordinal scale' Stevens accomplished another terminological stretch: 'if the property consists of a series of ordered categories, not only there is not measurement, but there is not also any comparison among objects ... Therefore, the label "ordinal measurement" seems completely inappropriate, and should be replaced by the label "allocation to ordered categories"' (Marradi, 1981, p. 601).

Scaling is not measurement

In scaling, the unit of measurement is established by the researcher, who divides (arbitrarily) the hypothetical continuum into discrete statuses, e.g., the response alternatives (such as 'strongly agree', 'fairly agree', 'fairly disagree' and 'strongly disagree'), before administering them (as a scale) to the research participants. Hence, on the one hand the property of the object is considered continuous; on the other, the statuses of the property are conceived as discrete. A blatant contradiction. By doing so, it happens that the distance among categories cannot be quantified. The only possible operation is to establish whether one status is greater or less than another; so the variables produced are only ordered categorically, i.e., ordinal scales, not a metric scale (necessary for measurement).

In fact, decades of methodological research on the social, pragmatic and cognitive aspects of the survey have documented that this approach has led to several biases (see Gobo and Mauceri, 2014 for an overview). Hence, it turns out that this (supposed) unit of measure is arbitrary, not intersubjective and not replicable due to the polysemy of meanings attributed by interviewees to the response alternatives (the discrete statuses on the scale crafted by the researchers).

In conclusion, in social sciences we have metric scales (ratio scales and interval scales, with a unit of measurement), absolute scales (the product of a count), scaling and classifications (Marradi, 1981, p. 608). Hence, in social research, we rarely **measure** (*unit of measure* or <how much>), sometimes we **count** (*unit of account* or <how many>), often we **scale** (*unit of scale or* <what is the most important ...>, <the degree of ...>) and more often we **classify** (<what> and <how>), as in Geertz's research example above, even if Geertz could go further by counting and scaling.

Sampling and generalization

Furthermore, for the two important key issues of 'sampling' and 'generalization', prominent Mixed Methods scholars (Collins et al., 2007; Onwuegbuzie & Collins, 2007), on the wave of pragmatism (Johnson & Onwuegbuzie, 2004), have accepted the (positivistic) received view, without problematizing its (highly questionable) basic concepts. For example, the 'basic MM sampling strategies, sequential MM sampling, concurrent MM sampling, and multilevel MM sampling' proposed by Teddlie and Yu (2007) are just a refinement and juxtaposition of both qualitative and quantitative received views, without any discussion of the epistemological, methodological and technical failings embodied in these two views.

No mention is made of at least three issues (see Gobo, 2008b for details):

1. The use of probability samples and statistical inference in social research often proves problematic and even impossible for a number of reasons: the *difficulty of finding sampling frames* for certain population subsets (drug users, sufferers of the rarest diseases, the unemployed, immigrants, domestic violence victims and so on), because these frames are often not available; the *phenomenon of nonresponse* which makes the final sample non-probabilistic – confined to individuals about whom we were able to obtain information – even if the initial sample was

probalistic; *representativeness and generalizability* are not two sides of the same coin, because the former is a property of the sample, whilst the latter concerns the findings of research.

2. There are numerous disciplines (paleontology, archaeology, geology, ethology, biology, astronomy, anthropology, cognitive science, linguistics), in both the social and human sciences, whose (general) theories are based exclusively on research conducted on only a few cases.

3. *Pace* the methodological orthodoxy, a significant part of sociological knowledge is idiographic. As Randall Collins (1988) stated, much of the best work in sociology has been carried out using qualitative methods without statistical tests. This has been true of research areas ranging from organizational and community studies to micro studies of face-to-face interaction and macro studies of the world system.

However, the serious rethinking of concepts of validity, generalizability and reliability demanded by Denzin and Lincoln (2005, p. 17) has been performed by few practitioners of Mixed Method research. Although reconceptualization of these terms, re-theorized in postpositivist, constructivist-naturalistic, feminist, interpretative, post-structural and critical approaches (Lincoln & Guba, 1985), has produced significant replacements of positivist concepts (e.g., 'credibility' for internal validity; 'transferability' for external validity; 'dependability' for reliability; 'confirmability' for objectivity), these conceptual changes still have little effect on Mixed Methods research practices and methodology. As Bryman (2007) has argued, the latter pays only lip service to combining results from the different methods and the replacements that Lincoln and Guba (1985) proposed are seldom used.

Yet, for some time now, theoretical and practical proposals have existed (see Gomm et al., 2000; Payne & Williams, 2005), which suggest abandoning the (statistical) principle of probability, recovering the (statistical) principle of variance, paying renewed attention to the units of analysis, identifying social regularities and sampling attitudes and behaviours instead of just individuals (Gobo, 2004, 2008b), sequences instead of instances (Silverman, 2005). These proposals could open the possibility to a real third approach.

An alternative classification of main methodologies

Creswell (1997) suggests that there are five approaches to qualitative research (and related research designs): narrative, phenomenological, grounded theory, ethnography and case study. Flick (2008) proposes an alternative classification: case study, comparative study, retrospective study, snapshot and longitudinal study. However, if we look at what researchers concretely do and how they practically act during the research process, we could envision another classification (see Table 3.2, from Gobo, 2008a, p. 24), based on the *main* cognitive modes activated when gathering information: survey (questioning), discursive interview (listening), ethnography (observing), documentary methodology (reading), transformative methodology (operationalizing) and speculative methodology (introspecting and reflecting). These cognitive modes build six related methodologies, which embody specific types of research, data collection and data analysis techniques (Table 3.2).

As mentioned in Chapter 2, each methodology has an actual driving force, a specific performativity, a particular agency. It embodies a distinct capacity to construct data, a defined methodological worldview. This has an impact on the research design, as we will see in Chapter 4.

Conclusion: repercussions and relapses

At this point, the reader might ask: what is the impact of these epistemological and methodological reflections on Merged Methods? What practical consequences might they have on research design, data collection and data analysis in Merged Methods? Will Merged Methods overcome or resolve the difficulties, contradictions, aporias existent in qualitative, quantitative and Mixed Methods?

The merged epistemology and methodology aims to give voice to those critical instances (regarding the three approaches) that have been neglected or left unheard. Such criticisms can reorient and re-establish empirical research, starting from the key concepts (recalled in this chapter) of the methodology of social research. This re-founding can have various consequences and practical repercussions.

First of all, a rethinking of the language (meanings) of social research, without necessarily changing the whole lexicon. The latter in fact can be largely borrowed from previous approaches (where, however, often some of these terms and concepts were mutually excluded and banned; this is a novelty of Merged Methods), amalgamated and integrated in a coherent and epistemologically more advanced vision.

Second, some terms and concepts (such as 'qualitative', properties', 'characteristics' etc.) could be abandoned and replaced by others that are more epistemologically grounded, in order to build a different methodological mindset. While other terms, such as 'measurement', should fall within their original riverbed, confined in its use only to certain and specific cognitive operations, processes and practices. This would

Table 3.2 Main methodologies and techniques in qualitative research

Methodologies	Pivotal cognitive modes	Research types	Gathering structure	Data collection techniques	Data management techniques	Data analysis techniques
SURVEY	Questioning	Market Motivational Survey Poll	Structured	Questionnaire + Random probe technique	Matrix	Covariance
DISCURSIVE INTERVIEW	Listening	Biographic	Little or partly structured	**Individual interview** (in-depth, narrative, open-ended, semi-structured, topical, problem-centred, with the double, realistic, interview control question, ecocultural family interview, ethnographic interview) **Collective interview** (group, focus and Delphi)	Transcription and coding	Narrative analysis; Discourse analysis; Thematic analysis; Grounded theory
		Hermeneutic				
ETHNOGRAPHY	Observing	Hermeneutic	Non-structured	Participant (e.g. cool hunting, Mystery Shopping, shadowing)	Fieldnotes	Fieldnote analysis
					Grid	Grounded theory
		Ergonomic	Structured	Non-participant	Matrix	Factor analysis
DOCUMENTARY	Reading	Textual	Little or partly structured	Letters, diaries Documents Images (photo, video) Class projects Transcripts	Coding	Thematic analysis; Narrative analysis; Discourse analysis; Foucauldian discourse analysis; Grounded theory; Conversation analysis

Category	Process	Approach	Structure	Data collection	Data format	Analysis
		Archive	Structured	Large textual dataset (newspapers, magazines); Ecological files; Census and register office; Database	Matrix; Matrix	Content Analysis; Covariance
		Action-research; Intervention-research; Participatory research; Cooperative research; Socio-analysis	Little or partly structured	Individual interview; Collective interview; Sociodrama; Candid camera; Breaching studies	Transcription/coding; Fieldnotes; Matrix	Thematic analysis; Fieldnote analysis; Covariance; Sociography
TRANSFORMATIVE	Operationalizing	Psychoanalysis; Systemic	Structured	Individual colloquium; Couple colloquium; Family colloquium	Grid	
		Experimental; Computational		Experiment; Simulation	Vector	Causal analysis
		Evaluation		Test	Matrix	Covariance; Sociography
SPECULATIVE	Introspecting	Phenomenological	Non-structured	Individual experience (thought experiments, breaching studies, inverted lenses)	Personal notes	Category analysis; Autoethnography
	Reflecting	Comparative	Structured	Database	Truth tables (dichotomous variables)	Causal analysis (formal logic); Rating

remove some romanticism from qualitative research and some scientism from quantitative research.

Third, the reflection carried out in this chapter would also involve a change in some research procedures, both of data collection (e.g., sampling) and of data analysis (e.g., generalization).

Fourth, a common methodological basis would thus be reinvented, as a premise from which the various methodologies and research methods would unravel like braids from the same hair.

Fifth, an alternative classification of the current methodologies would allow us to identify (as we will see better in the next chapter) which research practices are compatible and integrable (within a Mixed Methods logic) and which ones are instead problematic.

A final consequence, (as will be more evident in Part Two of the book) is the proposal of new Merged Methods and techniques, the re-proposition of little-known Merged Methods and the re-evaluation of those that have fallen into disuse.

Obviously, Merged Methods do not have behind them the tradition, practice and reflection (in some cases secular, if we consider the First Wave; in others 40 years, if we consider the Second Wave) of Mixed Methods. Therefore, they cannot be required to solve every problem that other approaches suffer. However, a process has begun and many perplexities, weaknesses and gaps of Merged Methods can be improved and overcome with the contribution of those who believe in them.

4

MERGED METHODS RESEARCH DESIGN: A THEORY-DRIVEN APPROACH

Contents

In the previous chapters efforts have been made to integrate the quantitative 'approach' and the qualitative 'approach' into a new, distinctively merged approach. A Merged Methods methodology takes seriously the aim of a full integration, proposing theoretically and practically how to build a new framework for understanding social phenomena where quantitative and qualitative can be reconciled in a merged research design.

Introduction

Given that all Mixed Methods approaches keep the qualitative and quantitative components separate in practice, Greene (2008) rightly questions whether Mixed Methods is a *distinct* methodology.

Distinct methodology, theory-based design orientation

We have argued that Merged Methods (see Chapters 1–3) is based on its own notions of ontology and epistemology. Merged Methods seeks to capture both the interpretative and the structural dimensions of a phenomenon in one research procedure, leading to *one single, valid outcome.* When the idea of Merged Methods is further developed and explicitly utilized in practice, this notion will be put to the test as regards how often Merged Methods in research practice is indeed the most adequate approach to studying a certain phenomenon. The current chapter shows that its applicability for a certain research problem starts with its theoretical approach. A researcher will decide to use Merged Methods only when prompted by the theoretical framework of the study. Designing a Merged Methods study is – quite differently from designing a Mixed Methods study – heavily theory-based.

There are no ready-made standardized Merged Methods designs that function as a basic vantage point, as is much more often the case in Mixed Methods (despite the theory-driven and tailor-made approaches that Mixed Methods sometimes encompasses). Consequently, all practical design decisions – like on sampling and selection, operationalizing concepts, choice of methods of data collection and data-analysis – will have the same *universal* concerns regarding validity, reliability, credibility and authenticity (there is no exclusion here of either neo-positivist or interpretivist standards) – as in other studies. However, as a methodology, Merged Methods adds criteria as specified in Chapter 3 and designing Merged Methods studies is characterized by particular principles as will be formulated in the current chapter. The future will show to what extent – and perhaps for which (social) domains and phenomena – more specific Merged Methods research procedures can be explicated.

Below we will deal with the background ideas, research stances and considerations that precede and inform the choice and elaboration of design characteristics of any specific Merged Methods study. Given that there are no standardized Merged Methods designs, it is up to researchers' theoretical focus, ability and creativity to make their own choices.

Such a basic design approach is not superfluous, as we have seen in Chapter 2: review studies demonstrated that in much Mixed Methods research its rationale and its basic design features were hardly traceable (Bryman, 2007; O'Cathain et al., 2007). A similar picture arises from Plano Clark et al. (2015, p. 315), who offer recommendations for implementing longitudinal Mixed Methods studies. Their review of 33 longitudinal Mixed Methods studies found that many articles lacked quite basic argumentation for incorporating longitudinal and Mixed Methods components. This provides a rather discouraging picture of these studies, considering that their recommendations, though very adequate, are of an utterly common sense character, particularly considering that their advice to 'articulate how time is conceptualized and measured' is their most general recommendation, that being the most basic and obvious feature of a longitudinal Mixed Methods approach. A thoroughly *conceptualized* design may not be necessary for all studies, or may not even be common, but is very much at the heart of Merged Methods.

In an early study, Mason (2006, p. 10) had already noticed the 'limited engagement with the methodological or theoretical underpinnings and implications of integrative research strategies. … The value of such approaches must be judged in relation to their theoretical logic, and the kinds of questions about the social world they enable us to ask and answer.' Such appraisals inform what we see as Merged Methods, as will be taken up later in this chapter.

Complexity-sensitive, adaptive procedures, clear purpose of integration

Conceptually, our approach to Merged Methods has much in common with how Poth (2018) approaches 'integrative thinking with complexity' in the context of Mixed Methods research. Her approach aims to be complexity-sensitive and to grasp dynamic realities in an adaptive, responsive manner. As Poth (2018, p. 18) describes it: 'The adaptive Mixed Methods research practices involve diagnosing the complexity of research conditions, framing complex research problems, defining interrelated research contexts, developing emergence in research interactions, realizing agile research integrations, and assessing the quality of research outcomes.' The complexity of research conditions is portrayed in five dimensions (Poth, 2018, pp. 86–89):

1. The intent of research *problem*: focus on integration.
2. The system of research *contexts*: dynamic and involving interconnected personal, social, and societal systems.
3. Designs of research *integration*: complexity-sensitive and supporting responsive procedures.

4. *Capacity* of research interactions: necessary skills and experiences for undertaking a study.
5. *Evidence* of research outcomes: specific to the integration processes and products.

Particularly valuable in this complexity-sensitive approach is the notion that research procedures need to be 'responsive' on the spot (dimension 3) and the explicit recognition that the 'outcomes' need to be specific to the integration (dimension 5). The former requirement means at a minimum that *procedures* must be flexible, and the latter entails that – to establish outcomes – indicators of integration (processes) are needed.

However, unlike Poth (2018), Merged Methods does not stress responsiveness in the sense of adapting to dynamic influences during the research procedure. While a Merged Methods research design must be adapted to the unique conditions at hand, it should involve a procedure that *embeds* the dynamic interaction between different steps in its procedures as well as with the respondents. Moreover, Merged Methods does not see the integration procedure as combining two separate methods or approaches. The vantage point is quite different: Merged Methods focuses on *one phenomenon* that can only be assessed by *one integrated data collection and analysis procedure* (hereafter '*assessment*' will be used to refer to this procedure).

These comments stem from the ontological principles of Merged Methods that were depicted by Box 1.1 (Chapter 1) and can be put now as:

- the core of phenomena studied through Merged Methods is the dependency between 'interpretative experience' and 'structural' external influences;
- assessing this means combining interpretative and structural approaches in data collection and analysis, and keeping both in balance, as tailored to the complexity of the empirical phenomenon that is being studied;
- in practice, the merging of interpretative and structural data collection requires paying attention to an adequate balance between openness and direction to prevent bias and enhance validity.

This focus on complexity and the ontology of phenomena can also be found in salient new developments in research methodology that stem from the field of Indigenous Research (cf., Chapter 11, Conclusions). Despite their localized roots, these new paradigms have been found to be quite similar across the world, putting interconnectedness and interdependence at centre stage (Held, 2019; Goodyear-Smith & 'Ofanoa, 2021). Simultaneously, these new views are specifically 'complexity sensitive', as trying to reach Indigenous peoples with their specific cultural profile, and research designs are needed that are able to connect to these peoples (Haitana et al., 2020). Given that those populations in particular have been subject to the ongoing process of colonization, they have a history of being researched 'on' rather than 'with' or 'for' (Haitana et al., 2020). Thus research designs that are capable of combining Western and traditional Indigenous ways of knowing, and that seek to integrate Indigenous and non-Indigenous approaches through collaboration, may '**decolonize**' research (Reid, 2020). The resulting new views in research methodology – that stress the integration of a holistic and complexity-sensitive approach – connect to the orientation that Merged Methods takes in seeking to reconcile interpretative and structural influences.

This orientation stretches further than the 'complexity-sensitive' approach of Poth (2018) and also differs in its theoretical, conceptual base. Poth (2018, p. 121) bases her approach on the idea that 'lack of understanding of background influences on the problems [demands that] adaptive practice for framing the intention of problems is more appropriate, given the uncertainty of the purposes for integration'. In fact this narrows the approach to an *application* of Mixed Methods to responsive studies. While this is an interesting Mixed Methods application, similar to Ivankova's (2015) Mixed Methods application to action research, it will seldom characterize a full Mixed Methods study given certain requirements that its quantitative component imposes.

In Merged Methods the responsive part of the design has a different orientation, not an emergent one. Precisely because of the complexity of phenomena, Merged Methods is based on theory-driven procedures with a *clear purpose of integration*. It is the theory-based Merged Method procedure that embodies responsiveness on a procedural level, fitting to the complexity of the target phenomenon. The focus is on enabling the respondent (or participant) to integrate external influences on a given issue with their own apperceptions, evaluations, judgements, explanations and attitudes. This requires substantial knowledge from which an appropriate research design and data collection procedure is created that facilitates the respondent's construction of their response.

Research designs from Mixed to Merged Methods

'Research designs represent an organizing logic for collecting, analysing, interpreting, and reporting data in mixed methods projects' (Creswell & Plano Clark, 2018, p. 98). A design thus gives direction to both the methods decisions and the interpretations that researchers make.

Mixed Methods designs and integration

To make clear how Merged Methods designs can be positioned, we will first sketch some main lines of Mixed Methods designs, so as to demonstrate the conceptual commonalities and differences between them and Merged Methods. Our focus in this section is mainly the issue of *integration* (where, why, how) and how Merged Methods can learn from Mixed Methods research to articulate its design properties.

The three most basic and well-known Mixed Methods designs are presented in a typology by Creswell and Plano Clark (2018, pp. 51–99) that adds a fourth category of complex applications of these core designs. The core designs perfectly display the contrast to Merged Methods, i.e., the fundamental separation of qualitative from quantitative in any Mixed Methods study:

- the *convergent design* combines simultaneously quantitative and qualitative databases to compare results and/or transform data;
- the *explanatory sequential design* includes a quantitative phase followed up with a second, qualitative phase to help explain the initial results;
- the *exploratory sequential design* starts with a qualitative explorative phase that builds to a second quantitative development phase, followed by testing the thus-developed quantitative feature in a third phase.

Designs in the fourth category of 'complex applications' *add* a core design to another design (similarly as regards a methodology or theoretical framework; Creswell & Plano Clark, 2018, p. 104). The authors present four exemplars of such applications: (a) an *experiment or intervention trial*, (b) a *single or multiple case study*, (c) a *participatory and/or social justice theoretical or conceptual framework*, (d) an *evaluation procedure* (Creswell & Plano Clark, 2018, pp. 101–141). Other complex applications are conceivable, like the familiar *nested* or *embedded designs* that the authors included in earlier versions of their typology and others often singled out as an integrated design (Greene, 2007; Nastasi et al., 2010). But, in every case qualitative and quantitative data are processed separately, even though this may be in a dependent, interactive manner. This is also true in other Mixed Methods typologies, like the 15 typologies published between 1989 and 2016 (in Creswell and Plano Clark, 2018, pp. 54–57). Each emphasizes different discriminating design features, like the *purpose* or intent (e.g., explanatory), relative *timing* or sequencing of strands, their relative *priority or weight*, and their level of *interaction or integration* (see Hall & Howard, 2008; Ivankova, 2015, pp. 119–124; Bazeley, 2018a, p. 22). In some views of Mixed Methods designs the degree of integration is more extensive. Teddlie and Tashakkori (2010, pp. 22–25), for example, distinguish *fully integrated designs* as one design family next to three basic Mixed Methods design families (parallel, sequential and conversion designs), representing a complex, iterative type that may include combinations of the other three but also integrates methods throughout the study.

Closer to Merged Methods is a *research-process approach* to design typologies (cf., Maxwell & Loomis, 2003; Hall & Howard, 2008; Nastasi et al., 2010; Maxwell, 2013), as opposed to the above described *modular or methods-focused* design approaches. Research-process design approaches – put forward by Maxwell and Loomis (2003) for Mixed Methods research but also applied by Maxwell (2013) to qualitative designs – do not just mix methods throughout the research design and implementation processes, but take a *systemic* view. Their focus is on the interaction and (cyclic) interconnection of (five) main components of a *research process*: goals, conceptual framework, research questions, methods and validity considerations (as well as the researcher's skills, situational constraints, ethical standards, funding agendas and prior research). While these interactive, system-based designs stress the interrelationships within and across these components, they still distinguish qualitative and quantitative elements.

From synergetic to Merged Methods

Pushing the idea of integration further, coming yet closer to Merged Methods, Hall and Howard (2008) suggest a *synergistic approach to designs*. This seeks to combine the principle of the above discussed typological and systemic design approaches. The synergetic perspective can be depicted as a *dynamic* approach that shares similarities with the interactive, system-based approaches yet strives for balance between a design that provides *structure* while remaining *flexible*. Perhaps most distinctive is its principle that both qualitative and quantitative approaches have equal value – conceptual, experiential and inferential – despite variations in weighting during any particular stage. While this promotes a full and extended degree of integration, distinguishing qualitative and quantitative perspectives still marks a sharp difference to Merged Methods. On the other hand, the shared issue of combining structure and flexibility is essential, since through that Merged Methods seeks to unite structural and interpretative facets of a phenomenon.

To clarify the balance between *structure and flexibility* of designs, we should distinguish between Merged Methods as an approach and a concrete research design. The approach is by definition flexible, given that Merged Methods can be applied in and adapted to almost any kind of study design and has no standard applications. Regarding Merged Methods as a research design, it is helpful to utilize the distinction between *fixed designs* – prescribed before the empirical research starts – and *emergent designs*

– applied in response to issues during research (Robson, 2011, p. 46; Creswell & Plano Clark, 2018, p. 52) – along with *evolving designs* that develop further as the research progresses (Poth, 2018, p. 177).

In these terms a Merged Methods research design would foremost be a fixed design: due to its theory-driven base, the design must be elaborated before the empirical research phase starts. This includes the layout of data construction procedures. But, within these procedures flexibility and interaction (between interpretative and structural features) is core. Thus a Merged Methods research design is *fixed* at a procedural level and is *flexible* (not emergent or evolving) in its consequences for data construction during the research.

A contribution to design orientation that might form a bridge between (integrated) Mixed Methods designs and Merged Methods is the well-known notion of *point of interface*. Starting with Morse and Niehaus (2009, p. 25), this was described as 'the position in which the core and supplement component meet during the conduct of the research'. With this, they referred to the 'results point of interface' (in writing up research results) and the 'analytic point of interface' (during data analysis) in a mixed-methods study. Guest (2013) gave this idea another twist by proposing the point of interface as the defining characteristic of a design approach, moreover being restricted to the point of interface between two *data sets*. As Guest (2013, p. 146) defines it: 'The point of interface refers to any point in a study where two or more data sets are mixed or connected in some way.' Though this perspective is still based on two distinct components, the focus on data as the decisive characteristic of a full integration fits a merged approach.

In Part Two of this book, we present research approaches and methods – like Q-Methodology, Calendar Methodology and Multimodal Content Analysis – that have this specific focus on merging data. Bazeley (2018a, p. 242) also recognizes that some methods combine qualitative and quantitative data in a procedure that is 'integral to these methods rather than an add-on possibility, and both forms of the data are integral to analytic interpretation and reporting'. Current Mixed Methods literature does not get closer to Merged Methods than this description. However, her explanation is still limited, picturing the procedure as a 'transformation from qualitative data to quantitative or "qualiquant" analyses' (Bazeley, 2018a, p. 242). An underlying *holistic* view on data construction – given the phenomenon that is to be assessed – is lacking, still putting the emphasis on two types of data and on combined analysis. Whereas all Mixed Methods designs are about *separate* methods and separate data or outcomes that have to be linked, transformed, added or confronted *after* data collection – Merged Methods is about one method that integrates interpretive and structural meanings *during* data collection in one datum.

Translating these ideas on design approaches and integration, one might say that a Merged Methods perspective entails a dynamic, synergistic approach – balancing structure and flexibility in its design – while leaving out the distinction between qualitative and quantitative perspectives and explicitly focusing on a 'data point of interface', where the merging culminates in data construction.

Theory-driven design orientation

Whether method-focused or research-process focused, Mixed Methods typologies are predominantly conceived around a distinction between quantitative and qualitative (cf., Bazeley, 2018a: 62). As Biesta (2010, p. 100) states, this 'reinforces the rather crude distinction between the two approaches [qual and quant], and little work is done to unpack the cluster of ideas behind these notions.' This may explain why these typologies are 'hardly embedded in theoretical and philosophical perspectives that might inform if not justify [them], ending up with a rather eclectic view about the paradigms researchers might select for their research' (Biesta, 2010, p. 100). Merged Methods distinguishes itself by the crucial role of a theoretical and substantial rationale for *uniting* structural information and interpretative information.

A theoretical rationale: the conceptual framework at centre stage

Depending on the ontology of the target phenomena, this rationale may include different *levels of abstraction* (micro, meso, macro) that together define data construction. As such, the Merged Methods orientation is influenced by Giddens (1984) **structuration theory**, as indicated regularly in this chapter by the various contributions of authors relating to notions of structure–agency and micro–macro intersections. This is not surprising given that the qualitative–quantitative duality often refers to similar dimensions in terms like individual – aggregate, or humanistic and societal. Here Merged Methods again takes a stance that is akin to the new Indigenous paradigms mentioned, that also stress dynamic understandings that encompass socioemotional, cultural, sociocultural, economic and historical interrelatedness (Gerlach, 2018). Clearly these views stem from Indigenous philosophies with their specific backgrounds, but it shares with Merged Methods a focus on a holistic ontology and dynamic integrations of macro-processes and micro-processes.

The position that any merging requires a strong theoretical base is underlined when inspecting the six main methodologies presented in Chapter 3 (Table 3.2, from 'survey' to 'speculative'). These methodologies each entail different 'cognitive modes', different research types, and different procedures for data collection and data analysis, that potentially reflect the Merged Methods approach. Moreover, in Merged Methods the integration is not just in the data collection and analysis, but also in the *assessment* itself: assessment typically involves an *extended procedure* that unites different types and/ or levels of information. It is the conceptual framework of the study that is essential to the rationale behind these procedures, which in turn is translated into the Merged Method research design. In line with Niglas' (2010) holistic multidimensional model, Yanchar and Williams (2006, p. 4) argue for such theoretically informed inquiry practices, stating: '… if a method were not based on certain assumptions about the phenomena to be investigated, it would not possess the unique characteristics required to study them. Thus – contrary to both the **compatibility thesis** and methodological eclecticism – methods cannot be extricated from theoretical concerns, because they are, at bottom, theories about how to systematically study a given subject matter and generate particular results.'

The 'intermezzo' in Box 4.1, based on our example in Chapter 2, may elucidate what a theoretical drive means for Merged Methods as a design orientation.

Box 4.1 Intermezzo: Applying the Merged Methods idea

Chapter 2 offered an example concerning the impact of societal conceptualizations of growing old on how older people experience their meaning in life. Assuming that societal conceptualizations also affect societal policy and institutions (like provisions for elderly care) the study may want to include micro (individual), meso (institutions) and macro (society) influences. In a Merged Methods study, the interaction between these levels forms ontologically the heart of the phenomenon and the aim of data collection, i.e., data construction. Defining and 'measuring' such complex phenomena requires a strong theory-driven approach, meaning that the conceptual framework (encompassing problem statement and research question) is pivotal.

When, as per our example, 65-year-olds retire, sell their spacious houses and move to a retirement home because they feel this fits the (tacit) cultural image of how 'older persons' should live, then we learn much from their interpretation of that cultural image and the relationship it may have with life circumstances, biographical life events (like 'buying a house') and standardized life events (like 'retirement').

Thus in this case the researcher's conceptual framework could be on how life events and biography go together with personal perceptions. This framework will shape the researcher's decisions in a '*synergetic*' manner regarding design, operationalization, data collection, analyses and interpretation, so as to define the meaning of the respondents' combined considerations that merge into their final judgement/ evaluation of the decision to move.

In this case, the structural dimensions are the 'facts, events and transitions' in respondents' life course; the *interpretive* dimensions are the subjective explanations and evaluations made by the respondent of relationships between such biographical elements. Both dimensions interact and result in the final report by respondents of why they moved now. Hence the layout of the data collection procedure and construction of the assessment tool will be theory-laden in order to create a single datum that incorporates the meaning of 'this context' and 'these conditions' that are taken into account. The basic layout of this design might be a fixed, predefined and structured scheme that provides an overview of life course events and trajectories. In addition, systematic instructions may guide the respondent in a flexible way through in-depth considerations of related personal perceptions, evaluations and explanations.

Such procedures can be designed in a number of ways, depending on the study at hand. Our example might best fit a Calendar Methods approach (see Chapter 6), but other Merged Methods strategies – as represented in Part Two of this book (like the Delphi Method, Intervey, Symlog) – have their corresponding affordances.

Interpretative framework: emic and etic

The balance in Merged Methods between flexibility and structure, and its combining of interpretive and structural influences in data construction, fit well to a broad conception of *interpretative* inquiry. As Morehouse (2011, p. 4) states: '[interpretative research] may include qualitative, quantitative, and mixed data as long as the interpretation is contextual, creative, conceptual aware, coherent and critically reflective' (cf., Yanchar & Williams, 2006). The defining orientations of interpretative research (Morehouse, 2011, pp. 2–3) – *agency* (agents instead of subjects), *action* (as opposed to behaviour) and *meaning* (rather than information) – inform and apply to Merged Methods designs. They entail the crucial notion that a phenomenon is seen as a process and that agents may play a part in explaining causal processes. Interpretative stances stress inquiry into the meaning of people's 'words and actions', in particular as understood by participants in the study. This entails a typical *emic* (actor-centred) rather than *etic* (observer-centred) viewpoint (Collier & Elman, 2008). It is important to be aware that Merged Methods explicitly include an etic view, stemming from contextual and structural data that may be distant or invisible to people (e.g., being at macro level). It is not only the respondent's understanding of contextual and structural data that counts, but also the researcher's scientific goal to examine the interaction between 'meanings understood' and structural patterns within the chosen theoretical framework.

Multidimensional, holistic

In line with these views, Mason (2006, p. 10) provides basic notions *of 'multidimensional research strategies'* that transcend the qualitative–quantitative divide and fit well to Merged Methods as organizing principles. The first is that social experience and lived realities are best conceived as multidimensional, meaning that examining only one dimension would not do justice to a phenomenon. The second basic notion is that lives are lived simultaneously on *macro and micro scales*. Since lived experience transcends these scales, research methods should adapt to that complexity. As Mason (2006, p. 14) states: 'although these macro-scale theories make claims about far-reaching, sometimes global phenomena, these are manifested in the everyday lives and cultures of people and populations. In this sense, they are wanting to be macro and micro, global and local, socio-cultural and individual, all at the same time, and it is something of a challenge to conceptualize what form of empirical "evidence" might be required to support this.'

A Merged Methods approach inherently incorporates a *holistic*, multidimensional understanding and thus transcends such a micro–macro distinction. Moreover, it has the advantage over a qualitative–quantitative differentiated view that it does not risk 'mimicking a micro–macro *distinction*', re-creating a duality. Juxtaposing the logics of qualitative and quantitative explanations is contrary to the core idea of Merged Methods that both logics are needed to understand phenomena and experiences fully. How precisely both logics are reconciled depends on the study at hand, but neither of the two logics has priority to begin with. What is needed is an overarching theory and a coherent worldview to conceptualize and assess a phenomenon.

Starting from the idea that the social world is multidimensional, Mason (2006) suggests that explanations need to do likewise and therefore proposes *'multinodal dialogic explanations'*. 'Multinodal' means that different dimensions of social experience are involved in the explanation, while 'dialogic' indicates that the ways in which these dimensions are conceptualized and seen to relate can be explained in more than one way, depending upon the theoretical orientation. The idea of multinodal dialogic explanations can be interpreted fruitfully from a Merged Methods perspective. Multinodal then refers to the *interpretative and structural dimensions* of the phenomenon: not *per se* 'dimensions of social experience' as such; it may also include societal and economic developments on the macro level to which experiences, attitudes and behaviour relate. 'Dialogical' in Merged Methods would mean the 'dialogue' that both *dimensions* undergo between each other *during* data collection, both in participants' considerations and in the assessment procedure the researcher has designed. This dialogue defines the essence of the explanation, i.e., the interaction between micro and macro shapes the individual's view/interpretation/response. How this dialogue works out is ultimately the core of a 'multinodal' explanation in a 'holistic' perspective.

Explanation and causation

We might ask how to further approach this 'multinodal' explanation? To begin with, we need a research design that embodies the 'mechanisms underlying causation' (Bazeley, 2018a: 288) that may capture the target phenomenon, as conceptualized in the study. Second we need procedures that lead to proper data construction, integrating outcomes of these mechanisms in making up the phenomenon for this specific case/participant under these specific conditions.

A trigonometrical view on assessment

As Kelle (2001, p. 12) puts it from a sociological perspective: 'methodological reflections on the integration of methods have to be based on theoretical considerations about the social processes under investigation. Thereby one must pay attention to the nature of social structures and social actions in the empirical field and to the ways that structures and actions are related to each other.' Certainly, the development of complex, Merged Methods designs and procedures require much *substantive knowledge* and understanding of the *theoretical notions* on how external influences interact and how this relates to intra-personal processes (cf., Poth, 2018, ch. 6).

Given the importance of interaction between micro, meso and macro levels, theorizing may include a *process-oriented* approach on how *multilevel interactions* take place – for what populations, institutions and structures – and to identify causal relations between the different levels (Baur, 2017). It is crucial to recognize what this requires methodologically and develop methods that are adequate to capture this interaction. *Structural* perspectives and facts as well as social *microprocesses* may remain hidden, and thus their theoretically assumed interdependency, if they are not embedded in the research design. This would limit the explanatory power of the research results.

In line with such process-orientated, multilevel social theory, a biographical approach requires both intensive and extensive lenses (micro–macro) to explain phenomena (Nilsen & Brannen, 2010). Furthermore, the distinction between *interpretative* and *contextual* biographical approaches emphasizes two main lines that Merged Methods seeks to unite. In a contextual approach, individual accounts are understood as interpretations, but it is recognized that they are set within a social context of factual events. On the other side, an interpretative approach pays more attention to single stories, focusing more inwardly on individual narratives than outwardly on the wider social context.

In Merged Methods both the contextual and interpretative approaches are combined, whether context is provided by structural information (Event History Calendar) or views of other people (Q-Methodology) or discourses (Multimodal Content Analysis). The context feeds into the interpretation (and recursively) and both can be placed against a structural background. Like notions of context varying between the interpretative and contextual biographical approaches (Nilsen & Brannen, 2010, p. 686), different Merged Methods orientations with different theoretical frameworks will lead to different choices and applications, but all seek a holistic explanation.

According to Kelle (2001) the best way to obtain valid explanations of phenomena is by combining types of information using a **trigonometrical** understanding of the well-known triangulation metaphor. The trigonometrical meaning (from the fields of navigation and land surveying) contends that the same phenomenon – not different parts, but the whole 'triangle' – can only be assessed with the help of different methods. It is a strong version of a complementarity model of triangulation – in which different phenomena supplement each other – and quite distinct from triangulation as validation by mutual checking of results. The trigonometric understanding concerns an *ontological* view on a phenomenon and thus provides an adequate simile for the integration that takes place in Merged Methods. Where Kelle (2001) applies it as a methodological model that combines quantitative surveys with ethnographic investigation, in Merged Methods it is inherent in one methodological procedure (as per Box 4.1).

What is integration?

But what does merging into a holistic picture mean from a design perspective? We may recognize much of a Merged Methods design orientation in the highly integrated approach presented by Mertens and Hesse-Biber (2013).

A holistic integration

Writing in the context of evaluation research, Mertens and Hesse-Biber (2013) ask how a *synergistic* endeavour of Mixed Methods can be given substance by evaluators, and how this can enhance credibility of the evaluation. The answer lies in their view of methodology as 'the theoretical and procedural link that brings epistemology and method together: defining the type of evaluation, how the evaluation process should proceed, what methods to select, and how they are employed to get at the evaluation problem' (p. 6). Evaluators thus combine theory and methods during the evaluation process and precisely by doing this they attain credible evidence. Mertens and Hesse-Biber (2013) thus stress that *integration* is not just about combining methods, but that any method is tightly linked to epistemological and theoretical viewpoints. Moreover, they indicate that these stances and viewpoint are being incorporated into the research design. Merged Methods has close affinity with this view on integration but embeds it in a unifying paradigm that – above all — underlies the full research process, including data construction.

Concerning data construction, we may recognize Merged Methods stances in integrated Mixed Methods studies where *joint data* are produced, like in quantification of qualitative data. Lieber (2009) states that systematic strategies for such data transformation into reliable data are demanding. But 'where possible and appropriate, the resultant data *provide a mechanism* through which one can bring together the Qual and Quant approaches' (Lieber, 2009, p. 223; emphasis added). The framing of resultant data as 'providing a mechanism' is similar to the Merged Methods idea. However, even in this case of 'complete qualitative and quantitative method integration', the underlying strategy is not one of a unity but seeking a middle ground that works for (combined analysis of) both approaches. Moreover, complete integration' by quantitizing qualitative data only works for qualitative data of a binary yes/no or absent/present type. Once shades or degrees of a behavioural or attitudinal phenomenon are captured, qualitatively translating that into a quantitative form requires weighting and becomes highly questionable. For integration in Merged Methods, we must secure the *theoretical link* between design, method and data, explicating how the research design seeks to guarantee validity or credibility of the inferences.

Is integration real?

One may wonder whether full integration is attainable when studying highly *complex* empirical phenomena as in Merged Methods. Bazeley (2018a: 10) cites overview studies that demonstrate that relatively few Mixed Methods studies show explicit integration (in design and analysis). Moreover, the theory-driven Merged Methods approach actually entails the construction of *'unobserved'* (multidimension, multilevel) phenomena, which depend highly on inferences from conceptualization. Seeking full integration may be a pitfall where a phenomenon is mistakenly conceptualized as being merged. Alternatively, a phenomenon may be inherently merged but not recognized as such and thus not approached with adequate methods.

Similar warnings are also sounded by Uprichard and Dawney (2019), who challenge the assumption that integration in Mixed Methods research is possible and is a desirable outcome. They do not question the logic of data integration, but challenge the presupposition that it is necessarily the optimal outcome, since 'mixed data could equally reveal multiple phenomena that are entangled together, even though they appear to [be] singular or whole' (p. 22). Moreover, they posit that while complexity may be one of the main reasons to employ Mixed Methods, it could be expected that the different methods used show different aspects of a complex phenomenon without being able to grasp the unity. Uprichard and Dawney (2019) plead for a 'diffractive' approach that does justice to differentiated and even contradictory facets of a phenomenon. They present *diffraction* as an alternative to integration, emphasizing 'difference and entanglement'.

However, such an approach does not seem to oppose the idea of integration. Actually, in line with a Merged Methods stance, it stresses the crucial role of ontology, epistemology and theory in full integration. Not everything goes: because of the ontology of the object itself integration may not be adequate or may be hard to achieve. However, precisely the conception that there may be a phenomenon that is characterized by ontological complexity is a reason for developing approaches and methods that capture this. Yet, the idea of 'diffraction' does entail a valuable warning for Merged Methods, since social phenomena may be very much entangled with other social phenomena and lack of theorizing or analytic focus may lead to unwarranted applications of Merged Methods. Whereas Uprichard and Dawney (2019, p. 22) warn that Mixed Methods could 'multiply the partiality, increase the uncertainty and further entangle the subject', Merged Methods could risk unwarranted unifications, representing a spurious phenomenon. This leads us to matters of quality in a Merged Methods study and the validity of its inferences.

Quality assurance

The next question is how – in designing a Merged Methods study – one may ensure and assess the quality of the integrated assessment of an ontologically complex target phenomenon. In other words, what is *validity* or *credibility* in a Merged Methods study?

Integrated assessment

Since a Merged Methods understanding obviously builds on qualitative, quantitative and Mixed Methods approaches, general notions of quality and validity apply here as well. However, Merged Methods does add a new concept that is crucial for its approach: we will call this *procedural construct validity*, stressing the rationale and application of the fully composed assessment procedure.

Inference quality: specifications towards merging

To assess the integrated quality of a study, Tashakkori and Teddlie (2003b) introduced the validity-related notion of *inference quality*. It is defined as a joint assessment of *design quality*, i.e., the process of reaching the result through design and analysis, and *interpretation rigour*, i.e., the degree of consistency of conclusions in all facets of the study (Teddlie & Tashakkori, 2010, pp. 28–29). Inference quality thus refers both to the research *process* and to its *outcome*. This notion sparked many elaborations, mainly broadening its reach and applicability, rather than specifying the validity of full integration of data (cf., Dellinger & Leech, 2007; O'Cathain, 2010; Ivankova, 2014, p. 42).

Nevertheless, certain elaborations of inference quality add *specific* features that might inform Merged Methods, as is the case for the Mixed Methods 'legitimation model' of Onwuegbuzie and Johnson (2006). In their model the quality of inferences is assessed by the *legitimacy of the conclusions* along four main lines: (a) consistency within components of the study (including questions, design and inferences), (b) the representation of *an emic and an etic view*, (c) adequacy of integrating the qualitative and quantitative components of design and (d) a consequential component regarding the degree to which the consumers of Mixed Methods research value the meta-inferences obtained. The salient emphasis in this model on the emic and etic view is clarifying the *role of context* in establishing validity (Adcock & Collier, 2001), as discussed below. In Merged Methods both an emic and an etic view are explicitly part of the integration procedure, representing the *interpretive and structural* sides of a phenomenon that it aims to examine.

Also, Dellinger and Leech (2007) provide a specific view on integration by placing *construct validity* – core to validity in Merged Methods – in the centre of their *validation framework* (which covers all aspects of a study process, from preconceptions to utilization and consequences). They distinguish three elements of construct validity: design quality, legitimation and interpretive rigour. However, their interpretation of 'construct validity' does not differ from 'inference quality' as defined by Teddlie and Tashakkori (2010, pp. 28–29) and does not provide a further focus for integration. On the contrary, they understand construct validity as 'encompassing all validity evidence' and as 'the continuous process of negotiation of meaning' (Dellinger & Leech, 2007, pp. 316, 322). It is not wholly clear why the authors use the term 'construct validity' instead of 'inference quality' and what the use of this term adds. Still, their *stance* on construct validity reads as being very close to Merged Methods:

> Quantitative and qualitative research approaches measure constructs differently or create meaning from data differently, but this does not mean that they cannot measure, or are not measuring, the same constructs or meanings on the basis of the *systematic arrangement of perceptions, experiences, attitudes, and so on.* (Dellinger & Leech, 2007, p. 319; emphasis added)

However, their 'validation framework' does not utilize these ideas on construct validity to provide more depth to integration at a construct level but instead stretches it to a broad notion of quality.

Procedural construct validity

While the broader quality context is important (and well described) the unique Merged Methods design feature is the integration of assessment. Given the ontological complexity of the study phenomenon, this integration usually encompasses a rather complex, theory-based procedure. The validity or credibility of the *procedural rationale* by which the merged assessment of a phenomenon is motivated and legitimized can be labelled *procedural construct validity.*

The meaning of *construct validity* initially concerned the degree to which an instrument actually measures an intended concept or construct (Cronbach & Meehl, 1955; Ivankova, 2015, p. 262). Taking this concept apart from its quantitative or neo-positivist origin, it remains a very useful and clarifying concept by focusing fully on the meaning of a measure, i.e., one single outcome. Obviously other parts of a study contribute to the meaning of a measure and construct validity (cf., Dellinger & Leech, 2007, p. 311) and construct validity does not cover validity of all aspects of a study (like inferences on other facets of its conceptualization). Also, as Bazeley (2018a: 299) makes clear, validity – let alone construct validity – is not the same as *quality*: 'validity is a property of inferences. It is not a property of designs or methods'. Of course, designs and methods try to safeguard validity of inferences. Validity of inferences is 'evident in the way in which those inferences coherently reflect and convey an understanding of the subject matter they are about' (p. 299).

The focus on *procedural construct validity*, or data integration, does not mean we neglect the *context* of the phenomenon. While the assessment of the phenomenon might encompass a layered and complicated procedure, it still is performed in a wider context. The 'merge' might give valid inferences in one context but invalid ones in other circumstances (even though its theory-driven base ideally seeks to limit this risk). Moreover, multiple inferences may be valid, depending on the theoretical viewpoints taken (Mason, 2006). This is in line with the notion of *contextual specificity* of validity, defined by Adcock and Collier (2001, p. 534) as the 'fundamental concern that arises when differences in context potentially threaten the validity of measurement'. Contextual specificity is not just an issue in (international) comparative studies, but in many studies like those that include different social groups, different subcultures, or different historical periods. *Merged Methods* studies are by definition based on nonequivalent data that relate to different contexts: its procedures are directed at processing unstructured, interpretative data (regarding particular or micro contexts) and standardized or structural data (regarding more abstract or macro contexts).

An underlying challenge stems from the qualitative–quantitative divide in views on validity and assessment, and the persistent lack of common standards. This divide is related to the fact that 'qualitative' researchers tend to adhere to a *particularizing* approach, which stresses the specific context and contests measures that transcend these contexts. On the other hand, 'quantitative' researchers tend to follow a *universalizing* approach, which is less sensitive to contextual differences (Adcock & Collier, 2001, p. 530). This means that Merged Methods need to pay attention to establishing *equivalence of meanings* across diverse contexts, by constructing context-sensitive measures (Adcock & Collier, 2001, p. 535). To start with, Merged Methods thus need to create *context sensitive designs,* in such a manner that its application in research practice leads to equivalent procedures of data collection and data analysis (while keeping a good balance between particularizing and generalizing). The core question is whether the interpretative and structural components of the design meaningfully merge the data so as to capture the ideas contained in the central 'merged' concepts, i.e., phenomena.

While a main function of a research design is to guarantee the validity of the study inferences, Merged Methods studies require a *composed* (or process style) definition of *procedural construct validity,* uniting the 'particularizing' with the 'universalizing' meaning of validity. Procedural construct validity in Merged Methods then stands for the degree to which the merged procedure is legitimate and the meaning of the merged outcome is safeguarded as intended. The specific qualities and characteristics of such procedural construct validity is one of the main issues to be further developed. By having Merged Methods as a lens, future studies will undoubtedly lead to empirical and theoretical elaborations.

Developing Merged Methods design applications

The above-presented notions on quality assurance and procedural construct validity help determine how to develop a research design for a Merged Methods study. A Merged Methods approach does not entail or privilege a standard study design like a cross-sectional survey, case study, quasi-experiment, or action research. Also there is not a general type of research design that applies to all Merged Methods studies. However, it is the *principles* as depicted in this chapter that specify each particular research design.

Conceptual and organizing principles of design

Usually a design is seen to have two important functions, to which these principles may refer: safeguarding an optimal validity of the outcomes and inferences (foremost depending on its theoretical base) and providing an organizing logic to a research project (cf., Gorard, 2010, p. 239; Creswell & Plano Clark, 2018, p. 98). In this line we distinguish two types of principles underlying a Merged Methods design orientation: *conceptual principles*, that put analytic demands on a design, and *organizing principles*, that indicate the form and procedures of a design.

The principles, as discussed in the foregoing sections, are summarized in Table 4.1. There is a connection between the conceptual and organizing principles, as sketched in the table, but this is not a one-to-one relationship; neither need all ingredients be present in each research design. It is like Yanchar and Williams' (2006, p. 10) remark about a 'soft incompatibility thesis' that stresses the importance of theoretical assumptions behind methods but also recognizes that 'creative, reflective investigators can, at times, reconceptualize methods to cohere with a particular assumptive framework or develop the methodological resources needed'.

From concepts of understanding to practical design applications

While each Merged Methods research design may be different, there are some features that provide guidance to practical applications. To begin with, applications of these designs all have a *structured and flexible component*. These two sides of a design are related to the structural and interpretative features that are elicited during data collection and data construction. The structure–flexibility balance encompasses further design dimensions that clarify the function of the design and thus guide practical procedures.

Table 4.1 A merged methods design orientation: conceptual and organizing principles

Conceptual principles		Organizing principles
1 Theory-based	=>	Conceptualization, interpretative and structural dimensions
2 Complexity-sensitive	=>	Fixed procedural design and flexible data construction
3 Systemic, research-process approach	=>	Adaptive procedures, clear purpose of integration
4 Multilevel, multidimensional, 'multinodal'	=>	Micro – meso – macro data
5 Interpretative – structural 'dialogue' (particularizing – universalizing)	=>	Etic–emic viewpoint Balance structured and flexible design
6 Contextual	=>	Context-sensitive design
7 Synergistic approach	=>	Interaction/interpretative and structural data construction
8 Holistic data construction, trigonometrical stance	=>	Phased and compound assessment of phenomenon Merging data as decisive characterization
9 Procedural construct validity	=>	Validity – credibility of inferences re. full procedure of assessing phenomenon Contextual specificity of validity

First, it obviously relates to the dimension of *fixed versus flexible designs*, as discussed earlier in this chapter in the section on research designs. This dimension, as Robson (2011, p. 46) puts it: 'captures many of the procedural differences between traditional quantitative and qualitative research. It is, however, an essentially atheoretical approach.' Second, a more theoretically based alternative is the dimension of *variable versus case oriented* designs (Della Porta & Keating, 2008, p. 207; Robson, 2011, p. 46), where variable oriented designs are common in standardized or structured research, case-oriented designs are typical for naturalist, interpretative research. The same dimension is sometimes labelled as 'extensive versus intensive' designs. Third, this distinction also entails differences in the level of *predetermination of concepts*: they are defined and operationalized beforehand in a variable-oriented design and constructed during the research process in a case-oriented design. Characteristic of a concrete Merged Methods design is that it encompasses *both sides* of these dimensions in one design: the *fixed–flexible* balanced design is both *variable and case-oriented* and it is *partially conceptually predetermined*.

These features have practical consequences for design procedures because – as is important to realize – the dimensions are related to different *concepts of understanding and explanation*: i.e., a variance approach and a process approach respectively

(Robson, 2011, p. 47; Maxwell, 2013, p. 29). The variance approach deals with relationships between variables and can be said to fit to *successionist or instrumentalist causation* (explanation based on associations and the order of events). The process approach deals with people, situations and events and the processes that connect them and is consonant with *generative causation* (explanation based on mechanisms and influences) (Robson, 2011, p. 47). Thus, each can be said to lead to different types of knowledge: *generalizable* knowledge of relations among variables versus *dense* knowledge of cases or phenomena (Della Porta and Keating, 2008, p. 207). Each will lead to different conceptions of explanation within one design framework.

As can be seen in the new Indigenous methodologies – which similarly combine different manners of understanding – such abstract philosophical–methodological views can be tied to practical research designs in particular by tailoring research processes to local contexts, perspectives and norms (Forbes et al., 2020). This leads to common types of study designs and research approaches – often participatory, collaborative and community-based (Peltier, 2018) – that fit to these Indigenous views. Moreover, they also lead to specific applications, as in focus group designs (Ferrazzi et al., 2019), text analysis (Lee et al., 2018) and photovoice methods (Mark & Boulton, 2017). Merged Methods employs this same way of integrating abstract views with tailor-made applications but in addition explicitly provides a link between both by its theoretical and conceptual rationale.

Decisions regarding practical elaborations of a Merged Methods research design are influenced by organizing principles and different ways of explaining. This pertains to issues that refer to conceptualization, operationalization, sampling and case selection, data construction procedures, analysis and the very conception of explanation and inference. The researchers get to these decisions only by first making judgements about what the ontology of a phenomenon is, what thus counts as valid, credible inferences and how to get there through adequate empirical procedures.

Part Two of this book describes several concrete Merged Methods strategies that all have their own translation of these dimensions and features. However, some general guidelines for typical Merged Methods requirements can be given from the perspective of a research process.

Merged Methods design as embedded in the research process

Maxwell (2013, p. 4; cf., Maxwell & Loomis, 2003) describes design as interaction between *five main components* of a research process: (1) research goal, (2) conceptual framework, (3) research questions, (4) methods (including relationship with participants, sampling/selection, data collection, and analysis) and (5) validity.

For Merged Methods as an approach, no standard prescriptions can be given for how to focus each of these five components. They depend on the substantive study at hand: Merged Methods can be a focus for all kinds of research designs, all kinds of sampling/ selecting and so on. However, sharing Maxwell's **systemic approach**, we take this model as a reference to elucidate *specific, inherent features* that the five components may have in a Merged Methods design.

1. *Goals.* In Merged Methods, research goals focus on providing in-depth insight into a complex phenomenon that is defined by (multidimensional or multilevel) interactions between interpretative and structural features. Interactions between individual experiences and actions and social or societal influences are key to understanding.
2. *Conceptual framework.* Given the complexity of the phenomenon of study a Merged Methods approach is strongly motivated by (interdisciplinary) theory. Elaborating how individual, contextual and multilevel features interact and form the target phenomenon provides the rationale for the research design. Extensive knowledge of the substantial field of study is required to construct (interactive) interpretative and structural design components. The conceptual framework therefore has a crucial role in the research design.
3. *Research questions.* A Merged Method research question usually consists of a rich description of the kind of interaction between interpretative and structural influences that is to be examined for whom or what, in what kind of context. The question will encompass both variance formulations (how much, how do variables relate) and process formulations (how, what mechanisms). The (subsidiary) questions may focus on specific aspects like a development in time, or contrasts between locations, conditions etc. Typically, the main research questions will be formulated before the main phase of data collection, since they are guided by the conceptual framework. However, in addition questions will be specified during the research process, in particular if the Merged Methods approach is embedded in longitudinal study designs, action research designs or evaluation studies and the like.
4. *Methods.* The crucial aspect of the methods part in a Merged Methods design is how the conceptual framework is operationalized into procedures for data construction, since the 'merge' of the study culminates in this research phase. Given the (multidimension or multilevel) complexity of the phenomenon, this entails the deduction and construction of an 'unobserved' phenomenon. The

operationalization of procedures that seek to merge the interpretative and structural features into one holistic representation usually will result in phased and compound data collection measures. While these measures will be largely pre-structured, at least as a procedure, the data construction necessarily involves sizable interactive, open components. Analysis may take place after or alternating with phases of data collection, depending on the specific design of the study. The aforementioned composite measures may entail in-between analysis, as part of the procedure.

In case the Merged Methods study is embedded in an overarching study design (like a field experiment or longitudinal survey) this, of course, may put constraints on choices regarding the relationship of the research(er) with participants, the sampling/selection, data collection and analysis. But within these constraints similar Merged Methods operationalization approaches are conceivable.

5. *Validity.* General definitions of validity apply to Merged Methods as well, like Maxwell's (2013, p. 122) description of validity as 'the correctness or credibility of a description, conclusion, explanation or other sort of account'. But given the specific phased and compound measures that are employed in Merged Methods, we introduced the concept of procedural construct validity to denote the validity and credibility of the inferences regarding the multi-phased assessment procedure with which the target phenomenon is assessed. Given the reasoning that Merged Methods deal with **unobserved phenomena**, its construction – that depends on inferences in conceptualization and operationalization and on composite assessment – risks leading to unwarranted conclusions.

In order to minimize such risks, Merged Methods may apply the usual strategies to rule out alternative explanations. In Merged Methods both 'advance controls' (common in standardized research) – like forming control groups, controlled sampling, or statistical controls – are applicable, as well as controls 'during the research' (common in naturalist or interpretative research) – by collecting evidence in the open, interactive parts of fieldwork, and respondent validation. Procedural construct validity can be seen as referring to similar strategies, applied specifically to the target phenomenon and emphatically along the theoretical (trigonometrical) rationale that underlies its construction.

Conclusion

Merged Methods designs have their own distinct methodology and theory-based orientation. While their specific design feature is the focus on integration during assessment,

the underlying conceptual and organizing principles may lead to quite different applications, some of which are presented in Part Two of this book. Merged Methods may
be embedded well in existing study designs, whether cross-sectional or longitudinal
designs, prospective or retrospective, it is a matter of elaborating the research design.
The framework presented in this chapter is not rigid; Merged Methods designs are built
on many different choices with regard to the features and options that are presented.
The aim that most Merged Methods study designs share is to provide a valid and credible understanding of a complex phenomenon in which personal experiences and external influences of events, organizations, communities and/or societal trends interact.

PART TWO
METHODS

PART TWO

5

THE DELPHI METHOD: FORECASTING SCENARIOS

The Delphi Method (DM) merges in one method the three main features of three traditional methods usually practised separately, one quantitative and two qualitative: respectively, closed-ended questions in questionnaires (Survey Method), open-ended questions (discursive or in-depth interview method) and group discussions (focus group methods).

Hence, the merged character of Delphi lies in its combination of three elements: qualitative elicitation; quantitative summarization and representation of what is elicited; and the use of an iterative process to distill and refine points of agreement and disagreement. Distillation and refinement is the key stage, and it is also where the quantitative and qualitative elements confront each other, through the use of measures of agreement for consideration by the expert panel. The distillation and refinement seeks to derive increasing precision around exactly what constitutes the points of consensus amongst the participants and the exact boundaries between the consensus and the points about which consensus is lacking.

Definition

The *Delphi Method* owes its name to Abraham Kaplan, an associate professor who worked at **RAND Corporation**, a research institute with its headquarters in Santa Monica, California. The institute was founded in 1964 with the financial support of the American Department of Defense, which commissioned a Cold War study to forecast American industries that might be targeted by Soviet strategists and to estimate how many atomic bombs would be required by Soviet forces to reduce the American arsenal by a specific quantity. In essence, the brief was to collect the opinions of experts about how a Soviet strategist might imagine an attack on the USA in order to forecast it.

In 1969, Norman Dalkey in his book *The Delphi Method: An Experimental Study of Group Opinion* described it as follows:

> (1) Anonymous response – opinions of members of the group are obtained by formal questionnaire. (2) Iteration and controlled feedback – interaction is affected by a systematic controlled feedback between rounds. (3) Statistical group response – the group opinion is defined as an appropriate aggregate of individual opinions on the final round. (Dalkey, 1969, V)

The definition provided by Dalkey summarizes the method's applications by the RAND Corporation through numerous experiments. Today the method is used in various sectors: technology, health, education, the environment and the initial statistical procedures – based on the calculation of the interquartile range – have been extended by probabilistic calculations and Markov matrices.

Over the years, the initial definition has therefore undergone changes or enlargements, which – today – allow us to consider the Delphi Method as:

- a systematic, interactive forecasting method which relies on a panel of experts;
- a method for achieving consensual agreement among expert panellists, through repeated (two or more rounds) iterations (now, usually by email or Web) of

anonymized opinions and of proposed compromise statements from the group moderator;

- a method seeking to 'obtain the most reliable consensus of opinion of a group of experts' through 'a series of intensive questionnaires interspersed with controlled opinion feedback' (Dalkey & Helmer, 1963, p. 458);
- a method designed to establish agreed policy recommendations;
- a method about which a large number of modifications and uses have prompted some researchers to speak of the 'Delphi approach' rather than the more specific term 'method' (Mead & Moseley, 2001).

To ensure the achievement of reliable forecasts, the Delphi Method has some essential features:

1. Participants' anonymity: unlike focus groups, a participant's identity is never revealed to the others.
   o This prevents the authority, personality, or reputation of some participants from dominating others in the process (to allow free expression, open critique, admission of errors when revising earlier judgements).
2. Structuring of information flow: initially data are collected in the form of open-ended answers to questionnaires and participants' comments on these answers.
   o The panel director controls the interactions among the participants by processing the information and filtering out irrelevant content.
   o This avoids the negative effects of face-to-face panel discussions and solves the typical problems of group dynamics.
3. Regular feedback: participants comment on their own forecasts, the responses of others and on the progress of the panel as a whole.
   o At any moment they can revise their earlier statements.
   o Unlike conventional regular group meetings, where participants tend to stick to previously stated opinions and often conform too much to the group leader, the Delphi Method prevents this.
4. Role of the facilitator: s/he facilitates the responses of the *panel of experts*.
   o The facilitator sends out questionnaires, surveys etc.
   o Responses are collected and analysed, then common and conflicting viewpoints are identified.
   o If consensus is not reached, the process continues through thesis and antithesis, to gradually work towards synthesis, and building consensus.

The workflow is a mechanism to be made to work perfectly, like a Swiss watch. A feature of the workflow is the iterations or rounds, which allow researchers – step by step – to arrive at a forecast shared by the experts.

The selected panel of experts is subjected to multiple rounds of investigation to obtain consensus on a particular problem or question.

1. First round: 'exploration', in which the topic is fully explored using broad or open-ended questions.
2. Second round: 'evaluation', in which the results of the previous round are used to frame another set of questions.
3. Third round: 'consensus'. Over multiple rounds, the process can gradually lead to consensus or near-consensus.
   o Each round provides an opportunity for the experts to respond and to revise their answers in light of the (virtual) group members' previous responses.
   o It is believed that during this process the range of the answers will decrease, and the group will converge towards a shared opinion.

Brief history of the Delphi Method

The method's name obviously was inspired by the oracle of Delphi, whose forecasts were not falsifiable. The oracle made statements that had the characteristic of being neither true nor false.

At the origins of the method we find the RAND Corporation, and the scientists who worked there were the main protagonists. Indeed:

- in 1944, General H.H. Arnold ordered the preparation of a report for the US Army Air Corps on future technological capabilities and to identify potential American industrial targets and their vulnerability to Soviet munitions (Dalkey & Helmer, 1963).
- Project DELPHI was developed by the RAND Corporation during the 1950s–1960s by Olaf Helmer and Nicholas Rescher (1959), and Norman Dalkey and Helmer (1963) (see also Helmer, 1963, 1964, 1966, 1967a, 1967b, 1967c).

The authors of the method were not happy with its name, because it implied 'something oracular, smacking a little of the occult' (Dalkey, 1968, p. 8). Dalkey declared that 'In some ways, it [the name] is unfortunate' because its oracular connotation implied 'precisely the opposite [of what] is involved'.

Over time, the method has undergone several variations in procedure and operational modalities by different authors.

Among these variations, the Policy Delphi, introduced in 1969 by Murray Turoff and published in 1970, claimed to be a break with the previous technique. The author considers it so because in contrast with conventional Delphi, it uses a group of heterogenous experts, it does not deal exclusively with technical topics, and it does not aim at reaching a consensus. A variant of Policy Delphi is Public Delphi, which permits participation by any citizen who shows an interest. A form of real-time Delphi is the Mini Delphi (Helmer, 1972) which – in Helmer's formulation – is a faster, shorter procedure than conventional Delphi, since it can be used in face-to-face meetings. It is summarized as **Estimate-talk-Estimate (ETE)**.

The procedural development of the Delphi Method displays a trend towards greater emphasis on the discussion, the composition of the panel of experts and the probabilistic nature of the forecasts themselves. More attention to statistical-probabilistic procedures to make forecasts with Delphi can be found in the Markov–Delphi Method (De Groot, 1974), where the changes in the subjective evaluations made by a forecaster/expert are connected to the linear combination of the remaining evaluations. The calculation of the probabilities is here made within a stochastic matrix that controls a Markov chain, hypothesizing that all the experts use the same law of probability to change their opinions. In this approach, the convergence of the opinions is derived from the development of the matrix.

Alongside are the following approaches.

- The Decision Delphi (Rauch, 1979) dates back to 1979. In this technique the participants are public figures with senior institutional/decision-making roles, who are asked to discuss a theme/issue.
- The Abacus-Delphi Method (Régnier, 1986) aims at reaching a decision. Discussion is focused by using colours to indicate the level of agreement/disagreement in the evaluations.
- The one-day 'group' Delphi (Webler et al., 1991) aims to reach results quickly in the formulation of opinions concerning risks about which there is uncertainty (e.g., environmental issues).
- Following the introduction of technologies that allow synchronous interactions among the participants, the Real Time Delphi (Gordon & Pease, 2006) and Internet Delphi were created.
- A final procedural innovation, dating from 2011, was Spatial Delphi (Di Zio & Pacinelli, 2011), which introduced into the Delphi world what can be called localization. If a decision-making problem requires identifying a place where a future event could occur, a panel of experts is used to identify/geo-locate a small area most likely for its occurrence.

The different techniques and approaches to the Delphi Method fall into four main categories according to their aims: decision-making; explorative and predictive analysis of the context; policy evaluation; and argument development.

A case study

One of the first studies in which the Delphi Method was used is the *Report on a Long-Range Forecasting Study* by Theodore Gordon and Helmer (1964). It remains an excellent example to understand the operative modalities of this approach.

The objective of the research was to forecast, in the next 50 years, general development trends in six specific areas: scientific breakthroughs, population growth, space exploration, probability and prevention of war, and future weapon systems. The use of this study, as a basis to understand how the method is applied, is interesting because the report contains many inherent procedural indications: the contents of the forecast itself; the bases according to which the interviewees declare they have made their forecasts; the convergence of the forecasts after the feedback of the data in the various rounds has been received; the experts' criticisms of the various opinions; and especially, the weaknesses of the method and possible ways of improving it (see the 'Practical tips' section). When describing how and why the method was used, Gordon and Helmer provide other extremely useful information, clarifying why they decided to use the Delphi Method to make forecasts. Furthermore, they were aware of the difficulty of formulating forecasts on the subjects they had identified, but also realized that the uncertainty could be resolved by identifying the right level of reliability of predictions.

The authors selected six groups of experts, one for each topic area. There were approximately 150 data points, depending on how many of the questionnaires the sample of 82 respondents completed. Of these: 35 came from RAND, seven were RAND consultants and the remaining 40 had some contacts with RAND. Some participants also voluntarily responded to questionnaires sent to other panels. Each group of experts answered four questionnaires, each questionnaire after the first being sent 2 months after the preceding questionnaire. The average number of questionnaires received and filled in by each panel every round was 14.5.

In order to understand how the administration, analysis and feeding back of the results was organized, let's follow the application of the method in the topic 'Scientific breakthroughs'.

The first item of the questionnaire aimed at introducing and explaining the reasons for the forecasting study, asking the experts to provide a list of the main inventions and scientific discoveries whose development was considered necessary and urgent within the ensuing 50 years (Table 5.1). In this case, the item was an open-ended question.

The collection and the analysis of the open-ended answers led the researchers to make a list of 49 items, presented to the experts in a second round questionnaire, as shown in Table 5.2.

Table 5.1 Opening question of the questionnaire

One of the major problems of conducting a predictive study which poses its questions on the basis of extrapolations of current technology is the almost unavoidable exclusion of discontinuous state-of-the-art advances.
In this current study a period of 50 years is being considered. (…)
Therefore, you are asked to list below major inventions and scientific breakthroughs in areas of special concern to you which you regard as both urgently needed and feasible within the next 50 years.

Source: Data from Gordon & Helmer, 1964, p. 7. www.rand.org/pubs/papers/P2982.html

Table 5.2 Three examples of the 49 items presented in the second round

B1	Chemical control over heredity – molecular biology
S8	Popular use of personality control drugs
P10	Reliable weather forecasts

Source: Gordon & Helmer, 1964, p. 7. www.rand.org/pubs/papers/P2982.html.

In the same questionnaire (second round) the experts were asked to indicate the probability of an effective implementation of the technologies in a list with time intervals. Table 5.3 gives an example of a closed-ended question.

Table 5.3 Time intervals for technology implementation

1963–65	1972–78	1997–2013
1965–68	1978–86	Later than 2013
1968–72	1986–97	Never

Source: Gordon & Helmer, 1964, p. 7. www.rand.org/pubs/papers/P2982.html

In the second questionnaire each respondent was invited to indicate for each item the time interval inside which the technological innovation would have had a 50% probability of becoming reality. This distribution was later summarized with the calculation of the median and the quartiles. Given an orderable quantitative or qualitative distribution, quartiles are the values/modalities that divide the object under observation into four equal parts; they are indices of position and belong to the field of descriptive statistics.

The values collected and here shown in Table 5.4 reveal how for the item P10 there already was reasonable agreement about the date range in which it could occur. A quarter of the interviewees thought that the date by which P10 would probably occur was before 1972 (the lower quartile); another quarter thought that it would occur before 1975 (the median); and another quarter that it would happen later than 1988 (the upper quartile).

Table 5.4 Distribution of median and quartiles for each of the items considered

	Median	Quartiles
B1	1993	1982–2033
S8	2050	1984–2050
P10	1975	1972–1988

Source: Gordon & Helmer, 1964, p. 8. www.rand.org/pubs/papers/P2982.html

The consensus prediction for item P10 (and for the others on which the researchers were already agreed) was communicated in questionnaire number 3 (third round), asking the experts to make a further evaluation, namely, if they agreed with this prediction or not, and to justify their choice (Table 5.5).

Table 5.5 Questions concerning reasons for agreement or disagreement

P10 (Reliable weather forecasts): Not within 5 but within 35 years.
Do you, by and large, agree with the opinion represented by the consensus [...]? If you disagree [...], briefly state your reason for your differing opinion.

Source: Data from Gordon & Helmer, 1964, p. 8. www.rand.org/pubs/papers/P2982.html

On the basis of results such as these the researchers believed that for 10 out of 49 items there already was reasonable consensus among the interviewees. Of the remaining 39 items, on which consensus was weak, the researchers discretionally selected 17 for further study. The new questionnaire contained, therefore, a reduced number of items, an indication of the level of consensus reached up to that moment and the request to justify one's opinion if it diverged from that of the majority (see Table 5.6). Furthermore, some of the questions were reformulated because it was thought that the lack of consensus depended on an ambiguous formulation of the questions themselves; this thesis was confirmed by comments from some panel members.

Following the return of the questionnaires, the researchers used the same procedures to single out the items on which there was already consensus, and then calculated the quartiles. This cycle included the reduction of items by eliminating those on which consensus is reached, an announcement to the panel that a sufficient consensus had been reached for some items, and reformulation of the text of the items on which no consensus had been found. When drafting the new questionnaire for this fourth round the researchers included both the reasons behind the opinion of the majority and an indication of the divergent opinions expressed by the minority (see Tables 5.7 and 5.8). The timing of these innovations was forecast as in Table 5.8.

Table 5.6   Questionnaire with requests for further study

	Description of potential breakthroughs	Consensus or dissensus to date	In your opinion, by what year does the probability of occurrence reach 50% 90%		If your 50% estimate falls within either the earlier or the later period indicated, briefly state your reason for this opinion
B1	Feasibility of chemical control over hereditary defects through molecular engineering	Consensus that it will occur, disagreement as to when			Why before 1987 or after 2013?
S8	Widespread socially accepted use of non-narcotic drugs producing specific psychological reactions	Divergent opinions, possibly due to differing interpretations of the original question			Why before 1987 or after 2013 (or never)?

Source: Gordon & Helmer, 1964, p. 9. : www.rand.org/pubs/papers/P2982.html

Table 5.7   Questionnaire with requests for further study

	Description of potential breakthroughs	Majority consensus to date	Minority opinion	50%-year	90%-year
B1	Feasibility (not necessarily acceptance) of chemical control over some hereditary defects by modification of genes through molecular engineering	By 2000	Will take longer or never occur, because it would necessitate intervention during embryonic development, when the fetus is inaccessible, hence would require prior development of techniques of gestation in vitro		
S8	Widespread and socially widely accepted use of non-narcotic drugs (other than alcohol) for the purpose of producing specific changes in personality characteristics	By 2000	Will take 50 years or more, because research on psycho-pharmaceuticals has barely begun, and negative social reaction will cause delay		

Source: Gordon & Helmer, 1964, p. 10. www.rand.org/pubs/papers/P2982.html

Table 5.8 Distribution of median and quartiles for each of the items considered

	Median	Quartiles
B1	2000	1990–2010
S8	1983	1980–2000

Source: Gordon & Helmer, 1964, p. 10. www.rand.org/pubs/papers/P2982.html

Following the sending of new information for item B1, the median remained the same and the quartile range declined slightly. However, on item S8 the median moved forward and the quartile range shrank. In this way the researchers reached what they deemed a 'reasonably narrow consensus'.

The results were summarized in a graph representing the 'break-even' date, the date when the event was expected to occur. Every bar on the graph extends from the lower quartile to the highest one indicating the answers; the peak represents the median. The events were ordered according to the median date.

Gordon and Helmer stated that the data they present are always the result of the opinions of experts, who may possess more knowledge of one sector than another. However, through what they define as retrospective wisdom, Gordon and Helmer demonstrate how such an exercise can be improved to the point of becoming a more reliable and valid planning tool (see 'Advantages and Disadvantages' section below).

Knowing and know-how

In order to understand how to develop a study based on the Delphi Method or one of its particular applications, we use the study by Simone van Zolingen and Cees Klaassen (2003), 'Selection processes in a Delphi study about key qualifications in Senior Secondary Vocational Education', interspersing it with appropriate clarifications. The study reports the selection processes and the assessments carried out in the field of vocational education in a Senior Secondary school in the Netherlands using a Policy Delphi and a one-day group conference.

When developing research based on the Delphi Method, we can identify the following phases:

1. selection of the Delphi approach to use;
2. recognition of the criteria of validity and reliability;
3. selection of the panel experts;

4. research design;
5. preparation of the first-round questionnaire and its distribution;
6. first-round questionnaire collection and analysis;
7. feedback to respondents and distribution of the second questionnaire;
8. iterative cycle.

Selection of the Delphi approach to use

The selection of the approach to use depends on the research question and on the goals the research wishes to satisfy. The Delphi Method is generally used when historical data are insufficient/inappropriate (Rowe et al., 1991) or when the problem to be addressed cannot benefit from or be solved using primary empirical analysis, thus requiring the formulation of opinions by experts whose roles mean they cannot meet together (Linstone & Turoff, 2002). van Zolingen and Klaassen (2003, p. 330) allowed themselves to be guided by their research questions in order to select among the various approaches: 'what key qualifications are important in the future, can they be acquired in Senior Secondary Vocational Education and how can this best be done?' They therefore decided that the objective was not to single out strategies to develop new curricula, but to identify which professional qualifications would be more in demand in the future. Theirs is a forecasting study aiming for clear impact on training and educational policies. The experts, bearers of interests and knowledge about the questions covered, were chosen either from the world of education or from the world of work. What is important here is not whether these panel members reach agreement on all the questions, but that the opinions and arguments of all the parties involved are represented. For these reasons, they decided to work with Policy Delphi, culminating in a one-day group meeting to share the results.

Recognition of the criteria of validity and reliability

Questions of validity and reliability are fundamental because they are tightly connected to the criteria of research development, the selection of the panel of experts and the preparation of the questionnaire. External validity within the Delphi Method considers the characteristics of the expert members of the panel, such as the argumentative skills of the group leader, the motivation of the participants, and their level of education. These characteristics capture the external validity of the forecasting method (Woudenberg, 1991). Internal validity in the Delphi Method refers to its capacity to identify future trajectories, in other words, to make truthful forecasts. Some (Rowe et al., 1991) think that internal validity depends on the number of experts, their average individual validity (that is their competence) and the average intercorrelation of their opinions (the extent to which the experts have a similar or different knowledge). However, these aspects are under-researched and the issue of reliability remains controversial and also under-researched.

The term 'reliability' is normally used to indicate that the repetition of the study will produce the same results. As we have noted, there are different Delphi approaches and numerous adjustments are required according to the research goals and the fields of application. In addition, as noted at the outset (see paragraphs 1 and 2), the Delphi Method was created to skim knowledge, speculations and opinions, taking on board the judgements of the panel experts. This led Harold Sackman (1975) to claim that the method's reliability is limited. In response to this criticism, Irene Jillson (1975) identified some criteria to aspire to. These are guidelines, protocols about the applicability of the method to a specific problem, the selection of respondents and the definition of the criteria in order to recognize their competencies, the planning and management of the questionnaire, the feedback and consensus, and the group meeting, that is, the sharing of opinions between the majority and the minority, whether they are convergent or divergent.

Selection of the panel experts

The criterion to follow when creating a panel of experts is to build a 'reasoned' and non-probabilistic group, representative of the sector to which the forecasting study is addressed. In van Zolingen and Klaassen's case (2003), two different panels were created: one in the world of work and the other in education. In the 'work panel', the experts came from industrial, banking and insurance sectors. The characteristics singled out for the selection of the experts belonging to the bank/insurance sectors were to have had managerial functions and training roles or to be the head of a department, while for the experts belonging to the industrial sector, the selection was based on their coming from large, medium- and small-size enterprises (over 500 employees; between 100 and 500 employees; 100 employees or fewer, respectively).

To this end, they approached the Electronic Components and Systems subdivision of Holland Elektronica (the Netherlands Association for Electronics and Industrial Automation). This is a sector organization of the FME employers' federation, of which larger companies, in particular, are members. They also approached UNETO (Federation of Electronic Entrepreneurs), in which, in particular, small and medium-size businesses are represented. While the membership list of Holland Elektronica supplied 38 enterprises using new technologies or techniques, from the UNETO membership 10 enterprises were selected. Four big industrial companies that had taken part in the preliminary study were also asked for further cooperation. A total number of 17 companies promised to cooperate in the study (10 from Holland Elektronica, three from UNETO and four from the preliminary study; van Zolingen & Klaassen, 2003, p. 333).

Teachers/educators who already had experience in the creation of curricula, including those of educational support, were contacted to constitute the 'educational panel'. The panel was made up of experts of the educational sector who had been teachers in a high-secondary vocational school, were policy consultants, or were the head of department in an institute working in the field of educational support. To assess and select the expertise of teachers, the following criteria were used: having worked on a curriculum development committee for at least six months, and being a Senior Secondary Vocational Education teacher. The expertise of respondents from the educational support field had to meet the following criteria: involvement in the development of vocational (training) profiles and/or courses, and having worked in this function for at least two years (van Zolingen & Klaassen, 2003, p. 335).

The research design

After selecting the Delphi approach to follow, the research question and the panel of experts, the next step was to envisage the various phases of the research.

The two researchers identified the 'key qualifications' of the young people who drop out of a high-secondary vocational school by reviewing the studies carried out in that sector. The specializations that could be useful sources of information for the study of key qualifications emerged from the exploratory examination of the literature about the work-educational issue in high-secondary vocational schools. This was followed by interviews with 18 experts in education, from which it became evident that the first key qualifications could not be those their interest might have been focused on because the students who had dropped out worked in very different sectors. For this reason, they decided to focus only on four relevant jobs for the graduating class in the specializations they had selected: service mechanic, bank clerk, claim acceptor and claims assessor in an insurance company. They added an extra round of 18 interviews addressed to students who had dropped out of a high-secondary vocational school and worked in one of the four key qualifications identified in order to track possible qualification issues in their passage from school to work. On the basis of all the data collected, a questionnaire was then sent to 53 education and employment experts. After sending the questionnaire to the panel of experts and the analysis of the results, some one-day group conferences were organized for each sector (work/education) to facilitate the discussion among the experts. At the end of the study, on the basis of the analysis of the results of the one-day group conferences, a short questionnaire was sent to all the panel members to reach a definition of the key qualifications on which everybody could agree (see Figure 5.1).

Preparing the first-round questionnaire and circulating it

The preparation of the questionnaire was described above. The questionnaire can, in fact, be created with open- and closed-ended questions. In the preparation of the questionnaires for the first Delphi round (see Figure 5.1), van Zolingen and Klaassen made different questionnaires for the various groups of experts with a number of items between 47 and 25. The questions in the work panel and educational panel questionnaires of the same sector contained some common items and other tailored ones according to the experience of each expert. While the majority of the questions were in part open-ended, some of them were multiple choice and others were fully open-ended. Reminder letters were sent two weeks after the questionnaires were circulated, followed up where necessary by phone calls.

First-round questionnaire collection and analysis

Since the questionnaire consists of closed-ended, multiple-choice, open-ended and partly open questions, the researcher must make methodological choices. As Gordon and Helmer (1964) have already shown, descriptive statistics, summary indices (mode, mean, median, quartiles, interquartile ranges) are a good solution to identify the space, the range within which consensus is concentrated and/or dissented from. The reduction of the number of items between one round and another derives exactly from the analysis of the first results, allowing reduction of the questions on the questionnaire, formulation of new ones and revision of pre-existing ones. The results are compiled into a report, which is used in the next step as feedback, or as in the case of van Zolingen and Klaassen, convening one-day group conferences for each sector (industry, banking and insurance sectors), to which were invited 28 of the 44 experts. During these one-day conferences the discussion focused on the results coming from the first-round administration of the questionnaires and especially on the differences between the work and educational panels in their answers.

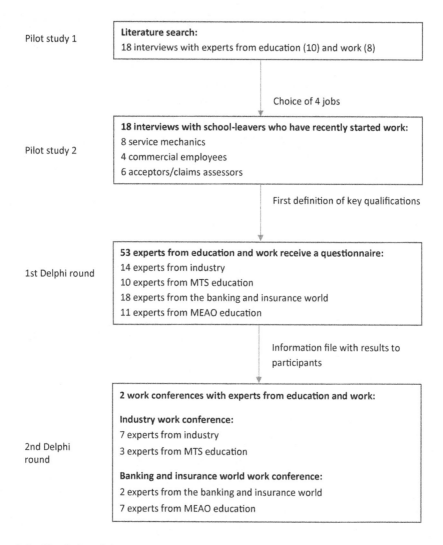

Figure 5.1 The design of the research.
Note: MTS = technical secondary school; MEAO = senior vocational secondary school in business administration
(*Source:* van Zolingen & Klaassen, 2003, p. 332)

Feedback to respondents and sending the second questionnaire

Giving feedback together with the second questionnaire or during a group discussion helps to increase the level of consensus (Rowe et al., 2005). The feedback can be given with a summary report that accompanies the questionnaire, or as done by Gordon and Helmer (1964), be directly inserted in the second questionnaire. Another way of proceeding is to revise the open-ended questions from the first questionnaire into closed-ended ones that use classification or assessment methods (Powell, 2003), for example, a Likert scale (Likert, 1932), in which the participants are asked to rank their answers in a scale from 'one to five', where 'one' can indicate 'agreement' and 'five' 'disagreement'.

It is recommended that the second-round questionnaire be given exclusively to interviewees who participated in the first round. The interviewees are then automatically selected from the second round onwards.

Iterative cycle

The preparation of the questionnaire, the analysis of the answers and the feedback given to the interviewees are repeated in the following rounds until the desired level of consensus or the required number of rounds have been reached. The consensus, the points of agreement, generally increase in consecutive rounds. After reaching the desired level of consensus or the final number of rounds (decided beforehand), the interviewees are shown the final report together with their personal answers, and it is possible to continue to discuss asynchronously with the experts or to organize a one-day group conference.

The merging point

The Delphi Method is an investigative technique based on the opinions collected with a questionnaire about a problem to be solved, and administered to a group of experts as members of a panel (see Table 5.9). Consensual agreement amongst them is pursued through repeated iterations (two or more rounds), now usually by email, of anonymized opinions and of proposed compromise statements from the group moderator. The first round is based on open-ended questions (like those used in an in-depth interview). The last round is conducted with closed-ended questions (like survey questionnaire items). Between the administration of each questionnaire, summaries of responses are circulated, and participants comment on them. The method constantly uses quantitative and qualitative data analysis techniques: written closed-ended questions of the questionnaire (survey), written open-ended questions (discursive or in-depth interview) discussion (focus group) and statistical analysis (distribution of median and quartiles).

Table 5.9 Identikit of the Delphi Method as a Merged Method

Characteristics of the researchers' work in the Merged Method	Identification in the Delphi Method
Data are co-constructed	Data are expert opinions, continuously constructed and co-constructed through the rounds
Data are relational and interactional outcomes	Data are the result of the relationships between: the opinions of each expert, the researcher's analyses, the interaction between the panel participants (the latter guaranteed by the feedback)
Methods predetermine the way the world is assembled	The Delphi approach chosen determines the way of looking at the problem and social reality
Abandoning the concept of validity (true-value), and rediscovery of fidelity	Validity is represented by the correct way of carrying out the interactions (Delphi per Delphi, round per round)
The researcher's orientation is not to find an out-there truth but to create the best (social and relational) conditions for gathering information	The intent with which the Delphi Method is already born is to identify opinions that are the result of knowledge, skimming between speculations and opinions that are the fruit of value judgements
Social actors under study are participants	Panel participants are holders of expert knowledge and information
The main aim is to guarantee participants' free expression	Freedom of expression is essential to the Delphi Method and is guaranteed by anonymity
Researchers' active listening should be pursued	Researchers express their active listening in considering the opinions expressed by the experts and by re-modulating – consequently – the content of the questionnaire
Results/findings are interpretations	The results arise from the interpretations provided by the experts. Researchers look at them cumulatively, distinguishing the orientation of the majority and minority. They return their analyses through feedback reports or one-day group meetings

Advantages and disadvantages

Earlier we made reference to Gordon and Helmer's (1964) retrospective wisdom in their understanding the limits of the Delphi Method and in time other scholars have also stressed its strengths and weaknesses (Linstone & Turoff, 1975; Sackman, 1975; Goodman, 1987; McKenna, 1994; Adler & Ziglio, 1995; Murry & Hammons, 1995; Powell, 2003; Keeney et al., 2006). Some have underlined how the method strains consensus, how it encourages conformity, and flattens the divergences and the dissent about certain opinions, or how it enables rushed judgements due to anonymity (Sackman, 1975; Goodman, 1987). Other critical elements were already mentioned in considering validity and reliability.

The following weaknesses have been identified by Gordon and Helmer (1964).

- Instability of panel membership may be unstable because there can be a fluctuation in the number of participants in the panel, and therefore a falling rate in terms of participation. After the first round, they would not be replaced. In this regard, the *Shang* approach eliminates the iterations.
- The time lapse between one round and another should not be longer than two months. Sometimes the length of the questionnaire administration period can result in a fall in the number of respondents and in changes of opinion.
- Ambiguous questions, especially when they concern very technical arguments and the panel/panels are heterogenous.
- Respondent competence, especially when the questions, or items refer to wide-ranging issues.
- Self-fulfilling and self-defeating prophecies, the consensus and opinions about somebody/something can vary according to how news from official sources, from the media or other authoritative sources of information changes or is filtered.
- Consensus by undue averaging because the use of medians and quartiles to measure the level of consensus can distort the assessment of an event distant in time. In this regard, the Markov–Delphi approach uses probability matrices.
- Substantive breadth, because even if we select experts belonging to the field of research, we often forget that the world is an interconnected system and we should not exclude the opinions/forecasts of experts close to the research sector. Gordon and Helmer, for example, admit that in their analysis on the future, they could have added experts coming from the area of international relations.
- The approach has been criticized for its potential to force consensus: it encourages conformity and neglects potentially illuminating information from alternative or outlying opinions (Goodman, 1987; Sackman, 1974):
  o 'quick and dirty' reputation;
  o panel recruitment bias;
  o high rates of panel attrition;
  o problematic consensus, where it is unclear what actually constitutes consensus;
  o 'specious consensus', where panellists conform out of sheer boredom.

The strengths, on the other hand, consist in favouring dialogue among experts, even if anonymously and asynchronously, and enabling exchange of opinions among those who are not geographically close to one another (Ziglio, 1995; Linstone & Turoff, 2002). In contrast to focus groups, for example, the participants in Delphi-based research remain anonymous, and this prevents the occurrence of two effects:

- a leadership distortion, which is possible when one of the participants occupies a prestigious position and is considered more authoritative by the others, so that when he/she expresses his/her opinion, the others feel 'forced' to follow suit;
- a spiral of silence, which occurs when one participant, fearing that his/her opinion might diverge from that of the majority, ends up not expressing it, and this opinion is therefore swallowed up inside a spiral of silence.

The Delphi Method allows the selected participants to express their thoughts and then re-organize them.

Practical tips

As we have seen, there are different types of Delphi. Therefore, the first thing to do is to specify the goal of your analysis and then to choose which of the Delphi approaches is the most appropriate to reach it.

Once the research question is identified, the best thing to do, as always, is to analyse the existing literature. Next, it is necessary to start selecting the members of the panel of experts, bearing in mind the objectives of the research on the one hand and the expertise of the experts on the other.

At this point, you ought to start preparing the questionnaire, which can consist of both open-ended questions and closed-ended ones. It is preferable for the first questionnaire to have more open-ended questions than closed-ended ones, so that it can collect as many opinions as possible. In the analysis of the results of the first round, the researcher should use content or category analysis techniques in order to close the answers and derive fixed response items. Alternatively, to analyse the level of consensus, you can use descriptive statistics and summary indices. The results obtained can then be graphically visualized with specific software packages such as Excel, **SPSS**, **Stata** and **R**.

It is important to give feedback to the participants through a specific report or by adding nuances to the new questions of the second questionnaire.

It is advisable to collect a strong consensus among the panel's participants since the Delphi Method requires various rounds, and thus, a relatively long engagement time. The experts need to be motivated; otherwise, the percentage of non-respondents will be high from the first round onwards.

Feedback and consensus are two fundamental elements for those who wish to use this approach. Also, it is important for the final discussion of the results to verify the quality of the consensus reached.

Further reading

In order to understand the philosophy of the Delphi Method, we recommend you read the documents created by the RAND Corporation. However, if you do not feel like going back so far in time, a good source is the manual by Linstone and Turoff (2002).

Linstone, H. A. & Turoff, M. (Eds.), (2002). *The Delphi Method: Techniques and applications*. Reading, MA: Addison-Wesley Publ. Co.

In the following you will find references for each single technique:

Di Zio, S., & Pacinelli, A. (2011). Opinion convergence in location: A spatial version of the Delphi method. *Technological Forecasting & Social Change*, *78*(9), 1565–1578.

Olsen, J. (2019). The Nominal Group Technique (NGT) as a tool for facilitating pan-disability focus groups and as a new method for quantifying changes in qualitative data. *International Journal of Qualitative Methods*, *18*, 1–10.

Rauch, W. (1979). The decision Delphi. *Technological Forecasting & Social Change*, *15*(3), 159–169.

Webler, T., Levine, D., Rakel, H., & Renn, O. (1991). A novel approach to reducing uncertainty: The group Delphi. *Technological Forecasting & Social Change*, *39*(3), 253–263.

Furthermore, it is suggested that you study use of the Delphi Method in the field in which you are carrying out your research, for example, to analyse the application of this method in sectors such as health, the environment and technology.

6

THE EVENT HISTORY CALENDAR AND INTERVEY METHODS: INTERACTION AT WORK IN SURVEYS

The Event History Calendar and the Intervey are two data collection methods that share common ground by placing interaction between the interviewer/researcher and the participant at centre stage in producing survey data. Though they are quite different in their procedures, both seek to generate – as a precondition for obtaining valid data – a kind of hermeneutic understanding that is produced in a full cooperation between the interviewer and the participant, whereas the Delphi Method pursues hermeneutic understanding between participants, through the interventions of the researcher.

The rationale of the Event History Calendar and the Intervey as Merged Methods lies in their combined employment of standardized but flexible data collection in one procedure. Grounded in a standardized questionnaire and/or calendar protocol, a cooperative and open interview phase leads the interviewee to the construction of quantifiable responses.

Definitions

The *Event History Calendar (EHC)* is a visual data collection tool that is applied by an interviewer in a flexible way to administer and record the answers of participants about (sequences of) past events within multiple life domains. It is the main representative of the calendar methodology approach that emerged from the wish of social researchers to gather in-depth retrospective data on life course trajectories in large populations (e.g., Freedman et al., 1988). Calendar methodology aims to stimulate participants to recall their autobiographical past, assuming that obtaining valid retrospective reports depends on a flexible interviewing style and conversational interaction (Belli et al., 2009, p. 32). Combining conversational interviewing (Conrad & Schober, 2005) with scripted questions and going through the participant's various life history domains in a flexible way (Belli, 1998; Belli et al., 2007) is central to most calendar studies.

The Intervey is a new term that Gobo (2011a) uses to revitalize both Likert's practice and Galtung's (1967, p. 120) interview method, in which the interviewer poses closed questions as if they were open-ended questions and – after a short conversation – classifies the respondent's answer in one of several predetermined categories. The neologism 'Intervey' puts together two characteristics: 'int' indicates the conversational component drawn from the (qualitative) in-depth interview; 'vey' transfers this dialogic component into the (quantitative) survey.

Brief history of the methods
The Event History Calendar

The rise of calendar methodology came alongside the emergence of research into autobiographical memory (e.g., Barsalou, 1988; Conway, 1996) and the growth of the CASM-movement of 'cognitive aspects of survey measurement' that developed quickly in the 1980s (e.g., Moss & Goldstein, 1979; Tanur, 1992; Schwarz & Sudman, 1994).

After some early studies (e.g., Balán et al., 1969; Blum et al., 1969) the development of calendar studies really started in the 1990s and continued in the decades that followed (see Glasner & Van der Vaart, 2009). Even the authors of the first study known to apply calendar methodology in this vein, dating back more than half a century ago (Balán et al., 1969), emphasized that their approach was a cooperative effort between interviewers and participants. This cooperative effort is still one of the central challenges, lying at the heart of what calendar methodology makes a Merged Method.

While the calendar methodology has its main roots in attempts to enhance recall in life history studies, its scope more generally includes the problem of validity of recall data in surveys. In the social sciences many empirical studies are based on retrospective surveys and it is well known that retrospective data often suffer from recall errors compromising data quality (Schwarz & Sudman, 1994; Dex, 1995; Grémy, 2007). Collection of retrospective data gets even more error-prone if additional threats arise due to communicative, cognitive and/or motivational disabilities, like when participants experience high task difficulty in recollecting information (Tourangeau et al., 2000). This can be the case if lengthy recall periods are applied (e.g., life histories), detailed information is requested (e.g., dates or characteristics of event), or if data are collected among vulnerable groups like the elderly, people with low literacy, or refugees who live in complex circumstances (cf., James & Burke, 2000; Quetulio-Navarra et al., 2015). In such studies it is seldom possible – and can be detrimental for data quality – to use fully standardized data collection methods (e.g., Harkness et al., 2010).

Calendar methods were one of the major innovations in survey research that sought to address such problems (see for reviews: Belli et al., 2009; Glasner & Van der Vaart, 2009) by combining a structured survey questionnaire approach with (visual) recall aids and conversational interaction to gather – ultimately – quantitative recall data (Belli & Callegaro, 2009). Recently they have also been applied in a qualitative manner (e.g., Harris & Parisi, 2007; Nelson, 2010). In the Merged Methods context our focus is on calendar methods that integrate qualitative and quantitative data.

The Intervey

The origins of the Intervey emerged during the methodological debate before and during World War II on the dilemma between open-ended and closed-ended response alternatives. In that period Likert pleaded for the idea that an interview should be more like a conversation and suggested posing survey questions without presenting the pre-established answer categories. Interviewers transcribed the interviewee's open answers and then (on conclusion of the interview) chose the response alternative which they considered to be the closest match with the interviewee's comment.

For decades, the dilemma between open-ended and closed-ended response alternatives dominated methodological debate (Schuman & Presser, 1979). But like all dilemmas it found no solution, for 'the closed questions did not capture the same dimensions of meaning that (are) revealed by the open question' (Groves et al., 1992, p. 60).

Over the years, survey researchers have resolved the dilemma by opting for the closed-ended alternative: as still prescribed by research handbooks today, the fixed-response alternatives are commonly presented to the respondents, who are asked to choose the response that fits them best. Most Mixed Methods researchers still follow this tradition. In the Intervey the interaction is put back at centre stage again.

In contrast to what is common in a standardized survey, the Intervey method approaches a research interview more like a natural conversation. As mentioned, the Intervey originated from Likert's procedure and the interviewee's comments are transcribed by the interviewer and later located in one of the pre-coded answer categories. Likert's procedure fell into disuse, but nevertheless, a few decades later, the Norwegian methodologist Johan Galtung (1967, p. 120) reprised Likert's ideas and devised a variant of his procedure which he called 'open question/closed answer'. Although this sounds like the reverse of Likert's technique, in fact both procedures were guided by the same principle: make the interview into a conversation, let the interviewees answer freely in their own words, and thus release them from the researcher's perspective (Galtung, 1967, p. 120). Galtung's version differed from Likert's to the extent that the interviewer does not transcribe the respondent's answers but classifies them on the spot, during the interview, in one of the predetermined categories. This made Likert's technique more agile, less time-consuming and economically less costly. However, Galtung soon lost interest in methodology, turning to substantive fields such as Peace Studies. Hence, his proposal never took off. For this purpose, the neologism 'Intervey' was coined (see Gobo, 2011a) to make the method more independent and distinct.

Approach to data collection and organization I: the EHC

Central to Event History Calendar methods is the use of a graphical time frame or grid that aims to facilitate access to long-term memory and enhance participant motivation during data collection (see Figure 6.1 for an example). By placing different activities within one time frame, the participant is helped to relate, visually and/or mentally,

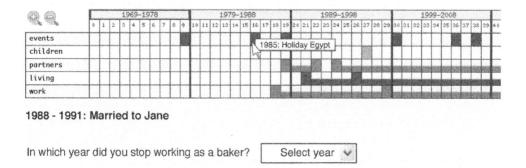

1988 - 1991: Married to Jane

In which year did you stop working as a baker?   [Select year ☑]

[<< Back | Continue >>]

Figure 6.1   A truncated example of a filled-out computer-assisted life history calendar.

(*Source:* Glasner et al., 2015)

the timing and content of several kinds of events or domains (Belli et al., 2013). The methodology takes advantage of narrative-like structures in autobiographical memory about causally or thematically related events (Burt et al., 2008). Moreover, the main applications of calendar methods utilize a standardized questionnaire in combination with a flexible interviewing approach, involving extended conversational interaction in which there is no strict adherence to asking scripted questions (Van der Vaart, 2004; Belli et al., 2013). Thus these methods grant a central and active role to the interviewer in enhancing recall.

Methodological studies report both positive and mixed outcomes regarding the impact of calendar methods on (quantitative) data quality (Goldman et al., 1989; Engel et al., 2001; Van der Vaart, 2004; Van der Vaart & Glasner, 2007; Sayles et al., 2010; Belli et al., 2013). Interviewer and participant evaluations of usage are largely positive (Belli et al., 2009; Glasner & Van der Vaart, 2009). Calendar methods are less common than regular standardized surveys but are generally accepted in both cross-sectional and longitudinal studies as an alternative to the standard survey data collection method with chronologically ordered question lists.

Although different versions of these instruments were developed relatively independently from each other in different fields of research, they share at least three important characteristics (for a review see Glasner & Van der Vaart, 2009).

1. The instrument includes a graphical display of the time dimension. Usually, the reference period is divided into smaller time units, such as years, months or days. The size of those time units largely depends on the length of the reference period.
2. The graphical display encompasses one or more themes or domains regarding which data are collected. Usually, the display consists of a grid in which life domains are listed horizontally and time units are presented along the top of the matrix.
3. The participant is provided with temporal bounding cues, such as public or idiosyncratic **landmark events**.

Figure 6.1 provides an example of a web-based calendar instrument in which the time dimension (a 40-year reference period) is presented on top and is divided into years, four life domains are listed horizontally (work, living, partners, children) and the first horizontal line is allocated for administering 'landmark events'.

Given the aforementioned three core characteristics, many different designs of calendar methods are possible regarding: (a) instrument design (choice of substantive domains, time units, type of landmark events); (b) mode of data collection (ranging from face-to-face paper-and-pencil interviews to self-administered web-based questionnaires); (c) structuring and flexibility of the questioning procedures (Glasner & Van der Vaart, 2009).

Of course, design choices also depend on the research field and the study of application. Currently, calendar methods are used in a wide array of domains with a great diversity in populations, ranging from life course research (e.g., Smith & Thomas, 2003; Reimer & Matthes, 2007; Drasch & Matthes, 2013), epidemiology (e.g., Colt et al., 2001; Engel et al., 2001), family planning studies (e.g., Becker & Diop-Sidibe, 2003) to domestic violence (Yoshihama et al., 2005). Also the Calendar Method has been applied in face-to-face, telephone and self-administered modes, and has been administered by paper-and-pencil, computer assisted and online tools (Glasner & Van der Vaart, 2009; Glasner et al., 2015).

The Calendar Method is most commonly known as the Event History Calendar (Belli, 1998), but the terminology is not standardized and alternative names are used, including life history calendar (Freedman et al., 1988), Timeline (Van der Vaart, 1996), life history matrix and time axes (Brückner & Mayer, 1998), life events calendar (Hoppin et al., 1998) and – in the medical sciences – the 'timeline follow-back' method (Sobell et al., 1988). In this chapter, we will use the terms 'Calendar Method' and 'Event History Calendar' (EHC) interchangeably to denote the generic 'calendar' approach.

Knowing and know-how I: the rationale of the EHC

The Calendar Method originated largely from two classic questioning procedures that have long been known to enhance long-term recall in survey studies (Sudman & Bradburn, 1974), i.e., **aided recall** and **bounding**. Aided recall refers to procedures that aim to improve the completeness of retrospective accounts, e.g., by providing participants with contextual information or memory cues, such as other events that occurred in the same time period (Eisenhower et al., 1991; Van der Vaart, 1996, 2004). Aided recall procedures may help people recall single events, the number of events, as well as substantive attributes of events (like the price of a purchase, Van der Vaart & Glasner, 2007). Bounding procedures aim to enhance the accuracy of dating past events by demarcating the borders of a recall period, e.g., by referring to specific dates – 'since July 1st' – or providing participants with other anchor points in time ('since your birthday', 'since the previous election', etc.). Bounding procedures that are applied in calendar methods, like relating the target event to 'landmark events' or to autobiographical episodes, have been shown to enhance the dating of past events (Loftus & Marburger, 1983; Tourangeau et al., 2000; Van der Vaart & Glasner, 2011).

The existing practice of using aided recall and bounding procedures – and combining both in (more extended) visual displays – was provided with a first theoretical underpinning and rationale by Belli (1998). This rationale, based on theories of autobiographical memory, proved to be essential for calendar methodology and hugely enhanced its further development and application. Belli (1998) grounded his rationale on multilevel models of autobiographical memory that give a central role to narrative-like structures in memory, which embed causally or thematically related events (Barsalou, 1988; Conway & Pleydell-Pearce, 2000; Brown, 2005; Burt et al., 2008). According to multilevel models, thematically organized lifetime periods (like housing, education, etc.) and their constituting life events serve as the primary organizational units of autobiographical knowledge. As we will see, Belli (1998) built in particular on Conway's (1996) multilevel model. Central to Conway's model, referring in turn to Barsalou (1988), is that autobiographical events are embedded in a context of ongoing life experiences. Conway (1996) distinguishes three highly interrelated memory structures in which autobiographical information is stored at different levels of abstraction:

- the highest level refers to thematically organized lifetime periods: they consist of long-term extended events, such as time periods studying at a college, or living together with a certain partner etc. Themes that can be distinguished within those lifetime periods (e.g., education, relationships) are considered to be central to the self;

- on a lower level, memories of 'general' or 'summarized' events are situated which took place during those lifetime periods. Such 'events' do not concern 'individual events' but draw together information from similar events or extended periods. They thus may differ in specificity (e.g., having health problems, going on holiday). General events are important in autobiographical memory, because they work as organizing representations for specific memories as well as providing access to thematic knowledge (Conway & Pleydell-Pearce, 2000; Burt et al., 2003);
- thirdly, memories of these general or summarized events are rooted in the 'phenomenological record', the memory structure in which **phenomenological experiences** are stored (in the case of events this is also known as episodical memory).

Designs of calendar instruments often (may) 'mimic' these three structures and thus provide a rich context for recall (Belli, 1998). The most elaborated calendar instruments, designed as data collection tools to record participants' answers about the sequencing and timing of past events within multiple life domains, were already explicitly designed to aid recall and enhance cross-references between life domains (Freedman et al., 1988). Belli's rationale (1998) demonstrates that the above-mentioned structures of autobiographical memory can be explicitly utilized to enhance data quality. In line with hierarchical memory models, Belli describes three types of (often interrelated) retrieval processes:

- top-down retrieval, which occurs when thematic and temporal information from higher order memory structures cue the recall of more specific memories; for example, when a participant recalls an episode of health problems within the context of his/her first job;
- parallel retrieval, taking place when one chronology of extended events on one theme cues the remembering of events that occurred contemporaneously on a second theme, while both are not hierarchically related. An example is when remembering a work history during a certain period cues recall of sports activities in that period;
- sequential retrieval, meaning that events or episodes are recalled as part of the same sequence. Thus temporal order and thematic information about events that are part of the same chronological sequence cues recall of information on single

events, like when remembering a certain job cues recall of the job that followed. The use of landmarks particularly enhances sequential retrieval.

As Belli (1998, p. 385) states: 'the success of the event history calendar is largely traceable to the use of many facets of autobiographical memory structure to improve the quality of retrospective reports'. Through the thematic and temporal organization of EHCs they encourage each of these retrieval strategies, which is largely enhanced by the visual display of an EHC that help participants to link events across different life domains and cross-check the reported information (Glasner et al., 2015). In comparison to the regular survey question-list method (in which sequential retrieval is common), the EHC indeed enhances the use of top-down and parallel retrieval (Belli et al., 2004; Bilgen & Belli, 2010; Belli & Al Baghal, 2016). In addition, the flexible EHC interviewing style allows for more cueing across periods and themes, and active probing by the interviewer based on such EHC features, as also confirmed in empirical evaluations (Bilgen & Belli, 2010).

Approach to data collection and organization II: the Intervey

The core of the Intervey procedure is that questions are phrased with an open format as if they were open-ended questions. As the interviewees answer, the interviewer tries (*during* the interview) to locate their answer within the pre-set range of answers, which only the interviewer knows. An example is presented in 'Question 5' shown in Figure 6.2.

'Question 5' is on motives (which guided the participant's choice of the Master in Political Science) and contains a long list of items, too long for the interviewer to handle straightforwardly. To help the interviewer, the motive-items are then divided into three areas,[1] matching the researcher's classification:

1. instrumental motives (items 1–8);
2. vocational motives (items 9–17);
3. social influence (items 18–19).

The interviewers are thus helped in their task. Then, if they are not immediately able to locate the interviewee's answer in the range of the pre-established items, they continue to talk to the interviewees until they understand which pre-coded item best

---

[1] These three categories have also been used as recodes in order to deal with the problem of statistical significance.

Question 5

What were the main reasons for your decision to enrol in the Master's in Political Science?

(instruction for the interviewer: *RESPONDENT'S FREE ANSWER, BUT MARK THREE REASONS AT MOST*)

1.	No entrance test	○
2.	Relatively easy degree course	○
3.	Attendance not compulsory	○
4.	Compatible with work. Possible to work and study at the same time	○
5.	Not accepted by faculty of first choice	○
6.	Subjects not excessively technical; it is a non-specialist degree course	○
7.	Close to home	○
8.	Wanted to go to university but did not know which degree course to select (choice by exclusion)	○
9.	Multidisciplinary programme	○
10.	To address political, social and cultural issues	○
11.	Because s/he liked it	○
12.	Because of the subjects taught	○
13.	The good reputation of the faculty	○
14.	The prestige of certain lecturers	○
15.	Useful for job	○
16.	Because of employment prospects	○
17.	To find a culturally stimulating environment	○
18.	Because some of his/her friends had enrolled	○
19.	Persuaded to do so by parents	○
20.	Other …	○
	....	
	....	
98.	Doesn't know/Can't remember	○

(*Source:* Gobo, 2011a)

Figure 6.2 An example of Intervey procedure.

matches their case. If there is still no matching item, they mark 'Other', noting down key words from the reply. They then write a brief note (two to three lines) upon completion of the interview, which will be classified according to the conventional double coding procedure.

Likert was aware that if the interviewer was to perform these tasks correctly, s/he had to be adequately trained in both how to conduct the probes and how to understand the meanings of the interviewee's statements. Accordingly, in 1942 Likert asked the psychologist Carl Rogers (1902–1987), known at the time for his use of 'nondirective' techniques[2] in psychotherapy sessions, to train interviewers in how to communicate with their interviewees and how to understand their emotions and reactions. The members of Likert's staff (in particular Charles F. Cannell and Victor C. Raimy) learned from Rogers how to formulate interviewee-centred probes and how to use pauses and silences as communication devices.

Knowing and know-how II: the rationale of the Intervey

The debate underlying the Intervey regarding open-ended versus closed-ended response, which already started before World War II (see the 'Brief History' section above), provides further insight into its rationale. The dispute culminated in the mid-1940s when conflict erupted between two opposing methodological factions: the *Division of Polls* headed by Elmo C. Wilson and the *Division of Program Surveys* headed by Rensis Likert (1903–1981), both of which were research divisions of the US Bureau of Intelligence, then directed by Keith R. Kane (see Converse, 1987, pp. 195–201). In the spring of 1942, Kane asked Paul F. Lazarsfeld (1901–1976), a methodologist of Austrian origin, to examine the controversy and to find a methodological solution for it. Lazarsfeld's famous article of 1944 ('The controversy over detailed interviews – an offer for negotiation) was a re-working of the report that he submitted to Kane in 1942.

Besides personal issues, the conflict between Wilson and Likert was provoked by the different research techniques employed in the two divisions. The interviewers used by Wilson's Division of Polls, for example, asked respondents to choose one of the fixed response alternatives – as still is common today. Instead, the interviewers who worked for Likert were instructed first to transcribe the interviewee's statements and then (after the interview) to select the response alternative which they considered to be the closest match with the interviewee's comment. Hence, in Wilson's case it was the interviewee who directly chose the answer; in Likert's case, it was the interviewer who chose the answer, doing so on the interviewee's behalf. The researchers at Likert's Division of Program Surveys also paid close attention to the procedures for codifying the narrative materials collected by open-ended questions. But they soon discovered the long-drawn-out and laborious nature of these procedures. Obviously, the criterion adopted by Likert still required more time and money than the criterion used by Wilson.

---

[2] Rogers originally called his approach 'non-directive therapy' but later replaced the term 'non-directive' with the term 'client-centred' and then later used the term 'person-centred'.

Although Likert's procedure was not proof against distortions (principal among which were misunderstandings of the interviewee's opinions), it nevertheless made it possible to avoid numerous other distortions that might arise during the interview, which according to Likert should as closely as possible resemble a conversation. This manner of administering questionnaires thus came to be baptized the 'fixed question/free answers' technique.

Regarding the long-standing dispute on open-ended *versus* closed-ended response alternatives, there are those who believe that fixed-response alternatives have considerable advantages (e.g., Selltiz & Jahoda, 1963, p.262; Oppenheim, 1966, p. 41; Bailey, 1978, p. 105). Other scholars object that open-ended answers are much more valid than fixed-response alternatives, which force interviewees to think in the same way as the researcher because pre-established categories suggest the answer to respondents who in fact have no opinion on the matter (Converse, 1964, 1970; Selltiz & Jahoda, 1963, p. 261; Noelle-Neumann, 1970, p. 193). The standardized survey interview is certainly easier to administer, but (through the close-ended response categories) it produces numerous biases well known in the literature. The principal ones are (see Gobo, 2011a for details):

1. *misunderstanding of the response alternatives* by the interviewees;
2. *the multiple word meanings of response alternatives;*
3. *the invented opinions* (or lies) phenomenon: fixed formats lead respondents to select an answer-opinion even if they do not have any opinions;
4. *the influence of the response alternatives* on formation of the judgement;
5. *social desirability* effects;
6. the *yea-saying* and *response set* phenomena: fixed formats lead respondents to always select the same response alternatives.

These are not biases (produced mainly by the close-ended response categories) of marginal importance. Indeed, at times their effect can be devastating (see Gobo, 2006, pp. 286–287, table 2). Researchers sincerely concerned with the quality of their data must necessarily seek remedies and try solutions able to reduce these biases. In our view, the remedy is to empower the interviewers, let them act flexibly and select the response categories on behalf of the participant.

The merging point

The two methods described embody the merging of qualitative and quantitative techniques in a single, unique and integrated method (see Table 6.1). Unlike using

Table 6.1 Identikit of the Event History Calendar and the Intervey as Merged Methods

Characteristics of the researchers' work in the Merged Method	Identification in the EHC and the Intervey
Data are co-constructed	Data are verbal or written responses of participants, expressed as replies to prompts and probes offered by the researcher/tool/interviewer
Data are relational and interactional outcomes	Data are the result of conversational interactions between the participant and the researcher/interviewer, and the relationships between autobiographical themes, life events and the participant's perceptions
Methods predetermine the way the world is assembled	The EHC and Intervey procedures determine the way of looking at the problem and social reality, in terms of contexts, meanings, relationships with external influences
Abandoning the concept of validity (true-value), and rediscovery of fidelity	Validity is represented by the credibility of the participants' judgements in relation to contextual information, by the correct way of interacting during data collection and the fidelity of interpretative data construction given the deductive categories employed
The researcher's orientation is not to find an out-there truth but to create the best (social and relational) conditions for gathering information	The EHC and Intervey procedures provide contextual information and interactive procedures that facilitate data construction by the participants
Social actors under study are participants	The actors/participants reconstruct in the interactional context their own attitudes, behaviour, decisions, evaluations, life events
The main aim is to guarantee participants' free expression	To guarantee a communicative climate which enables freedom of expression is crucial to validity and fidelity of the data construction and is ensured by anonymity
Researchers' active listening should be pursued	Researchers perform their active listening in considering the opinions expressed by the participant and providing facilitating prompts and probes
Results/findings are interpretations	The results arise from the participants' contextual and interactional interpretations that at the end of the data construction procedure are categorized by the researcher/ interviewer

different methodologies (survey, discursive interviews, focus groups, etc.) separately within the same research project (with all the problems of integration and epistemological incompatibility described in this book), the **Intervey** and Event History Calendar appear to be more compact, less costly and time-consuming. Hence, by combining both qualitative and quantitative approaches *in a single instrument* (in the wake of other methods described in the book), they seem a valid alternative to contemporary Mixed Methods practices. These two methods not only improve the integration of Mixed Methods, but also the quality of data. The core characteristic of EHC and Interveys as Merged Methods is the combination of standardized but flexible data collection: the cooperative, open style of data collection produces in the end quantifiable or at least categorizable responses. There have been substantive, general debates on the advantages and challenges of standardized versus flexible manners of data collection (see above: Fowler & Mangione, 1990; Schober & Conrad, 1997; Maynard et al., 2002). Both the EHC and Intervey do provide opportunities to balance the pros and cons of flexibility and standardization. It depends on the researchers and their tailor-made EHC or Intervey design how much interaction and hermeneutic interviewing are allowed, and in which and how many parts of the questionnaire/ interview flexibility or standardization are applied. Thus, a researcher may decide to use flexible EHC or Intervey interviewing only in certain sections of the questionnaire, and standardized interviewing in other parts.

In EHC and Interveys the merging of data thus is where flexible interviewing is applied to the standardized questionnaire – and structured calendar grid for EHC – and the interviewer–interviewee interaction funnels down the outcome into a valid quantitative record.

Thus, the question procedure and interviewer's behaviour must be interviewee-centred and *really* tailored to participants and their sociological and psychological differences.

As Schaeffer reminds us:

> criticisms of traditional standardized interviewing are particularly effective when taken together with research which suggests that the recall of events may be improved by procedures that do not fit neatly within the linear structure of standardized interview (Means, Swan, Jobe and Esposito 1992), that a less formal style of standardized interviewing may be more motivating (e.g., Dijkstra 1987), and that interviewers do not always implement standardization well ... and a formal standardized interview may not be the best social environment for stimulating and motivating recall of complex topics. (1995, p. 83)

Hence, we can achieve data quality by giving the interviewer a more active role, in order to bridge questionnaire and interviewee, and to reduce the gap between researchers' and participants' meanings. In David Riesman's (1958, p. 305) words: 'the task of the interviewer, as I see it, [is] to adapt the standard questionnaire to the unstandardized respondents'.

The utmost challenge of EHC and Intervey interviewing is to further optimize the interactional merging process for different types of populations and studies.

Advantages and disadvantages

Both procedures require changing interviewers' actual role and broadening their tasks, which provides opportunities to enhance data quality but of course may also come with some disadvantages. The role of interviewer has long been discussed in the survey literature. As Converse (1987, p. 95) reminds us, in the 1920s and 1930s some academics, and especially a good deal of the market research literature, 'placed the interviewer in some sort of middle ground of freedom and responsibility, with questions less standardised … There was concern that trying to standardise the interview more fully might interfere with the communication process.'

The interviewer was advised to act responsibly, with the freedom to 'conversationalize' questions without modifying their meaning. The directors of market research studies believed that the standardization of interviewers' behaviour was mandatory in laboratory experiments, but that it could not work in interview situations, where constant adaptation of the questionnaire to respondents and social situations was necessary. This kind of interviewer autonomy is still fairly commonplace in market research, though seldom admitted.

Flexibility in EHC interviewing

The flexible style of interviewing in EHCs consists of conversational interaction – explaining concepts, creating rapport – and active probing behaviour by the interviewer to stimulate retrieval (Belli et al., 2001; Conrad & Schober, 2005). Based on participants' replies and considerations, and on information that is already filled out in the calendar tool, the interviewer may stimulate top-down retrieval (relating a reply to overarching or subordinate events), sequential retrieval (by referring to earlier or later events and landmarks) and parallel retrieval (asking what happened simultaneously) (Belli & Al Baghal, 2016). In administering the EHC the interviewer has considerable freedom and may use many specific kinds of probes. They may probe for changes, check for gaps, provide cues from earlier answers and – like the interviewee – may go back and forth through the domains (Dijkstra et al., 2009).

But of course the promotion of flexibility in calendar interviewing does not mean that interviewers are free to ask anything they want; they are constrained by the objectives of the data collection as defined by the researcher (Belli & Callegaro, 2009). Depending on the study, standardized probes and clarifying definitions may be available in/with the calendar instrument. In the end, responses need to be registered in a standardized questionnaire or in calendar categories. Flexibility also means that interviewers may be more likely to skip questions, probe insufficiently or suggestively, define key concepts in idiosyncratic ways, fail to read introductory texts or questions as worded, or enter data incorrectly etc. (Dijkstra et al., 2009, p. 259). Thus while the flexible and active role of the interviewer is aimed at eliminating internal inconsistencies, enhancing recall and creating rapport, it could also in itself distort accounts (Tagg, 1985). The interviewer may be steering too much and the participant may find the negotiations offensive.

Another aspect that creates risks for data quality is the difficulty of the interviewer task. As we have seen above, the interviewer has a complicated task in asking questions, cross-checking information, stimulating recall, keeping up rapport and administering the responses. Given that an EHC often consists of an extended and complicated instrument, coding errors may also easily occur. Further, working with an EHC on sensitive topics may on the one hand be beneficial for data quality (by more self-disclosure of participants in self-administered EHCs, see below) but may also evoke emotional reactions in both interviewers and interviewees caused by its detailed data collection and visual display of the information. For instance, Yoshihama (2009, p. 150) found in a Japanese study on intimate partner violence, that three out of six interviewers experienced emotional distress that was specifically heightened by the EHC. Debriefings suggested that the close attention in the EHC to duration and extent of violence played a role, but also the visualization of long duration and recurrence of violence over the women's life course. Therefore, EHC interviewing demands complex skills and requires intensive interviewer training (Van der Vaart, 2004; Dijkstra et al., 2009).

Many skills that are required for EHC interviewing (as well as in the Intervey) are less common for large-scale surveys. Regarding these skills – like how to listen well to the interviewee, how to create rapport, how to formulate questions appropriately in their own words, how to select the relevant events to probe with and how to probe adequately (Belli et al., 2009; Glasner & Van der Vaart, 2009) – lessons can be gathered from qualitative interviewing styles. Some studies already have shown that further qualitative interviewing techniques match well with calendar methodology.

One example is a small EHC study among welfare recipients in which Harris and Parisi (2007) added open-ended questions to follow up on some earlier reported EHC data. Their aim was to explore how changes in welfare recipiency were interpreted and shaped by personal and contextual circumstances. The open-ended questions demonstrated that some participants, who had almost equal life trajectories, had experienced very different lives.

A second example is a qualitative EHC application on working-class Latinos' educational trajectories for which Nelson (2010) designed a largely unstructured procedure. The domains and time units were co-constructed by interviewee and interviewer and the interviewee steered the interview sequence. Nelson (2010) reports that this approach not only allowed for more in-depth narratives, but that its visual and interactional aspects (grid, markers, stickers, colours) helped build rapport. Capturing narratives of emotionally sensitive events especially benefited from this open EHC variation.

Similar results were also obtained in another small-scale, qualitative EHC study on sexual behaviour of adolescents in the USA (Martyn, 2009). First, through a self-administered EHC, detailed 6–10-year histories were collected on life context such as significant events, health information, risk behaviour like substance use and sexual risks. After recording these sensitive data in the EHC, participants found it easier to discuss in-depth their risk behaviour histories with the interviewers. Thus the completed calendar tool served as a frame of reference for further in-depth interviewing, both by diminishing sensitivity and emotional burden for the participant as well as by enabling a more integrated, contextual interviewer approach.

These examples demonstrate that – if interviewers are trained thoroughly – the qualitative side of EHC methodology can help build rapport and enrich the data by opening up sensitive discussions and providing unforeseen explanations. The flexible and interactive interviewing style of EHCs is perfectly suited to taking more advantage of qualitative in-depth interviewing techniques.

One major, more general, advantage of flexible EHC interviewing is that events in many life domains not only serve as memory cues for the target phenomena but also (can) represent factors that are related to the target phenomena. So the occurrence and timing of both the target events and its antecedents and consequences can be related to each other. Also the navigation through contextual data permits a wide range of possibilities to collect data regarding (antecedents and consequences of) occurrence, duration, temporal sequencing and the perceptions of interrelationships (Nico & Van der Vaart, 2012). This advantage of EHCs is particularly useful in more complicated cases where life experiences make consistent recall difficult, e.g., psychiatric participants who lived chaotic lives marked by mental illness, substance use and violence. As Roberts and Mulvey (2009, p. 192) put it: '[the EHC] provides researchers with a richer set of data points. Instead of simply getting a summary measure of life changes over an extended recall period, the [EHC] places these events at specific points in time.' Providing this context allows for a richer picture of potential causal mechanisms.

Flexibility in Intervey interviewing

Many of the issues mentioned above apply also to the Intervey. The Intervey technique has the considerable advantage that it offers all the strengths of open-ended questions, particularly their greater fidelity compared with closed-ended questions (which force interviewees to think in the same way as the researcher and to use his/her cognitive categories), and the fact that such questions grasp more dimensions of meaning (Groves et al., 1992, p. 60). Thus, the major advantage of the Intervey is that it produces responses that (as data) are highly comparable in meaning among respondents. Since interviewers are trained in the intended 'meaning' of the questions it leads to less variation in meaning among respondents. It standardizes 'meaning' of questions to a greater extent. In addition, while retaining these conversational and interactional qualities, the procedure is still efficient since responses are categorized on the spot into the pre-existing categories.[3]

Therefore, it collects more valid answers without increasing the costs of administering the questionnaire. In fact, the conversation time (between interviewer and participant) lost in giving the answer compensates for the time taken by the interviewer (or by the interviewees, if they are given cards) to read the list of the response alternatives.

Of course, the flexibility of the Intervey technique also results in some risks and limitations.

Like all open procedures, the Intervey may give interviewers opportunities to frame the responses too closely or selectively and thus steer the outcome. Obviously, the Intervey procedure releases the interviewers from the obligation of standardizing their behaviours. But the standardization of meanings remains an irremovable obligation that, nevertheless, can be satisfied by flexible interviewing techniques.

Making up the balance

A central idea behind both EHC and Intervey interviewing is that their potential limitations are easily compensated for by their more essential advantages. To begin with, because an interviewer's error does not *necessarily* produce a response error, the crucial question is this: to what extent do the interviewer's errors really affect the data quality (Schober & Conrad, 2002, p. 69)? In this regard, it is important to recall Beatty's statement:

---

[3] The Intervey differs from the use of open-ended questions in the conventional survey because the categorization takes place on the spot, instead of after the data collection is finished.

We are, after all, interested in reducing *total* error in surveys. If attacking the slightest interviewer deviation brings about modest reduction of interviewer error – but simultaneously causes a *great increase* in error from the respondent, who is unable to draw on the communicative resources of an informed, intelligent interviewer – then the strategy is self-defeating. (1995, p. 154)

Directing too much attention to interviewer's effects is like, to use an old saying, 'not seeing the wood for the trees'. The wood is the long list of biases mainly imputable to the questionnaire (or to the researchers as its designers) and to respondents (see Gobo, 2006, pp. 286–287, table 2).

Several studies[4] have evidenced that standardizing the stimuli (i.e., questions, items, response alternatives and interviewer's behaviour), which is the main task of the conventional Survey Method, does not necessarily imply standardization of their meanings, which should remain the main aim of all data collection. Clearly, the aim of reducing respondent errors by broadening the interviewer's tasks will lead to an increase in interviewer effects. However, the dilemma is deciding which kind of errors we prefer to minimize. In addition, the magnitude of the interviewer's errors may be far smaller than those of respondents if:

a)   a trained interviewer knows the purpose and correct meaning of questions, items and response alternatives better than respondents;
b)   the consistency of the meanings in the (relatively small) 'interviewers community' is greater than amongst the mass of socially and culturally different respondents, as inter-rater reliability exercises seek to bring about. From this perspective, interviewers and respondents should work together to 'jointly construct' the meaning of questions and answers (Mishler, 1986). Surveys (in order to succeed) have to exploit the 'interactional resources that routinely mediate uncertainties of relevance and interpretation' (Suchman & Jordan, 1990, p. 241) in conversations. As Schober and Conrad (1997) have shown, in a laboratory experiment with trained telephone interviewers using both standardized techniques and flexible interviewing, there is no substantial difference in response accuracy when the concepts in the questions are clearly mapped onto the fictional situations of respondents. In addition, and even more interesting, when the mapping was less clear, flexible interviewing increased accuracy by almost 60%.

---

[4]   Nuckols (1953); Cicourel (1964, p. 108); Galtung (1967, p. 116); Bourdieu et al. (1968, p. 70); Gostkowski (1974, p. 19); Briggs (1984); Marradi (1984); Pitrone (1984, pp. 35–36); Mishler (1986); Suchman & Jordan (1990); Houtkoop-Steenstra (2000, pp. 180–184).

However, the opposition to flexible interviewing is widespread in the literature, even if it seems to be based more on a methodological narrative than on evidence (see Gobo, 2006 and 2011a). In fact, the magnitude of the (alleged) 'dangerousness' of the interviewer has still not been wholly quantified, given that interviewers' errors seem of secondary importance and far smaller than researchers' and respondents' errors. As Bradburn states, 'the characteristics of the task[s of the questionnaire] are the major source of response effects and are, in general, much larger than effects due to interviewer or respondent characteristics' (1983, p. 291). In addition, Sudman and Bradburn (1974, p. 138) believe that the biases introduced by social desirability, forgetting and so on, are more dangerous than the interviewer's behaviour. Hence, Bradburn, Sudman and Blair (1979, pp. 50 and 171–172) conclude that interviewer errors do not have significant effects on the quality of data. Nevertheless, the dogma of standardization is still alive.

Practical tips

The event history calendar

When designing and employing an EHC study it is important to build a data collection procedure – including the related EHC grid – that is both theory-based and tailored to the population and research themes at hand. In particular, close attention needs to be paid to the following practical issues:

- being well-informed about characteristics of the target population and the communicative and cognitive abilities of the participants;
- choosing an adequate mode of data collection – like (computer-assisted) face-to-face, self-administered, telephone or web-based – and adjust the calendar grid and aided recall tools accordingly;
- training interviewers regarding their flexible, interactive role, while adhering to the data collection procedures;
- optimizing the difficulty of the recall task in relation to the length of reference period;
- creating a graphical calendar grid that is user-friendly and motivating to fill out;
- providing a clear and practical instruction on how participants are expected to fill out the calendar grid and how to use landmark events; being aware of both the possible aided recall effects and possible bias that may be induced.

The Intervey

- This technique is best suited for telephone mode interview, since the interviewee should not look at the answer the interviewer chooses. In fact, the interviewee may not feel represented by the interviewer's chosen answer. For example, in surveys conducted traditionally, respondents sometimes insist that the interviewer tick an alternative response as 'completely satisfied' (for example in relation to an item on relationships with colleagues), while the comments preceding the answer indicated clearly that their relations are bad. In a telephone interview, the interviewer can remedy this distortion (dictated by conspiracy of silence) by choosing the alternative response closest to the interviewee's status as inferable from the comment. Instead, in a face-to-face interview, this would be more problematic because the interviewee could contest the interviewer's choice even if it is more truthful. Of course, this procedure can raise ethical problems, especially by those who endorse ethicism, an abstract approach (from desk methodology) and not practical to research, instead of adopting 'situational ethics' (see Gobo, 2008a).
- Interviewers must be trained to approach the interview more like a natural conversation; hence they should be flexible, interactive, active listeners, while adhering to the data collection procedures.

Further reading

The Event History Calendar

For broad reviews of fields of application, designs and data collection methods:

Belli, R.F., Stafford, R.P., & Alwin, D.F. (2009). *Calendar and time diary methods in life course research*. Thousand Oaks, CA: Sage.

Glasner, T.J., &. Van der Vaart, W. (2009). Applications of calendar instruments in social surveys: A review. *Quality and Quantity, 43*, 333–349.

For cognitive aspects of survey methodology, underlying calendar methods:

Belli, R.F. (1998). The structure of autobiographical memory and the event history calendar: Potential improvements in the quality of retrospective reports in surveys. *Memory, 6*(4), 383–406.

Tourangeau, R., Rips, L.J., & Rasinski, K. (2000). *The psychology of survey response*. Cambridge: Cambridge University Press.

For calendar design, aided recall and landmark events:

Freedman, D., Thornton, A., Camburn, D., Alwin, D., & Young-DeMarcco, L. (1988). The life history calendar: A technique for collecting retrospective data. *Sociological Methodology, 18*, 37–68.

Loftus, E.F., & Marburger, W. (1983). Since the eruption of Mt. St. Helens, did anyone beat you up? Improving the accuracy of retrospective reports with landmark events. *Memory & Cognition, 2*, 114–120.

Van der Vaart, W., & Glasner, T.J. (2011). Personal landmarks as recall aids in survey interviews. *Field Methods, 23*(1), 37–56.

The Intervey

A classic article that anticipated later developments on the problem of answer comparability consistent with the Intervey:

Lazarsfeld, P. F. (1935). The art of asking why. Three principles underlying the formulation of questionnaires. *The National Marketing Review, 1*(1), 32–43; reprinted in Lazarsfeld, P. F. (1972). *Qualitative analysis: Historical and critical essays* (pp. 26–39). Boston: Allyn and Bacon.

An (inadvertent) manifesto for the interactional survey approach:

Suchman, L., & Jordan, B. (1990). Interactional troubles in face-to-face survey interviews. *Journal of the American Statistical Association, 85*(409), 232–253.

A conversational analysis that shows the weakness of the assumptions of standardized interviewing:

Houtkoop-Steenstra, H. (2000). *Interaction and the standardized survey interview: The living questionnaire.* Cambridge: Cambridge University Press.

For an extended treatment of the Intervey see:

Gobo, G. (2011a). Back to Likert: Towards a conversational survey. In M. Williams and P. Vogt (Eds.), *The Sage handbook of innovation in social research methods* (pp. 228–248). London: Sage.

7

Q-METHODOLOGY: STUDYING PEOPLE'S VIEWPOINT

Contents

Q-Methodology, introduced by William Stephenson in 1935, is a method that aims at analysing in an objective way the subjective points of view of the individual, extending the interactional element of the methods discussed in Chapter 6 by techniques that involve task-completion by participants. In this sense it uses a series of techniques that converge in the same research and analysis procedure. It is useful when one wishes to identify the way in which different groups of people think systematically about a peculiar problem. Q-Methodology normally requires six steps. The first step is the development of the concourse, which is the necessary step to identify the flow of communication surrounding the research topic, finding the views, attitudes, perspectives and vantage points on an issue. The six steps can be grouped into three main phases:

- Q sample selection, which is the selection step of a representative sample of statements drawn for the Q study (emerging from concourse development);
- Q-sorters selection (Q-set), in which the number of participants and their characteristics (gender, age etc.) are chosen;
- Q-sort generation through Q-sorting, which is a phase of organization and analysis of all the individual Q-sorts which are analysed by person factor analysis) and begins the interpretation.

The path of a Q-sort study is: each of a sample of participants (the Q-set) sorts a sample of items into a subjectively meaningful pattern (the Q-sort). Resulting Q-sorts are factor analysed by person (Q-analysis), yielding a set of factors whose interpretation reveals a set of points of view. Along this path, Q-Methodology shows its merged character, because it combines: qualitative techniques in the creation of the cards and in listening to the opinions of the participants; quantitative techniques in the creation of the Q-sort and in the analysis of Q-sorts; and returns to a qualitative technique in the interpretation of the factor analysis and feeding back results to the participants.

Definition

Q-Methodology is an interdisciplinary approach comprising procedures and a conceptual framework that provide the basis for a science of subjectivity, and target phenomena consisting of ordinary conversation, commentary and discourse in everyday life (Brown, 1986, 1993).

In its analysis of subjective points of view, it uses both qualitative and quantitative resources. For its characteristics, the authors Pnina Shinebourne and Martin Adams (2007) have defined it as a phenomenological approach; this closeness is established following Stephenson's and Brown's declarations about procedures – of a statistical kind – thanks to the attribution of meaning they receive, and to the results this research method can reach. The issue is quite simple and is connected to the rationale behind the quantitative techniques used within this approach. In fact, even if a factor analysis is used, one must consider the purpose for which it is used and the interpretative modalities of the results themselves.

On one hand, Stephenson claims that 'Q-sorts really measure *nothing* if they are correctly applied, and their meaning-conferring and intentionality only emerges by way of factor analysis of several Q-sorts' (Stephenson, 1988, p. 211; emphasis in original).

On the other hand, there is a relevant element represented by the use in various applications of the Q-sort statistical technique to compare types of participants with an ideal Q-sort built up *a priori* (Rogers & Dymond, 1954), or to use factor analysis to make the single type factors emerge. Stephenson believes that 'Husserl's phenomenology and Q-Methodology are on the same footing, except for denial of consciousness as substantive and its replacement by communicability in Q' (p. 216). This communicability is traced by Shinebourne and Martin (2007) in Steven Brown's words (1980):

> Communicability in Q refers to the flows of ideas, statements, commentaries, beliefs, etc., surrounding any topic (Brown: 1980). The set of statements is envisaged as a 'launch pad for an investigation, an entré into a phenomenon' (ibid: 39), the researcher's 'best initial guess' (ibid) to start the process and engage in a collaborative manner in a dialogue with participants. Brown is in fact describing the Q set of statements as an entry point into a 'hermeneutic circle'. (Shinebourne & Martin, 2007, p. 107)

In fact, it is true that Q-Methodology makes use of quantitative techniques, but its connection with the phenomenological approach wishes to stress specific ways of using such statistical analyses to access the interpretation, and therefore the hermeneutics of a phenomenon, in the way it is interpreted and defined by a group of individuals. Q-Methodology aims at exploring the subjective narration of phenomena from the point of view of the participants and asks them to attribute a meaning by giving a score or expressing a scale of agreement/disagreement to the statements.

The researcher prepares the sentences or can use images, as **visual stimuli**, but it is for the participant to establish the number of elements to use and then to assign them a position in the ranking of the Symmetrical Q-grid (see Figure 7.2). This procedure, that allows the participants to control the ranking process, makes it possible for the factors to be derived statistically from the results of the distribution activities performed by the participants, rather than be determined by a researcher's topic ranking and analysis. In addition, the sentences themselves are created in a participative way. In what is defined as the 'concourse' (from the Latin *concursus*, which means running together, 'as when ideas run together in thought' (Brown, 1993, p. 94)), the researcher needs to take all points of view into account to create statements, use interviews and focus groups to understand and embrace the various perspectives on a phenomenon, while also bringing to bear an analysis of the literature from which to derive relevant statements. It is a bottom-up approach and not a top-down one; for these reasons 'the analysis involved in Q-methodology may incorporate less "researcher bias" than other interpretive techniques' (Cordingley et al., 1997).

Brief history of Q-Methodology

The possibility of using a quantitative technique to explain the subjectivity of points of view seems to be – from the very beginning – a feature of this methodology. This search for a merging point begins with a one-page publication 'Nature' by Stephenson in 1935, in which he announces a different way of working with factor analysis to open up new, interesting applications. 'The technique, however, can also be inverted. We begin with a population of n different tests (or essays, pictures, traits or other measurable material), each of which is measured or scaled by m individuals. The (m) (m − 1)/2 **intercorrelations** are then factorised in the usual way' (Stephenson, 1935, p. 297).

The proposition was to study factors in Q-Methodology such as categories of operant subjectivity (Stephenson, 1977). Subsequent studies will disclose these categories of subjectivity starting from the concourse phase, show themselves later in the ranking of the cards and finally reappear as factors.

From here onwards (see also Burt and Stephenson, 1939; Burt, 1972), the studies started being consolidated and a review of what this method is and what are its main characteristics can be found in a work published by Brown in 1993 called *A Primer on Q-Methodology*. It is a self-avowed introduction and a defining study for other more complete works; it is also, however, an essential step in the construction of the history of this methodology. In his research, Brown explores the responses to the question: 'tell me about a phenomenon that I cannot learn some other way' (see 'Knowing and know-how' section in this chapter). In fact, Brown's article is a revised compilation of a series of postings to QUALRS-L and Q-METHOD, which are Internet electronic conferences on qualitative research methods and Q-Methodology, respectively. The goal is to identify the specific characteristics of this methodology and to distinguish it from others that could seem apparently similar. The posts collected by Brown mostly tell the story of a debate focused on two themes: the use of factor analysis and the identification of an innovative feature for this method.

Stephenson's ideas have gained prominence outside psychology. Spurred initially by his own *The Play Theory of Mass Communication* (1967), several other books and articles have appeared which have served to clarify Q's presuppositions and to demonstrate its applicability in virtually every corner of human endeavour. In 1977, publication began of *Operant Subjectivity: The Q-Methodology Newsletter*, which in 1989 was adopted as the official journal of the newly created International Society for the Scientific Study of Subjectivity. The Society has met annually since 1985 and has generally pursued the implications and applicability of Stephenson's ideas in psychology, communication, political science, health, environmental and related areas.

Approaching Q-Methodology

Q-Methodology begins with the intention of making human subjectivity – represented by points of view – communicable, and subsequently synthesizing it through quantitative procedures. The starting point is the development of the concourse 'and it is from this concourse that a sample of statements is subsequently drown for administration in a Q sort' (Brown, 1993, p. 95).

The development of the concourse

In developing the concourse, the researcher must take into account all points of view to create statements that the researcher subsequently selects and records on sort cards. It represents an important phase and in order to capture all points of view several techniques are used, such as: interviews, focus groups, literature analysis and so on.

The researcher assigns a random numbering to the cards. As soon as the statement creation procedure is concluded, the statements are inserted in the Q-set and are generally placed on cards for participants to sort. They are then distributed to the participants who are asked to order them inside the Q-grid (see Figure 7.1). The researcher assigns a random numbering to the cards. Participants receive instructions to arrange the cards inside the matrix in what they see as a normal or quasi-normal shape (see the 'The Q-sorters selection and Q-sort generation' section below), such as: 'Sort the cards according to what is most like and most unlike your everyday feelings' or 'Sort the cards in accordance with what is most like/unlike your situation' (Ellingsen et al., 2014, p. 3).

The statements the participants are asked to classify concern opinions and not facts, and since they are opinions, there is nothing 'right' or 'wrong', being subjective points of view.

The Q-sample selection

Figure 7.2 shows a symmetric grid ordered with an agree/disagree scale from −5 to +5 and a neutral view represented by 0. The Q-grid has fewer rows at the furthermost ends

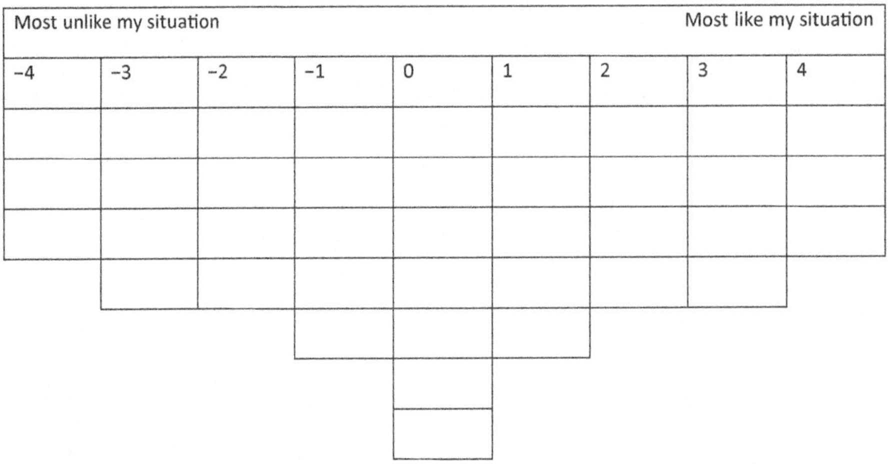

Most unlike my situation							Most like my situation	
−4	−3	−2	−1	0	1	2	3	4

Figure 7.1 Q-sort distribution grid used in the Ellingsen et al. study.
(*Source*: Ellingsen et al., 2014, p. 430)

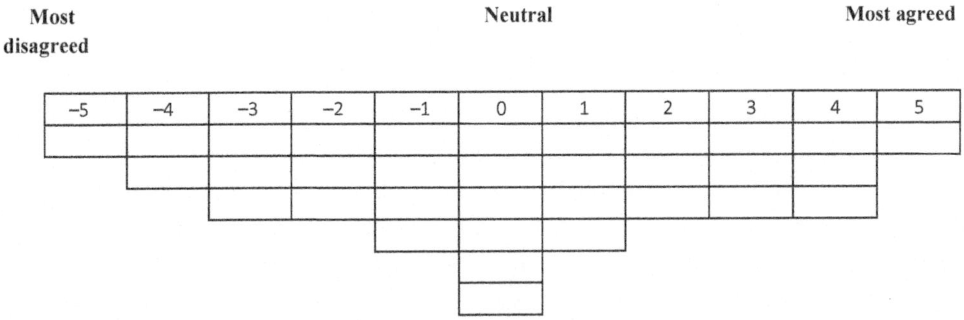

Most disagreed **Neutral** **Most agreed**

−5	−4	−3	−2	−1	0	1	2	3	4	5

Figure 7.2 Symmetrical Q-grid.

than it has in the neutral column and the pattern is symmetrical, in that if there is one row under the +5 column then there is one row under the −5 column and so on, with the majority of rows falling under the 0 column reflecting the neutral view.

In their study, Ingunn Ellingsen et al. (2014) applied Q-Methodology by creating cards with images, to be submitted to children to understand their point of view and the effects regarding divorce. Q-Methodology does not require that the items that are sorted are written statements. Stephenson (2005) proposed Q-sorting with sculpture, artwork, statements or images. Before creating the images, Ellingsen et al. conducted a range of qualitative studies not only among daycare staff, parents and family therapists, but also with the children themselves (development of the concourse). In the end, Ellingsen and colleagues collected a total of 20 statements that were then translated into images by illustrators and submitted for sorting (Q-sorts) to the children. An opinion statement or an image on the card is understood to be a kind of stimulus that triggers respondents' search for meaning (Glynos et al., 2009). The process of selecting the statements or images to be submitted to the participants is the phase Q-sample.

Given that the participants must compare each item with all other items, the Q-sample usually does not exceed 50 or 60 items (Davis & Michelle, 2011); studies using smaller Q-samples of around 35 items are common, while studies using Q-samples of more than 100 hundred items are rare.

The researcher may elect to use:

- an unstructured Q-sample, in which 'items presumed to be relevant to the topic at hand are chosen without undue effort made to ensure coverage of all possible sub-issues' or underlying factors (McKeown & Thomas, 1988, p. 28);
- or a structured Q-sample, which adopts a design that reflects categories the researcher apprehends in the concourse or which is based on prior theory.

The Q-sorters selection and Q-sort generation

It is also possible to develop a test-pilot with the aim of obtaining a final 'well-structured' Q-sample. Ellingsen et al. developed a pre-test phase with five children and then started the analysis with a larger group (37 children). The group of 37 children represents the group of respondents, known as the person-sample or P-set, but it is important to remember that in Q-Methodology, the design of the p – like the Q-sample set – has theoretical significance, not statistical significance.

In practical application, to fill in the grid with cards, participants are usually asked to create three piles with the aim of ordering items-statements: those with which they are in general agreement on the right, those with which they are in general disagreement on the left, and those about which they are neutral or indifferent in the middle.

Implementation of sorting can be in two ways:

- forced, in which participants/sorters are asked to choose from the agree pile only a specific number of cards and place them under the 'most agree' column. After the agreed pile is exhausted, the disagreed pile will be used to fill up the disagreed side of columns, starting with the 'most disagreed' column. Neutral cards can be used to complete the agreement column, they can be inserted in the disagreement column or in the neutral column;

- free distribution, in which participants/sorters are asked to place statements in the positive pile anywhere under the columns without any restraint, followed by negative statements and neutral statements. (Lee, 2017, pp. 73–75).

It is through this sorting that each Q-sorter gives subjective meaning to the statements.

As Byung Lee (2017, p. 73) explained, 'After dividing statements in three piles of "agree," "neutral," and "disagree," Q respondents are allowed either a fixed or free distribution matrix for further sorting. They can have a prearranged quasi-normal form of frequency distribution.' Regarding the quasi-normal form of frequency distribution, Lee refers – to explain it – to the work of Stephenson (1935):

> The forced distribution is based on one of Q-technique postulates: 'vi. Scores are approximately normally distributed with respect to the person-array' (Stephenson, 1953, p. 58). Regarding why it should take a quasi-normal distribution, Stephenson did not seem to clearly show any empirical evidence throughout his works. He just wrote, 'A normal curve is not likely. For certain reasons, however, it should be symmetrical. Therefore, we follow the practice of using a much flattened symmetrical distribution of scores for all Q-sorts' (p. 59). (Lee, 2017, p. 75).

Obviously, among the researchers who use Q-Methodology there has been a division between those who prefer forced distribution and those who prefer free distribution. Those who insist on forced distribution argue that it makes sorters think more deeply because they are forced to choose the most suitable statement out of many for one column and continue to do so one after another. On the other hand, those who prefer free distribution remark that the purpose of Q studies is to find thinking patterns or frameworks of people from their own viewpoints (Lee, 2017, p. 77). In fact, the importance of Q-Methodology remains as a procedure of a subjective classification, that is also a relative ranking, because the participant classifies the statements in relation to the ranking of the other statements, rather than evaluating them individually. Not less, this relative ranking has the advantage of reducing the risk of arbitrary or biased sorting, for example by the emotions of the participant, and thus enhances the replicability of the sort (Raadgever et al., 2008; Louah and Visser, 2016).

The researcher is with the participant when s/he sorts the cards in the grid (assisted Q-sorting). It is up to the researcher to:

- improve the internal consistency of the ranking;
- avoid contradictory statements receiving the same score;

- help the participant when it comes to discriminating between two closely spaced scores;
- collect and record qualitative data on how the participant interpreted the statements in their Q-sorting and what implications those statements have in the context of their overall view (Louah & Visser, 2016).

When the participants have finished positioning the statements, the grid is full and there are no more Q-cards to position, what is obtained from the completion of the grid are the participants' Q-sorts. It is also possible to ask participants to comment on their positioning of the statements after completing the Q-sort in 'post-sorting interviews'. The researcher can record them, and during these interviews ask the reasons for which some statements were placed on the right or left of the grid.

The Q-analysis

At the end of this process the researcher has as many Q-sorts as there were participants. It is possible to analyse the Q-sorts by using a factor analysis, where the objective is to place them in correlation. The use of correlation in Q-Methodology is different from R-type methods, which usually examine the correlation between a small number of variables observed across many subjects. In the survey the principle is that the greater the number and representativeness of subjects (respondents), the better each variable (question) is described by the data and the greater the validity of the results.

In Q-Methodology the relationship is reversed, and it is the correlation between subjects (sorters) that is important. This means that individual viewpoints are kept whole, rather than atomized across variables, and that a larger number of statements across a smaller number of sorters can provide the same validity in a statistical sense as the usual R-type approach (Eden et al., 2005, p. 416).

The participants' rankings are therefore subject to the factor analysis; these factors derive however from single subjectivities. The factor analysis reveals the similarities between the participants' rankings. This means that what is analysed is the overall image of the order attributed to the statements by the participants. In other words, similar orders are placed upon the same analysis factor, even if it is possible for some participants to have in common only the scores attributed to some statements and to differ instead for the others.

To be more specific, if two persons' Q-sorts are similar (but not identical), they will correlate highly and will end up on the same factor. These two people share central aspects of their subjectivity and will therefore influence the structure of the same general factor together with others sharing similar views. Factors are often also called views or viewpoints in Q methodological studies, since their content reveals general views that participants on this factor share (Ellingsen et al., 2014, p. 4).

The results from the analysis also reveal differences among the participants. So, bearing in mind these similarities/divergences in the Q-sorts analysis, it is important to point out two things:

- in the interpretation of emerging factors, central viewpoints among participants are disclosed in a systematic way;
- in the interpretation of emerging factors, 'we search for the overall configuration of meaning that lies in the factor, as well as what the different factors have in common and what distinguishes one factor from another' (Ellingsen et al., 2014, p. 4).

It is exactly for these reasons that what we obtain is an overall image, a general model inside which we find placed the card statements that define a factor. For what concerns the attributions of statements to factors, Joy Coogan and Neil Herrington (2011) inform us that:

> Generally, the higher the number of factors extracted from a study the lower the number of participants who will significantly load on these factors. Participants will only significantly load on a factor if their pattern of statements is (as a whole) different from the other patterns of statements shown by the participants who loaded on the other factors. The more factors there are, the more possibility there is of part of the pattern of an individual's sorting of the statements being similar to another factor. The number of factors extracted from the data is based on a decision made by the researcher, which is based on an evaluation of eigenvalues, distinguishing statements and number of participants loading on all factors. (Coogan & Herrington, 2011, p. 27)

The interest of Q-Methodology is in the nature of the segments and the extent to which they are similar or dissimilar. Statistical representativeness, so essential in social research, is in this case relatively irrelevant.

A case study

In his 1993 paper, Brown shows Q-Methodology's specificity by analysing the posts published by a public of experts during an electronic conference in which the characteristics of the method itself were discussed. Brown's article is also an illustrative exercise on how to apply Q-Methodology. He reminds us that it is the analysis of a subculture, that is the opinions of a group of experts about a specific topic, who work during the concourse phase putting together ideas and opinions. Hence, he begins by showing the *verbatim* comments (see Table 7.1) in the order in which they appeared during the conference and accompanying them with the authors' pseudonyms.

Table 7.1 lists different points of view on Q-Methodology, which consider different traits of it, now factor analysis, or the possibility of exploring subjective points of view and so on. This considers subjective points of view about what Q-Methodology is and what this methodology is not – in the opinion of experts – which become part of the concourse phase. When all the texts/opinions have been collected, categorizing activity begins on them, as happens in Content Analysis. The organization of the comments, in the sense of the texts, is carried out by the observer/researcher, who is sometimes forced to fall back (as in Content Analysis) on categories that are superimposed on the data.

Table 7.1 Some verbatim comments that appeared during discussion

It allows us to sort patterns of speech among speakers. (Follet)
It uses an ipsative technique of sorting a representative set of subjective statements drawn from a concourse of possible feelings or reactions about a subjective condition. (Martin)
In Q-factor techniques, a case by case matrix of some sort of similarity measure (usually an ipsatized correlation) is analyzed. (Kendig)
Q-factor analysis is a simple variation of factor analysis, actually component analysis. (Hoffer)
Q methodology is a set of procedures, theory, and philosophy supporting the study of the same kind of subjectivity that is the focal point of much qualitative research. (Brown)

Source: Data from Brown, 1993, p. 96

Brown proceeds by selecting from all the comments collected in the concourse phase a subset, which is the set of statements eventually presented to participants in the form of a Q-sort.

The goal of this subset selection procedure is 'to provide a miniature which, in major respects, contains the comprehensiveness of the larger process being modeled' (Brown, 1993, p. 98).

We here present some of the 20 statements that make up Brown's Q-sample (see Table 7.2).

When reading the statements, Brown noticed that some of them were methodological while others were more technical. So, all statements in the concourse were categorized as either (a) methodological or (b) technical, depending on their main thrust, all the time recognizing that few statements are ever exclusively one or the other. At this point it is necessary to organize the categories identified (a and b) to make them fairly represent the respondents' universe. The 'methodological' and the 'technical' categories are then divided *per* participants, who in Brown's research are: (c) Stephenson, (d) Burt and (e) neither, to take into account the intellectual heritage of the points of view at issue. What is obtained is a 2 × 3 table (see Table 7.3), in which an equal number of statements is selected for each cell (e.g., 8 of type ac statements, 8 of type ad, etc.) for a Q-sample size of N = (6)(8) = 48 statements for Q-sorting by respondents.

Table 7.2 Q-sample in Brown's article

(1) It permits the a priori structuring of hypotheses in the design of the Q-set to be sorted.	(12) Q can give some fascinating insight into underlying philosophic structures which comprise subjective phenomena.
(2) Q methodology is a set of procedures, theory, and philosophy supporting the study of the same kind of subjectivity that is the focal point of much qualitative research.	(14) It allows for the interpretive study of subjective behaviors without imposing the usual biases of structured survey questionnaires.
(5) Centroid factor analysis is recommended since its indeterminacy is compatible with quantum theory and, at the rotational stage, with inter behavioral principles.	(18) Q has never involved the correlation and factor analysis by rows of the same matrix of data that is analyzed by columns in R methodology.
(9) Cluster analysis is really something quite different and has no commitment to that subjectivity which is central to Q methodology.	(19) The frequencies in the piles must be restricted to the frequencies that would be expected if you had a normal curve, with each pile corresponding to an area of a normal curve.

Source: Data from Brown, 1993, pp. 98–99

Table 7.3 Q-sample structure

		(a) methodological	(b) technical
(c)	Stephenson	(ac)	(bc)
(d)	Burt	(ad)	(bd)
(e)	Neither	(ae)	(be)

Source: Brown, 1993, p. 100

To simplify the illustration of his work, which aims to explain how Q-Methodology is applied, Brown chooses only N = 20 statements, 10 from category (a) methodological and 10 from (b) technical (see Table 7.4).

Table 7.4 Number of statements by categories 'methodological' and 'technical'

methodological	2	5	6	8	9	12	14	17	18	20
technical	1	3	4	7	10	11	13	15	16	19

Source: Brown, 1993, p. 100

Brown (1993) then informs us of an important element that distinguishes this classification procedure with a score from what happens in the usage of scales. 'Before proceeding, it is important to note that, unlike scaling theory, no assumption is made that these 20 statements in any sense measure a "methodological" or "technical" position or stance or understanding per se' (Brown, 1993, p. 100).

This indication is useful because it highlights the work from the personal points of view of the individuals; in other words, the 'methodological' and 'technical' categories inside which the 20 statements have been organized are general *a priori* categories created by the researcher to summarize and divide the statements collected. Despite this, in the moment in which the participant orders them inside the grid, and therefore reads them, words and phrases can acquire a different meaning according to the participant's point of view, or better, view of the topic.

According to some authors, the categorization function is very important within the debate on Q-Methodology; in fact, Fred Kerlinger's work (1986) stresses the relevance of a correct categorization, presupposing that the statements can be inserted in only one category. However, according to other scholars, Kerlinger attributes too much importance to variance designs and their analysis and overlooks Stephenson's admonition that 'it is a mistake to regard a sample as a standardized set or test of statements, any more than one can hope to regard a particular set of children as a standard sample' (1953, p. 77). Hence, in the analysis of the results, the invitation is not to consider exclusively the categories created by the researcher, and therefore, the creation of *a priori* categories; rather it is to pay attention to how the participants organize their statements on the grid and how the latter can configure or reconfigure the overall image of a specific situation. (For this reason, in 'The Q-sorters selection and Q-sort generation' (see above) we underlined the importance of the researcher during the compilation of the participant's grid and the collection of comments in the post-sorting interviews.)

At this point the cards are given to the participants who must order them – according to their judgement or point of view – on the grid. The latter is created considering a maximum, a minimum and a neutral state of agreement/disagreement. In Brown's study the level of agreement/disagreement varies from +3 to −3. Each participant creates a Q-sort. 'These Q-sorts are formal models of my understanding of the points of view at issue, rendered ostensible through technique' (Brown, 1993, p. 106). With the aim of showing how we arrive at a compiled and therefore full grid (see Table 7.5) from an empty grid (see Figure 7.1), Brown creates his own Q-sort based on the 20 declarations. Inside the grid he has placed all 20 bids – the compiled grid on which the cards have been placed forms the Q-sort.

Table 7.5 Brown's Q-sort and Follet's Q-sort

Brown's position							Follet's position						
−3	−2	−1	0	1	2	3	−3	−2	−1	0	1	2	3
16	3	1	7	6	5	2	7	5	6	2	1	3	11
19	13	4	8	17	9	12	18	9	8	10	4	15	13
	15	11	10	18	14			14	12	17	20	16	
			20							19			

Source: Brown, 1993, pp. 102 and 105

The Q-sorts of all participants are to be compared. A calculation of the correlation (represented by the sign r) is made for the comparison. Still with the aim of explaining Q-Methodology, Brown compares his Q-sort and Follet's. 'The specific calculation in this case is achieved first by squaring all of the scores in the Follet and Brown Q-sorts and summing those squared numbers, which produces a sum of 66 for each, or 132 for the two combined' (Brown, 1993, pp. 107–108) (see Table 7.6). The correlation is calculated by forming the ratio of the sum of squares for Follet and Brown combined to the sum of the squared differences, and then subtracting this from 1.00. Or:

$$r = 1 - (\text{Sum n 2} / 132)$$
$$= 1 - (220/132)$$
$$= -0.67$$

If we consider that the perfect positive correlation is registered as +1.00, a perfect negative correlation is −1.00, and so the correlation between Follet and Brown of r = −0.67 indicates a quite high level of disagreement, the statements which one embraces tending to be the ones the other rejects.

Always with the aim of showing readers the procedures of Q-Methodology, Brown continues by expanding the analysis and entering the results (Q-sorts) of the other colleagues who participated in the study (the group or P-set is made up of 10 people in total). At this point it is possible to generate a correlation matrix 10x10 (see Table 7.7) for all 10 Q-sorts at stake.

For a reading of the data presented in Table 7.7 we rely on Brown's analysis (1993, 109–110):

As indicated, Brown (no. 10) correlates with Follet (no. 1) in the amount −0.67, and a quick perusal down column 10 shows that Brown correlates substantially and positively only with Q-sort no. 5 (Stephenson, his mentor) and no. 9 (quantum theory); otherwise, he correlates negatively with virtually everyone else save for Martin, although the positive correlation in that case ($r = 0.24$) is insubstantial. Follet on the other hand correlates quite highly with Kendig and Hoffer. To determine how large a correlation must be before it is considered substantial, we calculate the standard error (SE), a rough and ready estimate of which is given by the expression $SE = 1/\sqrt{N}$, where N is the number of statements (N = 20 in this case): the value is therefore $1/\sqrt{20} = 1/4.47 = 0.22$. As a rule of thumb, correlations are generally considered to be statistically

Table 7.6: Calculation of r

Item	Follet	Brown	D	D²
1	1	−1	2	4
2	0	3	−3	9
3	2	−2	4	16
4	1	−1	2	4
5	−2	2	−4	16
6	−1	1	−2	4
7	−3	0	−3	9
8	−1	0	−1	1
9	−2	2	−4	16
10	0	0	0	0
11	3	−1	4	16
12	−1	3	−4	16
13	3	−2	5	25
14	−2	2	−4	16
15	2	−2	4	16
16	2	−3	5	25
17	0	1	−1	1
18	−3	1	−4	16
19	0	−3	3	9
20	1	0	1	1
Sum	0	0	0	220

Source: Brown, 1993, p. 108

Table 7.7 Correlation matrix

Sort	1	2	3	4	5	6	7	8	9	10	
1	–	17	79	76	−70	86	48	85	−71	−67	Follet
2	17	–	14	−05	06	12	74	20	−08	24	Martin
3	79	14	–	73	−70	70	27	82	−53	−57	Kendig
4	76	−05	73	–	−85	80	23	82	−77	−81	Hoffer
5	−70	06	−70	−85	–	−82	−17	−76	73	76	Stephenson
6	86	12	70	80	−82	–	39	82	−65	−66	Burt–Cattell
7	48	74	27	23	−17	39	–	44	−48	−28	Kerlinger
8	85	20	82	82	−76	82	44	–	−74	−67	Textbook
9	−71	−08	−53	−77	73	−65	−48	−74	–	85	Quantum
10	−67	24	−56	−82	76	−65	−27	−67	85	–	Brown

Source: Brown, 1993, p. 109

significant if they are approximately 2 to 2.5 times the standard error – i.e., somewhere between 2(0.22) = 0.44 and 2.5(0.22) = 0.56 (irrespective of sign). Hence, in the above correlation matrix, Brown's '8 positive correlation with Stephenson is substantial (i.e., in excess of 0.56) as is his negative correlation with Follet (i.e., in excess of −0.56), whereas his correlation with Kerlinger is insignificant (i.e., is less than ± 0.44)'.

In Q-Methodology, the correlation matrix is of no interest in itself but represents a transition phase to reach the factor analysis. The total variance of the correlation matrix is divided into variance portions explainable through factors. After this the saturations and the correlations among factors are calculated. In the factor analysis the correlation level indicated in the matrix is calculated; what is obtained is an indication of how many different types of Q-sorts are present. Q-sorts that are highly correlated with one another may be considered to have a family resemblance, those belonging to one family being highly correlated with one another but uncorrelated with members of other families. Factor analysis tells us how many different families (factors) there are. The number of factors is therefore purely empirical and wholly dependent on how the Q-sorters performed. In some cases it is useful to rotate the factors. This is necessary to change their position in space so that we can find high levels of saturation only in a few observations/variables, while others have low levels of saturation, or almost close to zero. The final rotation is carried out to make sure that a single variable can correlate only with one factor and little or nothing with all the others, drawing a more defined picture of the connections observed. In Brown's case, the rotation produces what can be seen in Figure 7.3.

The consequence of this rotation – as Brown says – serves not only to focus Martin and Kerlinger on factor A, but also Stephenson (n. 5) and Brown (n. 10) on factor B (and Hoffer, n. 4, at the opposite pole of the same factor). This rotation changes the factor A and B loadings for all the Q-sorts, and these are registered in Table 7.8.

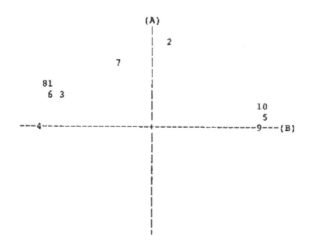

Figure 7.3 Rotated matrix.
(*Source*: Brown, 1993, p. 113)

Table 7.8 Rotated loadings, factors A and B

	Q-sorts	A2	B2	C	D	E	F	G
1	Follet	39	−83*	07	05	11	−06	−13
2	Martin	79*	13	−14	34	−10	13	12
3	Kendig	30	−72*	31	20	01	−24	07
4	Hoffer	01	−92*	05	11	−19	−06	08
5	Stephenson	05	89*	−10	−14	26	−13	02
6	Burt–Cattell	29	−84*	16	13	−01	11	−25
7	Kerlinger	62*	−31	−66	46	20	17	07
8	Textbook	39	−86*	09	03	−01	−08	10
9	Quantum	−13	85*	40	01	29	19	15
10	Brown	18	86*	13	−03	03	17	05

Significant loadings.

Source: Brown, 1993, p. 114

Knowing and know-how

In a 2008 study, Noori Akhtar-Danesh, Andrea Baumann and Lis Cordingley present Q-Methodology as useful for nursing researchers, with an illustration of its appropriate usage. They use this methodology to explore and compare the nurses' attitudes and subjectivities, proposing in their study suggestions taken from Cordingley's thesis (1999) on older women's health and social support, where Q-Methodology was used to investigate attitudes about social support and independence, and making use of the work by Brown (1993). Here, the phases of Q-Methodology are summarized, presenting its usage in various studies in order to understand its application in concrete cases (further information is provided in the 'Practical tips' section below).

Concourse

The first step is the development of the concourse, that is of a list of topics concerning the research theme. In the study by Akhtar-Danesh et al. (2008), there are more than 300 statements. Obviously, the number of statements varies from study to study and it should provide an exhaustive list to describe the different aspects of the theme being analysed (see Table 7.9). The authors have generated the statements using three sources: (1) interview material from 100 interviews about health, social support and independence conducted with older people living in the community; (2) a television documentary about three older people who lived alone and described how they managed their daily lives with and without the help of others (all statements from this source were comments by the participants); (3) literature on social support and independence.

The Q-sample

The next step is to represent the Q-sample, which collects the final statements that the participants will then position on the Q-grid. When organizing the statements, the researcher also carries out an analysis to eliminate duplicates or statements similar to one another and can consult experts to achieve this; then there is piloting to test the goodness of the statements. An initial list of 113 statements was reduced to 87 by identifying repetition within the statements (an example of statements used in the study can be found in Table 7.10) in the study of Cordingley (1999). After piloting the statements with 10 participants, the list was further reduced to 58 (Akhtar-Danesh et al., 2008, p. 768). If the statements are still too many, it is possible to create *a priori* some general categories within which to classify/group them; the statements are then extracted from these categories. These methods of Q-sampling are usually expressed in two more technical approaches (Brown, 1980; McKeown & Thomas, 1988): unstructured and structured (see 'The Q-sample selection'). An example of a deductive structured approach is that developed by Brown (1993) with the creation for his study of 'methodological'

Table 7.9 Examples of topics for Q methodological inquiry in nursing research

Attitudes, feelings, beliefs, values; perceptions related to these areas, separately or in combination:

Life experiences
   Living with chronic illness
   Coping
   Stress
   Attribution
   Quality of life
   Social support networks

Health beliefs
   Preventive health practices
   Cultural influences on health-seeking behaviours
   Cross-cultural value orientations
   Lifestyle changes (e.g., diet and exercise)
   Self-care

Intra-individual concerns
   Self-esteem
   Body image
   Efficacy
   Ageing
   Sexuality

Clients and providers
   Clients' needs within patient–provider relationships
   Satisfaction with care
   Quality of care
   Modes of nursing care delivery

Roles
   Family: marital dyad, sibling, parent–child
   Faculty: teaching, practice, research
   Student: role transition, professional socialization
   Nurses: image

Source: Akhtar-Danesh et al., 2008, p. 761, adapted from Dennis, 1986

Table 7.10 Some examples of statements in the Q-sample example

Sometimes I feel guilty for not wanting to accept help from people who are only trying to be kind.
It's easier to ask someone in my family for help than to go to friends or neighbours.
There are times when you sometimes just have to let go and let others do things for you.
Being on your own can bring you a lot of freedom from the demands of others.
Sometimes people assume I need help with something when in fact I can manage perfectly well myself.

Source: Akhtar-Danesh et al., 2008, p. 769

and 'technical' categories (as seen in the 'Case study' section), enter these two categories Brown classifies the collected statements; subsequently extracts them taking into account their representativeness per category. When instead a strong or structured theoretical picture is lacking, the categories emerge inductively from below.

The sample of participants, or P-Set

The group of participants who sort the Q-sample in a Q-study is called the P-set (McKeown & Thomas, 1988). A sample between 40 and 60 subjects is usually advised. What is critical, however, is not so much the number of participants as their representativeness with reference to the numerous points of view that the study aims at analysing. The P-set of Cordingley (1999) consisted of 34 women living in different household structures (married, single, with or without children) and with different levels of mental and physical health.

Q-sort table, or data collection table

Once the Q-sample has been created and the number of participants has been defined, it is necessary to ask the latter to place the cards on the grid, that as already specified, is organized *per* levels of agreement/disagreement (see Figure 7.2).

Data collection and data entry

The participants are invited to read the statements and then to place them on the Q-grid. The organization of the statements on the Q-grid generates the Q-sort, that is the file containing the subjective view of each participant to be analysed.

After the data collection, the rank-ordered scores are entered into an appropriate program for analysis. A frequently used program is the PQMethod 2.11 developed by Schmolck (2002), which is a free, user-friendly DOS program that can be downloaded from http://schmolck.org/qmethod

Analysis and interpretation

As we already know, each factor represents a group of individuals with similar views, feelings, or experiences in relation to the theme of the study. The original extracted factors from the Q-sort are customarily used as the raw material for further analysis. Only two methods of factor extraction are implemented in the aforementioned program: principal component method and **centroid** method. These original factors may be rotated to generate more relevant factors. Only two methods of rotation are currently available in the Q-method programs: varimax and manual (judgemental). It is worth noting that choosing a rotation method may be informed by theoretical reasoning rather than simply statistical criteria. In Cordingley's (1999) study a principal component technique followed by varimax rotation was used for factor analysis. Varimax rotation was selected because there was no theoretical justification for judgemental rotation. Five factors were eventually identified, representing five salient viewpoints among the participants. The labelling of the factors was facilitated by a group of domain experts. One of the factors was labelled Loneliness Versus Companionship. The strongest issues that emerged were related to fears about social isolation.

The most extreme responses to the statements were +4 or –4.
  Loneliness is the worst thing that can happen to anyone. (+4)
  I love being on my own. (–4)
The second factor was labelled Self-Reliance.
  The perspective highlighted by this factor stresses the importance of self-help.
  I have always had to be self-reliant. I'm used to helping myself. (+3)
  People often get help from social services when they don't really need it. (+4)
  I don't like to feel under obligation to anyone else. (+4)
The third factor was labelled Interdependence and Reciprocity. The importance of close social ties was emphasized. A key issue was the opportunity that social ties provide to develop mutual understanding. Like the Loneliness Versus Companionship factor, this factor revealed the central importance of close personal relationships. (Akhtar-Danesh et al., 2008, p. 770)

The merging point

Q-Methodology analyses subjective points of view, using quantitative analysis techniques for the synthesis of the results. Already in the work of Ellingsen et al., referring to the study of Good and Brown (2008), Q-Methodology is called 'merged', since 'it combines together quantitative and qualitative techniques, and some even claim that it goes beyond the quantitative and qualitative distinction. This is because the quantitative and qualitative aspects are merged into one approach' (2014, p. 4). Furthermore, we find inside it the usage of Content Analysis, fundamental to create general categories chosen *a priori* by the researcher. In the steps presented in this chapter we have seen a sequence of various research techniques: individual 'think-out-loud' narrative or a focus group discussion, plus card sorting, plus factor analysis or cluster analysis. In addition, during the compilation phase of the grid the role of the researcher remains substantial, in:

- providing indications to the participants;
- helping the participants to focus on their degree of agreement/disagreement with the statements;
- collecting the overall evaluations of the participants when they have finished filling in the grid and can have an overview of their personal point of view.

The data is co-constructed by researcher and participants; the data are both qualitative and quantitative (see Table 7.11).

In this regard, we can consider Brown's words (1993) about what is effectively a merge method:

> (1) The Q sample is comprised solely of things which people have said, and it is therefore indigenous to their understandings and forms of life. (2) The Q sorting operation is wholly subjective in the sense that it represents 'my point of view' …: issues of validity consequently fade since there is no external criterion by which to appraise a person's own perspective. (3) As a corollary, the factors which subsequently emerge – factors, that is, in the factor-analytic sense – must represent functional categories of the subjectivities at issue, i.e., categories of operant subjectivity. (p. 106).

In Q-Methodology, subjectivity is omnipresent since its goal is to measure it. The use of statistical techniques has this function by making it possible to identify connections/correlations which would otherwise remain latent.

Table 7.11   Identikit of Q-Methodology as a Merged Method

Characteristics of the researchers' work in the Merged Method	Identification in Q-Methodology
Data are co-constructed	Data are the viewpoints of the participants, collected in the Q-sorts; data are the notes that the researcher takes during and at the end of each construction of the Q-sorts
Data are relational and interactional outcomes	Data are the result of the relationships between: the opinions of each participant, the categories constructed by the researcher, the choice of sentences to be included in the categories, the notes of the researcher
Methods predetermine the way the world is assembled	Q-Methodology allows the communicability of subjective points of view regarding controversial issues
Abandoning the concept of validity (true-value), and rediscovery of fidelity	The validity of Q study is evaluated by content, face and Q-sorting validity
The researcher's orientation is not to find an out-there truth but to create the best (social and relational) conditions for gathering information	The intent with which Q-Methodology is conceived is to identify points of view that are the result of the way of looking at the world of the participants
Social actors under study are participants	Participants are holders of their own points of view
The main aim is to guarantee participants' free expression	Freedom of expression is crucial to Q-Methodology and is guaranteed by anonymity
Researchers' active listening should be pursued	Researchers express active listening in considering the points of view of the participants (during filling out and at the end of filling out) and consequently building the content of the categories starting from them
Results/findings are interpretations	The results arise from the interpretations provided by the participants. Researchers look at them cumulatively, using the Q-sorts. They return the interpretation of the Q-sorts through factor analysis and the interpretation and rotation of factors

It is important to remember that the results of a Q methodological study can be used to describe a population of viewpoints and not, like in R, a population of people (Risdon et al., 2003).

Validity of a Q-study is evaluated by content, face and Q-sorting validity. Content validity of statements is usually assessed by literature review and a team of domain experts, a common practice in qualitative research (Valenta & Wigger, 1997; Polit & Beck, 2008; Gallagher & Porock, 2010). The items selected for Q-sorting must be representative of the concourse. It can also be tested in one or more pilot studies. Furthermore, the results of the Q-sorting can be discussed with the participants. Regarding the reliability for Q, the most important type is replicability: will the same condition of instruction lead to factors that are schematically reliable – that is, represent similar viewpoints on the topic – across similarly structured yet different Q samples and when administered to different sets of persons (Brown, 1980; Dennis, 1992).

Advantages and disadvantages

Compared to purely qualitative methods – with interpretation processes often unclear – Q is attractive because it contains a rigorous analytical picture capable of minimizing distortions by the researcher (Brown, 1980) and of giving more defined and transparent steps. This gives the technique the strengths of both qualitative and quantitative methods (Dennis & Goldberg, 1996) and can be seen as a bridge between the two (Sell & Brown, 1984).

This is one of the first advantages of Q-Methodology. Alongside this, we find:

- a smaller sample size; thus, it is more cost-efficient than other methods (Dennis, 1986; Smith, 2001);
- questions pertaining to one and the same domain are not analysed as separate items of information but rather in their mutual coherence for the respondent (Brouwer, 1999).

Working on subjectivity, its disadvantages are connected precisely to this element:

- results from Q methodological studies have often been criticized for their reliability and hence the possibility for generalization (Thomas & Baas, 1992);
- the presence of statistical techniques within Q-Methodology has been seen as a weakness or disadvantage, because it ends up not being a pure qualitative technique.

Practical tips

- In the phase of statement creation, it is necessary to embrace all points of view; furthermore, it is desirable, when using interviews during the concourse stage, to secure the presence of some of the interviewees while the Q-sort is being completed so that their opinions can be properly considered. In addition, the interviews should be recorded and transcribed verbatim.

- When choosing the total number of statements to present to participants there are various conventions, from 20 statements to 100 (Dennis, 1986; Watts & Stenner, 2005). It needs to be considered that the greater the number of statements, the longer the time necessary to order them. Generally, a study with 50 statements requires from 30 to 60 minutes to be ordered.

- The researcher does not have to worry too much if some statements seem ambiguous because the interpretation and attribution of the meaning process is in the hands of the participants, who can give them various meanings inside the Q-grid.

- To favour the positioning of the Q-cards, it is possible to create instructions for the participants, in which they are advised to position first the statements they strongly agree or disagree with and then find a collocation for the other ones.

- For the factor analysis of Q-sorts it is possible to use the free software PQMethod 2.11 and its instruction manual. Remember that the software rotates the factors, but there could be other theoretical or practical reasons for a further rotation. In that case, such action can be performed only if it pursues a line of inquiry and rationale.

- Concerning the loading of the statements and hence of the Q-sorts on the factors, it is advisable to to consult the work of Coogan and Herrington (2011), who explain there are no firm rules on how many factors should be extracted from the analysis; however, there are several considerations to be made when making the final decisions. One such consideration is the eigenvalues of each factor loading.

Further reading

For further information on Q-Methodology, several texts can be noted. They are to be considered as handbooks:

Brown, S. R. (1980). *Political subjectivity.* New Haven, CT: Yale University Press. Available on the qmethod.org webpage: https://qmethod.org/portfolio/brown-1980-political-subjectivity.
McKeown, B., & Thomas, D. (2013). *Q methodology* (2nd ed.) Newbury Park, CA: Sage.
Watts, S., & Stenner, P. (2012). *Doing Q methodological research: Theory, method and interpretation.* London: Sage.

Social scientists with little knowledge of statistics to understand factor analysis will find these useful:

Adcock, C.J. (1954). *Factorial analysis for non-mathematicians.* Melbourne: Melbourne University Press.

Rust, J., & Golombok, S. (1989). *Modern psychometrics*. London: Routledge.

Stephenson, W. (1980). Factor analysis.. *Operant Subjectivity, 3*, 38–57.

Other, in-depth, publications are:

Black, C. (2013). Q methodology: Approach the newsletter from the Social Research Team at Ipsos MORI Scotland, April, 4–5. Available for download at http://schmolck.org/qmethod/Black_QMethodology_2013.pdf.

Müller, F. H., & Kals, E. (2004). Die Q-Methode. Ein innovatives Verfahren zur Erhebung subjektiver Einstellungen und Meinungen [Q-sort technique and Q-methodology: Innovative methods for examining attitudes and opinions]. Forum Qualitative Sozialforschung/Forum: Qualitative Social Research [On-line journal], *5*(2), Art. 34. Available at www.qualitative-research.net/fqs-texte/2-04/2-04muellerkals-d.htm.

For use of the software dedicated to Q-Methodology, consult:

http://schmolck.org/qmethod.

8

MULTIMODAL CONTENT ANALYSIS: TEXTS AND SENTIMENTS

One of the longest-established approaches to social science is the analysis of text. With Content Analysis we move to a method that does not work directly with the interaction of researcher and participants but with artefacts of interaction captured in text. 'Content Analysis' is established in the humanities (e.g., studies testing the disputed authorship of texts), media studies and political science (e.g., interpreting rhetorical strategies in politicians' speeches). Multimodal Content Analysis introduces techniques characteristic of the Digital Age, but still derives its essential heuristics from foundational approaches.

Definition

The essence of Content Analysis is an enumerative strategy based on listing, counting and categorizing the individual words in a text. It begins by counting the frequency of each unique word within the text, on the assumption that frequency reflects a word's salience to the topic. Routine words that recur across any text, like 'a' and 'the', are discounted. Content Analysis is one of the first social science methods to be supported by computer programs, and most programs have a feature for omitting words on the basis of their frequency. Once routine words are removed, the remainder are rank ordered.

Another basic tool is the 'index', a word list showing not only which words are present but the position of each. A 'concordance' lists all the words in a text, showing the immediate context within which it appears (users can usually set the extent of context). A common concordance is the key-words-in-context (KWIC) format, which shows each word, usually centred on a page, surrounded by the words which appear immediately before or after it. Analysing 'collocates' examines how words in a text associate with each other. In Britain's 1980s/1990s bovine spongiform encephalopathy outbreak Anders Hansen (1995) found that 'top', 'senior' and 'leading' were commonly collocated with 'scientist' and 'expert' in newspaper coverage, reinforcing the perceived authority of such commentators.

Brief history of Content Analysis

The techniques of mainstream Content Analysis have been practised since the mid-20th century but their roots long precede that time. Indeed, they did not originate in social science but in theology (Kelle, 1997), where biblical exegesis, the monastic tradition of hermeneutics as interpretation of seminal religious texts, gave rise to what is now called 'philosophy'. Similar exegetical traditions emerged in Islam and other world religions, finding their perhaps best-known modern form in Talmudic scholarship. Foundational principles for constructing rational arguments stem from such traditions.

Content Analysis, and associated methods of analysing words, is a broad church (to maintain the religious referent). It ranges from computer-based statistical methods to highly flexible qualitative approaches. In this chapter we treat Content Analysis as a compelling instance of Merged Methods, consisting in the systematic but adaptive combination of positivist and constructivist principles and procedures in techniques that are fully 'merged'. That is not where Content Analysis has come from, but it is, we argue, where it is going.

In several breaking areas of technique and method around text analysis a large part is played by the affordances of the online environment and born-digital research technologies. These breaking areas include *Sentiment Analysis*, a powerful technique in market research but also fruitfully practised in social research (see Chapter 9); the application of *Topic Models* to the analysis of text, with current applications ranging across linguistics, political science and social science; and *Multimodal Content Analysis*, which combines Content Analysis with multimodal discourse analysis to produce accounts of meaning that can be visualized in three-dimensional space. This chapter's major exposition is around Multimodal Content Analysis.

Approaches to data collection, organization and analysis

Content Analysis is mostly applied to 'found' texts like newspaper articles, political speeches, blogs and other online postings, i.e., by-product data. The content analyst's interest in word frequencies challenges the importance given to context in qualitative data analysis. Certainly the variation in meaning according to context can make interpretations based on simple counts unreliable. But content analysts devote much effort to 'disambiguation' procedures that search for signs of irony, *double entendre* and other features that would undermine interpretations that assume a word's intended meaning is always available on the surface. Frequency counts can also underestimate salience when they ignore synonyms or words like pronouns that can be substituted for other words and carry the same meaning. Nevertheless, Content Analysis can be a valuable 'front end' to interpretive work using qualitative data analysis techniques based on coding. Word frequencies can be a useful first step, providing initial insight into a text with limited effort. Counts also flag words that are used only once but are salient; they may reflect important ideas that an interview, say, has not sufficiently covered, or indicate an emerging rather than fully formed idea.

Just as work with words has a long lineage, so does the uneasiness of the relationship between quantitative and qualitative approaches to Content Analysis. Bernard Berelson's (1952, p. 18) definition of Content Analysis as 'a research technique for the objective, systematic and quantitative description of the manifest content of communication' is seminal and well-known, but it is not so well known that in the very same year Siegfried Kracauer (1952) criticized the limitations of a purely quantitative approach to Content

Analysis, rejecting the idea of confining attention to manifest content (thus excluding attention to latent structures of meaning) and of prioritizing coding frequencies (whereas the occurrence of a single word can be significant). Despite attempts to synthesize the two approaches (notably, in the context of psychology; Mayring, 1983, 2000), the division has not been bridged. Indeed, while the canonical principles of quantitative Content Analysis remained largely unchanged until the advent of digital and online resources, qualitative Content Analysis has developed with ever-increasing variety, such that some have deemed it 'very ambiguous' (Glaser & Laudel, 2013, paragraph 63).

Philipp Mayring (2012, p. 30) regards qualitative Content Analysis as 'neither a purely qualitative nor a purely quantitative method' and proposes 'category driven qualitative-oriented text analysis' as a more appropriate term. Some methodologists maintain that Content Analysis has a unique combination of qualitative and quantitative features (Fielding & Schreier, 2001; Burzan, 2016) and consequently exclude qualitative Content Analysis from qualitative methods, a view strongly held in German social science (see Schreier et al., 2019). There, the debate has been whether there should be a standalone paradigm of 'interpretative research' (Flick, 2008) and whether distinctive quality standards for qualitative Content Analysis apply (Reichertz, 2007), such that 'objectivity' and 'reliability' criteria from the quantitative paradigm would be applicable (Schreier, 2012). At an opposite pole are those who argue that the data volumes of qualitative Content Analysis, its strategy for sampling and the focus on data reduction by assigning text portions to categories and then performing cross-case analysis of the categories, all typify a quantitative orientation and cannot be considered qualitative at all. They reject categorization by pre-defined characteristics and the principle that categories must be mutually exclusive. Attempts to move beyond the analysis of categories alone pull qualitative Content Analysis back in a quantitative direction, an instance being Udo Kuckartz's (2019) 'cases-by-categories' matrix and thematic summaries. Behind these debates lie competing epistemologies, those of positivism versus hermeneutics. Margrit Schreier (2016) seeks to reconcile the poles of the debate by arguing for inductive, data-based categories which would have some predetermined characteristics and others derived from case-based, grounded theory codes.

Work with words as data is diverse. In sociology alone it includes conversation analysis, discourse analysis, dramaturgical analysis, ethnomethodology, narrative analysis, phenomenology, semiotics, structuralism and others. Each has its own techniques. Nevertheless, these hermeneutic approaches to text share a view that language cannot be treated as describing an external reality. Instead, social worlds are socially constructed in and through language. In Manning and Cullum-Swan's (1994, p. 464) summary, such approaches foreground 'the relationship between the "text" as a social construction and its form or its imputed audience-derived meanings'.

Narrative approaches

To establish connections between hermeneutical approaches and Content Analysis we will take the case of narrative analysis. Narratives are ubiquitous in everyday talk and interaction, and in reports of talk and interaction (second order 'talk about talk', e.g., social media commentaries). Narratives tend to have a beginning, middle and end, thus forming a distinct unit that can be analytically detached from surrounding discourse. They are also frequently organized chronologically. While stories can be thematically organized or have an episodic structure, the chronology remains dominant. Approaches like 'domain analysis' and 'account analysis' may focus on narrative-like structures or elements rather than a full chronological narrative but still attend to the diachronic dimension. A common format involves 'the temporal ordering of events that are associated with change of some kind' (Hyden, 1995), e.g., the 'first we sat down and then he told me he wanted a divorce, so I slapped him' structure. Within the format the degree varies to which the internal coherence of a narrative 'is defined in advance with reference to codes, syntax, grammar or forms' (Manning & Cullum-Swan, 1994, p. 464). Some hermeneutic approaches attend to such structural features whereas others refrain. Asking three practitioners of hermeneutic approaches to say what can be left out of a summary of transcribed speech or some other set of words is likely to produce three accounts of what is chaff and what is wheat. One individual's summary might address the plot of a given narrative by its principal features, another's may fixate on the sequence of events in detail, and the third's may be interested in the trigger events motivating the changes comprising the narrative.

This interpretive diversity contrasts with a structural approach to narrative. Inspired by William Labov's (1982) and James Paul Gee's (1991) approaches, Catherine Kohler Riessman (1993) was interested in the interplay between common structural features of a painful experience (specifically, divorce) and the experiential meaning associated with them. She used interview talk about a single topic (e.g., children in divorce) that was delivered at the same speech rate and 'tonality' to underpin an account that looked for commonalities despite their being experienced differently. Riessman's structural analysis related externally produced tensions the respondent encountered at given points in the process to their experiential meaning. Commonality and variation in the impact of the structural stages supported an empirically based theory.

Reissman's study is an intentional contrast to the code-based analysis prevalent in mainstream qualitative data analysis. Coding is done in narrative analysis but not to construct a theory from themes derived from data to which codes have been assigned. In narrative analysis the coding aims to delimit the narrative and its component parts while retaining its sequential character. Conventional coding chops discourse up into themes and diverts attention from their sequential development, fragmenting the text. In narrative analysis the codes are indicators of narrative functions, components that recur across narratives and can be pre-specified.

Attention to typical elements of narratives can alleviate what Paul Atkinson (2013) terms the 'Romantic version of the social actor' in qualitative analysis, which pursues 'authenticity' and at worst regurgitates in analytical language the account offered by the respondent. In reality, talk elicited in interaction draws on discursive resources to accomplish biographical, revelatory or therapeutic accounts (Whitaker & Atkinson, 2019, p. 621). Respondents construct themselves as 'narrative types' – heroes, victims, survivors, successes or failures. Focus on typical structure can be an antidote to the uncritical 'celebration' of what may be a motivated account. Thus, Whitaker and Atkinson (2019, p. 622) treat the narrative types as dictated by the requirements of form as much as by personal experiences, moving us towards treating talk-in-interaction as a series of rhetorical 'positioning' actions (Georgakopolou, 2000).

This stance can be illustrated in the study of occupations. Narratives of workplaces and workgroups often organize around the 'career', a diachronic trope often found in analyses of occupations, where they 'construct a professional biography that … warrants a distinctive kind of identity' (Whitaker & Atkinson, 2019, p. 626). The associated 'journey' trope can be applied to temporary roles, as in medical sociology's accounts of the illness career (the classic is Roth, 1963). These narratives involve a central figure who moves through adversity and adventures to eventual success, as in Fielding's 1749 comic novel *Tom Jones*. Accounts derived from life history and other forms of the long interview often adopt a picaresque narrative of 'survival, success and progression' (Whitaker & Atkinson, 2019, p. 626), punctuated by 'moments of revelation and confession'.

The career is not the only narrative form found in work with words. Human societies have increasingly embraced therapeutic telling, originally to priests, then psychoanalysts, latterly to the ever-expanding range of 'talking therapy' trades, and even to non-human agents, like the Student Dog found on university campuses as a corrective to first-year angst, second-year blues and final-year exam jitters, and the variants of the Sony Robot, the best-seller of which is, indeed, a robotic dog. The narrative forms of 'confessional culture' revolve around suffering and overcoming 'democratised through … multi-media outlets' (Whitaker & Atkinson, 2019, p. 630). It is thus possible for a social work manager to respond to questions about organizational decision-making and the policy dimension of welfare services in terms of his own biography and emotional life, as if the policy enterprise created by hundreds of politicians, managers, budget-holders and the legions of the urban poor were actually inscribed in his own very being.

The narrative approaches discussed above each move away from the empirical level of data to consider the structural relationships behind the data. As computational resources have improved, 'expert systems' that automate (or semi-automate) Content Analysis have appeared, alongside 'clause-based content analysis' (Popping, 2012), the linguistic parsing of text. Practitioners foresee the future of Content Analysis in Text Mining and Big Data, using semi-automation to handle large data volumes, with examples already emerging of automated Content Analysis (Hoxtell, 2019). This involves designing algorithms of certain word combinations using a coding frame and training software to search for such combinations, supervised by users.

Qualitative software programs like ATLAS.ti offer inter-coder agreement analysis tools that are designed to check consistency of coding but are also useful in Content Analysis. Inter-coder agreement is a quality check derived from quantitative Content Analysis. It is noteworthy that in designing the tool the ATLAS.ti programmers consulted Klaus Krippendorff, an authority on *quantitative* Content Analysis (Krippendorff, 1980, 2018; 'Krippendorff's alpha' is a standard coefficient for assessing inter-coder agreement). The collaboration involved understanding the requirements of code-based *qualitative* data analysis, rather than simply importing statistical tests. It developed a family of alpha coefficients to assess inter-coder agreement at various levels. Hybrid methodological approaches are increasingly prompted by the development of computer software to support data management and analysis.

Topic models

Automation can extend the range and scale of text analysis. Computers readily sort text but are challenged by determining meaning, which requires attention to context. This has long inhibited automated analysis. Topic Models offer a scalable way to summarize text while also handling context. Some combine familiar interpretive techniques with user-controlled automation to enhance generalizability, but topic modelling also supports new analytic procedures, particularly for discourse analysis.

Topic models provide a degree of automation for coding the content of texts into small sets of meaningful categories ('topics'). The topic is a group of words that frequently co-occur and represent a theme or coding category. As Grant Blank (2017, p. 639) puts it, 'the model of authorship for topic models is that authors have a bag of words that they use to write about a topic. As they write they reach into their bag and choose the most appropriate words. Different topics generally have different bags of words, although some words may be used in multiple topics. Topic models attempt to reconstruct the bags of words that authors use for each topic'. Topic models employ procedures for grouping things together. Classification algorithms include established procedures like Principal Components and Cluster Analysis and recent procedures like latent dirichlet allocation (Blei et al., 2003) and structural topic modelling (Roberts et al., 2014).

The principal output is a list of words associated with each topic, indicating the hidden structure of topics in the text. The algorithm that produces the list does not label the topics. The researcher looks in the lists for topics with a substantive meaning and that bear on the concepts being developed (see Mohr & Bogdanov, 2013), thus working backwards from the words to identify meaning – their representation of concepts and relationships between concepts, akin to Howard Becker's (2017) 'reasoning to the fact'. Topic modelling provides three main outputs. The 'topic-term matrix' assigns every word in the text a probability for each topic, by ranking them on their probability of representing the topic in the text. The rule of thumb is that the first 5–20 words (the 'top words') are roughly representative of the topic. The 'document–topic matrix' tabulates the proportion of each text that is made up of each topic. Combined with contextual data like the author and date this enables comparisons by social actor and by time. The third output provides an overview of which topic each word in each text has been assigned to (Jacobs & Tschötschel, 2019).

Topic models show particular promise for discourse analysis (Levy & Franklin, 2014; Jaworska & Nanda, 2016; Tornberg & Tornberg, 2016). Arguably, Content Analysis scores high on systematic methodology but low on revealing the process of making meaning, whereas discourse analysis is low on systematic procedure but high on inferring meaning. This limits the scope of discourse analysis, not just in terms of scale but the level of subtlety and nuance, and the shifts in language use, it can detect. Thomas Jacobs and Robin Tschötschel (2019, p. 470) maintain that topic modelling addresses these constraints while assisting verification but is also particularly suited to studying questions of 'hegemony', a central concept in discourse analysis. Hegemony is the most common and conventional meaning most speakers/readers would understand by a given set of words. Discourse analysts maintain that meaning-making is a 'relational open practice', i.e., concepts acquire meaning only in relation to other concepts rather than by correspondence to an external reality. Hegemony anchors what would otherwise be a free-for-all where anything could mean anything. It makes the dominant meaning seem both normal and natural. This is where topic modelling comes in. As artefacts, texts are the result of 'first selecting subjects, then selecting ways of speaking about them, and finally selecting some words associated with that way of speaking' (Jacobs & Tschötschel, 2019, p. 471–472). Topic modelling reverses this process. The algorithms use the distribution of words across texts to identify clusters of words that typically co-occur. Dominant clusters represent hegemonic (typical) ways of speaking/ writing about a given topic.

'Polysemy', the idea that words acquire multiple meanings depending on context, is explicitly addressed by topic modelling, since it traces the multiple contexts in which every word in the text is used. By modelling the relations between the words contained in topics, the relations the words in topics have to the topic, and co-occurrence of words with those in other topics, the relationality at the core of discourse analysis is respected.

Work with topic models requires a text corpus that has a degree of coherence around its theme and style. It also requires a relatively large number of topics so outputs will not simply list the themes covered in the corpus but contain more granular, nuanced aspects of language use which can be decomposed into word combinations representing the discursive units that are used to build up themes. Topic modelling is most useful where a corpus contains a large number of topics, the corpus comprises a single genre of texts, like speeches or newspaper articles, and the analysis focuses on one well-defined meta-subject (Jacobs & Tschötschel, 2019, p. 474). By examining the number of topics in the overall corpus and in a given document within it the analyst can examine how the discourses present in the corpus are constructed, and in what contexts a given discursive form appears. If the given document represents particular contexts or respondent groups the discourses present in the overall corpus can be related to component texts or respondent groups. Where the corpus comprises primary data 'we can reveal patterns of speech used at particular points in time by particular groups' (Jacobs & Tschötschel, 2019, p. 475). Topic modelling contrasts with Sentiment Analysis, whose categories or scales are pre-defined by the analyst (see Chapter 9). Rather, topic modelling represents patterns of language use in the corpus without imposing any pre-definition.

A case study

A case study of change in public attitudes towards economic growth during a fiscal crisis demonstrates how topic models merge qualitative and quantitative data (Jacobs & Tschötschel, 2019, pp. 480–482). A large corpus of newspaper articles related to economic growth in Austria and its changing salience over time was collected. Correlations between topics indicated how different elements of the discourses typically combined in the articles, identifying hegemonic and non-hegemonic discourses about economic growth. It was hypothesized that discourses with a pro-growth stance would dominate. At the crisis point of the financial crash keywords like 'dramatic', 'severe' and 'lost' featured, the antithesis of 'growth'. The correlated 'recovery' topic explicitly contrasted the crisis with a period of strong growth following a fiscal policy intervention (correlation coefficient = 0.28 between the frequency of words around the topic 'crisis' with the frequency of words around the topic 'recovery'). Semantic interpretation of the articles suggested topics labelled 'optimism' and 'prognosis'. Public discourse emphasized economic growth as a public good and a desirable result of the policy intervention. In later years non-hegemonic discourses emerged, questioning growth as a public good. The evidential base was the quantitative change in topic salience over time, measured by the changing composition of topics in the newspaper articles, changes that were recognized by semantic interpretations clustering associated keywords.

Topic model algorithms are available in qualitative analysis software, including SAS Institute's *Text Miner* and Provalis' *QDA Miner*, enabling qualitative analysis that scales to large amounts of text while being sensitive to context and meaning. As one of the earliest social science uses of computer software, Content Analysis has a long engagement with technology. We have profiled the role that qualitative software has had in supporting systematic analysis of text, and taken a brief look at topic modelling as a method that draws on digital technology to handle 'Big Data' with a degree of semi-automation. We now move to our principal focus, Multimodal Content Analysis, a field of Merged Methods that fundamentally depends on technological resources, and, as we will see, a field that often makes digital communication its topic of study.

Knowing and know-how

Multimodal Content Analysis is a Merged Method for working with the polysemic communications of social media. We consider, e.g., the hashtag as a concept. Whether it concerns an event, a protest, a social media star, or something else, it represents a semantic content of linguistic signs and mental images, redefined continuously through actions and interactions. Multimodal Content Analysis (MCA) provides a way to reconstruct sense and meaning contained in the hashtags.

Multimodal Content Analysis (La Rocca, 2018b) is a Merged Method (Driscoll et al., 2007) that enables decomposition and re-composition of polysemic communication. It merges Content Analysis and multimodal discourse analysis. Content Analysis features in the attention placed on the content of communication, text decomposition, the creation of categories and the reconstruction of frames. Multimodal discourse analysis features in the study of speech in combination with other resources, such as images, symbols and videos. Speech and other resources together create a meaning that is multimodal or multi-semiotic.

Emoticons, emojis, comments, references, photos, links, videos and other tools can stand in lieu of text, depending on the expository intentions of whoever created or shared them. We cannot ignore these resources when analysing social media and other digital contents, particularly when interpreting what is said about a certain topic or phenomenon on the Web. This opens up Content Analysis to considering the 'language' used as a technologized meta-resource and moves Content Analysis closer to ethnographic discourse analysis (Androutsopoulos, 2010, 2011) rather than simply an analysis of occurrences. This move is needed because it is not simple to reconstruct the path and the emotional element of an online topic, due to the grammatical structure and syntax of messages, the mix of colloquialisms and topic-specific terms, and the need to codify emoticons so as to incorporate their nuances into evaluating the text.

Multimodal Content Analysis extends thinking developed in the study of discourse (Kress & van Leeuwan, 2001; Jewitt, 2014), which attends to how language interacts with other semiotic systems. This approach partly reflects summative Content Analysis (Hsieh & Shannon, 2005), which goes beyond simple word counts to include latent content. Latent Content Analysis here refers to the description and interpretation of multimodal content. The reconstruction of meaning performed in Multimodal Content Analysis can be seen as retrospective sense-making, in the terms proposed by Karl Weick (1995), who defines sense-making as a process of continuous co-evolution between sense and meaning. If we consider the hashtag as equal to a speech act we need to investigate the denotative and connotative components of its semantic content.

Everything that is anchored to a single hashtag contributes to redefining its meaning. This new meaning – or perhaps better, this *affordance* – is created by users through their actions. Multimodal Content Analysis extrapolates sense and meaning from each tweet, considering not only the text but its accessory elements.

Multimodal Content Analysis: research experience

This case study of MCA's research application is based on tweets relating to two Italian television reality shows (La Rocca & Rinaldi, 2020), in particular, those about two characters, shown here as #namea and #nameb, representing the LGBTQI+ community. The goal is to extrapolate the emotional range linked to them. Posts by single users to support or denigrate these characters are considered, looking at how the points they make are substantiated in an emotional and personal way. The range of feelings expressed is wide and variegated. Our objective is to reconstruct and problematize LGBTQI+ typifications by analysing the different representations the members of the LGBTQI+ community, Character A and Character B, have received during their participation in reality shows.

Character A won the sixth edition of the reality show *L'isola dei famosi*, transmitted every Monday between September 15 and November 24, 2008 on Rai 2; she is a politically engaged person. Character B participated in *Grande Fratello VIP 2017*. He is a showman, known for his career as singer and songwriter. We have chosen to follow the evolution of hashtags related to reality shows because the format allows the characters to show themselves in relationship with others for a long period of time (provided they are not eliminated early). Furthermore, these shows are broadcast in several time slots: primetime or lunchtime. The audience is thus differentiated by gender, age and lifestyle.

We first download the tweets and all the multimodal resources about the two characters and their participation in the reality shows. Categories are then applied to these multimodal resources, whether *a priori*, created by the researcher using the conceptualization of hashtag above, or *ex post*, which emerges as the researcher works on the hashtag contents. Whether moving from concepts to categories, or from the content of multimodal resources to categories, the creation of categories is crucial to relocate the hashtag in the user's intentions. A hashtag can relate to a set of feelings that conforms to the label or contrasts with it.

Ex ante and *ex post* application of categories constitutes two distinct processes: deduction and induction. Category creation (deduction) is linked to the literal and figurative meaning of our hashtag. Literal meaning is the first road map to creating containers/labels (categories) of derivable meanings (deductive process). Figurative meaning involves using several expressive modes that refer to the literal meaning but reference it in a symbolic and translated way (inductive process). This way, under the # umbrella, different meanings accumulate and contribute to redesigning the global meaning of #. At this stage the researcher, while analysing the hashtags, must create new labels (La Rocca, 2018a).

This procedure integrates Content Analysis with discourse analysis (Feltham-King & Macleod, 2016) and can be regarded as Mixed Methods (Archibald et al., 2015), but it also goes beyond that by employing spatial analysis (Rucks-Ahidiana & Bierbaum, 2015) using computational techniques, thus becoming a Merged Method. Use of the Hamlet software supports multidimensional scaling (MDS) in application to texts, videos, emoticons, links, comments and mentions.

The case study research questions were:

- [RQ1] Considering the normalization and resistance processes present in public acceptance of the LGBTQI+ world, do these also affect TV characters? Or having become icons, are TV characters removed from these processes?
- [RQ2] Whether or not television characters are considered as LGBTQI+ icons, what kind of emotions do users express towards them under the hashtags #namea and #nameb?

Answering these questions to rebuild the intended sense and meanings requires all the resources attributed to #. To do that we create a data collection form organized in categories. The form collects texts (messages, sentences, paragraphs), descriptions of videos and of symbols. Making the description involves work on two levels: that of denotative and that of connotative meaning. In the case study we used systemic functional-multimodal discourse analysis (SF-MDA) (O'Halloran, 2008, 2011), but Content Analysis on the model of Frank Serafini and Stephanie Reid (2019) is also appropriate.

The first step in identifying the range of emotions expressed by the two hashtags selected as polysemic collectors is categorization of the texts, including their multimodal component. The categorization involves procedures through which information is codified in homogeneous sets containing portions of meaning. The categories must satisfy two criteria: mutual exclusiveness, that is each analysis unit is codified in only one way, i.e., each unit belongs to one and only one of the categories; and completeness, meaning that the whole data corpus must be codified.

The *a priori* categories identified for Character A represent a literal decomposition of the hashtag. In fact, they are categories about the character, the TV programme in which she appears, her politics and gender. Emergent *ex post* categories from analysis of the multimodal content include hate speech, activism and private life. (See Table 8.1.)

The *a priori* categories identified for Character B concern his character, the TV programme, the music world and gender identity. *Ex post* categories are ironic speech and private life. We should note that the gender identity category was little considered in the Multimodal Content Analysis of Character B (See Table 8.2.).

Specific terms associated with the categories come from the texts included in the hashtags, but also from the researcher's textual descriptions of the videos, images and emojis. Thus, we create a dictionary of the categories, which is uploaded to the software to extrapolate the keywords in context. In a quantitative representation they provide information on the presence in the text of the words in each specific category.

The computational part of the Content Analysis begins as soon as text codification is completed. The reduction of the data, their synthesis in an easily readable format that can be rendered in a graphic representation, allows us to summarize information from a large database. We used Mini-SSA Scaling (Brier et al., 2016), a form of multidimensional scaling per ordinal data, defined by Anthony Coxon (1982), also drawing on Chikio Hayashi's (1956) quantification scaling and Jean-Paul Benzécri's (1964) 'l'analyse des correspondences'. The MDS summarized the data by calculating the geometric distance between the dots, constrained to leave the positions taken by the categories one towards the other unaltered (Krippendorff, 2004).

In the resulting tri-dimensional MDS there is space for the categories elaborated to represent the communicative and emotional frame gathered under the hashtag #namea (see Figure 8.1). The dots summarize the emotions, images, videos and emojis used by the users, giving a complete picture of the semantic variability of the hashtag and of

Table 8.1 Main entry and associated words for Character A

Main entry	Associated words
Character	Politician*, representativ*, guest*, TV appearance*
TV programme	Island, famous, direct, evening, hunger, costum*, relationship*, competitor*
Politics	Party*, PD, profession*, famil*, comment*, election*, candidat*
Gender	Man, woman, identity*, exposure, spokesman, lov*, gay, gender
Hate speech	Excessive, inappropriate, transphob*, offending, discussion*
Activism	Fight*, battl*, arcigay[1], flag*, resist*, cultur*, life choic*
Private life	Partner*, past stor*, mom, dad, siblings, adolescence, coming out

[1] Arcigay is an Italian association that aims to protect LGBT rights in Italy.

Source: La Rocca & Rinaldi, 2020, p. 35

Table 8.2 Main entry and associated words for Character B

Main entry	Associated words
Character	Songwriter, showman, participation, appearance*, guest, columnist
TV programme	GF, disput*, show*, compet*, opinion*, strip*
Music world	Festival, song*, Sanremo, lyric*, author*, tour*
Ironic speech	Tuft, flashy, funny, danc*, movement*, boa*, jacket*, sequin*, glass*
Private life	Husband, Spain, toyboy, stori*, men

Source: La Rocca & Rinaldi, 2020, p. 36

how close they are to each other. Likewise with the tri-dimensional MDS for Character B (Figure 8.2).

These outputs show how, working from the deductive operationalization of the hashtag, it is possible to widen the semantic content through the induction process. Krippendorff (1980) invokes Pierce's abduction when describing the communicative frame obtained through MDS. Abductive reconstruction of the phenomenon represents the connection between the initial description of the texts and what actually emerges from the data. Before we conclude that findings that diverge from the habitual explanatory scheme for the phenomenon are valid we must devise hypotheses to validate them.

Regarding RQ1, with reference to Character A the MDS performed on a similarity matrix, using the Jaccard coefficient, shows us that some of the topics described with hashtags are close to one another. In fact, the themes of 'politics' and 'gender' both

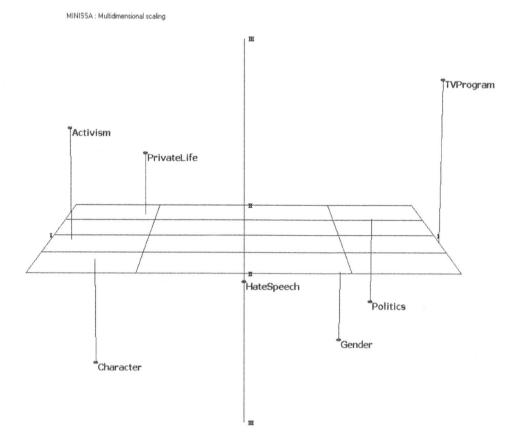

MINISSA : Multidimensional scaling

Figure 8.1 Multidimensional scaling for Character A.
(*Source*: La Rocca & Rinaldi, 2020, p. 36)

attract 'hate speech'. The character displays its value as a gay icon fighting for the rights of the LGBTQI+ community and attracting hate speech. On the other side, we find 'character', 'private life' and 'activism'. In Character B we find another type of division, where the representation concerns two aspects of the character's social life: on one hand, participation in such a programme and his being a TV character; on the other hand, aspects connected to his being an artist, such as 'music world', a sense of irony, and his private life. Overall we see the two characters' way of choosing to live out their sexual orientation and to fight or not fight for issues related to gender identity and LGBTQI+ communities.

RQ2 links their way of living and their gender identity to the classification of the emerging emotions. The emotions that gather around the hashtags for their names are different: for Character A the category of hate speech emerges, for Character B that of

MINISSA : Multidimensional scaling

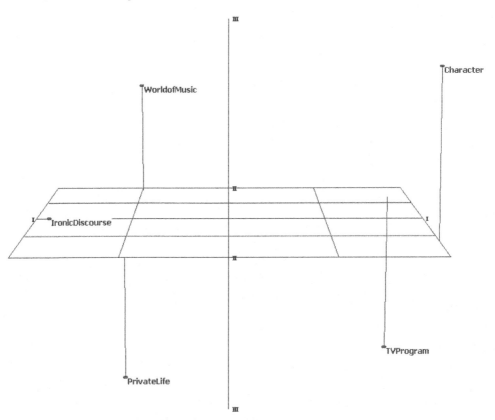

Figure 8.2 Multidimensional scaling for Character B.
(*Source*: La Rocca & Rinaldi, 2020, p. 37)

ironic speech. These are different emotional categories, linked – as shown by the MDS – to different thematic categories. In other words, with this type of analysis we not only find emotions, but also what they are related to, in this case, what gives rise to hatred or irony of the two characters.

The Multimodal Content Analysis also provides important information about how the mediatization of emotions emerges as an affordance (Gibson, 1979; Wells, 2002; Rathnayake & Suthers, 2018; Boccia Artieri & La Rocca, 2019; La Rocca, 2019) of the social media whose study implies attention to digital practices and the formation of a sense of public affection among the connected publics (boyd, 2010) that participate by expressing feelings (Papacharissi, 2015). These are stories of connection and expression, where hashtags are used as empty meanings waiting for an ideological identification with a wider polysemic orientation (Colleoni, 2013; Papacharissi, 2015; La Rocca, 2018a).

Hashtag analysis gathers the multiplicity of aspects one can trace of a character, attaching the feelings of those who look at the character. The hashtags and their polysemy reconfigure cognitive components such as hopes, fears, emotions and purposes built around a person or an event (Rathnayake & Suthers, 2018). When uptake by hashtag users occurs, the meaning of the hashtag also changes. We can see uptake as the 'most fundamental element of interaction'. 'Projected uptake' is based on the affordances of acts for future uptake; so, hashtags are affordances of the platform that organizes momentary connectedness into networks. Using MCA we can see that the best way to observe affordances is to evaluate their effects. Technologies show their affordances when actors are engaged in performing an action within the social system using them. Agency derives from an actor's knowledge of the frameworks and their ability to apply them to new contexts, working in a creative way with transformative actions. This transformation of the hashtag associated with social media features requires users to express their emotions within a hashtag, emerging here as hate speech for Character A and ironic speech for Character B. This momentary connection to users – in which the hashtags act as a bridge – becomes a tool to express emotions.

The merging point: MCA as Merged Method

The earlier discussion detailed the elements of classical Content Analysis and the debate over the status within it of qualitative data analysis that presage the emergence of Multimodal Content Analysis as a Merged Method. MCA is a Merged Method that looks at several elements: to Content Analysis for the attention it pays to the content of communication, to the analysis of texts, to the creation of categories and to the reconstruction of communication frames; to multimodal discourse analysis (MDA), because it extends the study of language *per se* to a study of language in combination with other resources, such as images, symbols, videos. MDA accepts that the language and other resources combine to create a meaning that is multimodal or multi-semiotic. And so does the Multimodal Content Analysis, which reconstructs the communication frame and visualizes the results in a three-dimensional space (See Table 8.3.).

Advantages and disadvantages

Multimodal Content Analysis offers ways to address what phenomena Big Data can explain and what they cannot (boyd & Crawford, 2012). Nevertheless, some questions remain: Are data representative of all tweets? Can the topic trends tell us what's inside

Table 8.3 Identikit of multimodal Content Analysis as a Merged Method

Characteristics of the researchers' work in the Merged Method	Identification in Multimodal Content Analysis
Data are co-constructed	Data are texts, images, graphic signs left by users such as comments, articles and other forms of expression. They are successively organized into categories by the researcher
Data are relational and interactional outcomes	Data are words, images, emojis, hashtags used in digital environments to exchange information, opinions, feelings, build a glossary of meanings
Methods predetermine the way the world is assembled	Multimodal Content Analysis determines the way of looking at the problem and social reality, in terms of contexts, meanings, relationships
Abandoning the concept of validity (true-value), and rediscovery of fidelity	Validity is represented by the correct method of coding and decoding the texts, the data collected, which must be faithful to the interpretative categories whether they are produced from top-down or emerge from the bottom-up process
The researcher's orientation is not to find an out-there truth but to create the best (social and relational) conditions for gathering information	The intent with which the Multimodal Content Analysis is conceived is to identify and categorize all manifestations of polysemic digital communication, whether they are manifest or latent
Social actors under study are participants	The work object of Multimodal Content Analysis are the traces left by any social actor in digital environments
The main aim is to guarantee participants' free expression	Freedom of expression is already guaranteed by digital environments in which polysemic digital communication develops itself. The researcher collects the traces of conversation after their expression
Researchers' active listening should be pursued	Researchers express their active listening in considering all the elements of the conversation, and interpreting them in the most faithful way to their original meaning
Results/findings are interpretations	The results are the fruit of the expression of free comments, posts and other elements of communication. Researchers look at them a posteriori, in search of categories of meaning, aimed at guaranteeing a mapping of the manifest and latent elements of communication. The researchers work to produce a categorization of all the elements present in the collected data

the hashtags? danah boyd and Kate Crawford (2012) claim that taken out of context, Big Data lose their meaning, because modelling processes reduce the data to what can adapt to and be interpreted in a mathematical model. It is therefore necessary to understand what one intends by the sense and meaning of a hashtag. The Multimodal

Content Analysis allows consideration of hashtags as cultural products that change meaning via human action and interaction.

Practical tips

When embarking on an MCA project your first task is to be clear about the goal of the analysis. Whether you design a formal hypothesis or simply state an aim it is important that you reflect on the research question(s) and how MCA will address them.

Before operationalizing the method, you should consider the balance between its components – the Content Analysis element and the multimodal discourse element. While you can look to creative thinking to guide you to what emerges from the data once it is characterized there are some strict guidelines for satisfying the definitional work for the classifications involved at the *ex ante* stage.

The primary computational techniques associated with MCA are supported by the Hamlet software package. Obtain the current version and familiarize yourself with it using a test dataset. Likewise, consult one of the practical guides to using MDS and, before you consider its techniques, ensure you understand its epistemological assumptions and satisfy yourself that they are consistent with your research question(s). When working with the three-dimensional graphical representations of the data relationships, review the *ex ante* classifications to identify tentative relationships that would violate or call into question these classifications.

Further reading

Content Analysis is a well-established method within the social sciences; many texts are listed in this chapter, such as the works of Berelson, Holsti (1969) and others. These texts have now become classics, to which you can add those produced by Krippendorff. To learn more about the multimodal characteristics of Content Analysis you can consult these works:

Androutsopoulos, J. (2011). From variation to heteroglossia in the study of computer-mediated discourse. In C. Thurlow & K. Mroczek (Eds.), *Digital discourse: Language in the new media* (pp. 277–298). London: Oxford University Press.

Feltham-King, T., & Macleod, C. (2016). How content analysis may complement and extend the insights of discourse analysis. *International Journal of Qualitative Methods*, 1(9), 1–9. DOI: 10.1177/1609406915624575.

Jewitt, C. (2014). *The Routledge handbook of multimodal analysis*. London: Routledge.

Kress, G., & Leeuwen, T. J. van (2001). *Multimodal discourse: The modes and media of contemporary communication.* London: Arnold.

O'Halloran, K. L. (2011). Multimodal discourse analysis. In K. Hyland & B. Paltridge (Eds.), *Companion to discourse.* London: Continuum.

Serafini, F. & Reid S. F. (2019). Multimodal content analysis. *Visual Communication*, 1–27.

For more information on multidimensional scaling or Hamlet software (http://apb.newmdsx.com/download.html) see these:

Brier, A., De Giorgi, E., & Hopp, B. (2016). Strategies in computer-assisted text analysis. Southampton: National Center for Research Methods Working Papers, 3/16.

Coxon, A. P. M. (1984). *The user's guide to multidimensional scaling.* London: Heinemann Educational Books.

For topic models:

Jacobs, T., & Tschötschel, R. (2019). Topic models meet discourse analysis: a quantitative tool for a qualitative approach. *International Journal of Social Research Methodology*, *22*(5), 469–485.

Levy, K., & Franklin, M. (2014). Driving regulation: Using topic models to examine political contention. *Social Science Computer Review*, *32*(2), 182–194.

9

TEXT MINING: FROM TACIT TO EXPLICIT KNOWLEDGE

Contents

- Definition
- Brief history of Text Mining
- A case study
- Knowing and know-how
- The merging point
- Advantages and disadvantages
- Practical tips
- Further reading

Text Mining (TM) is a close relative of Multimodal Content Analysis. Ronen Feldman and Hirshi (1996) place Text Mining within the field of Knowledge Discovery in Databases (**KDD**). TM aims to discover previously unknown knowledge that can be found in text collections. A non-trivial process of identifying valid, new, potentially useful and ultimately comprehensible textual data patterns is the goal of the TM process, which can be said to be achieved when the pattern does not represent the texts but the phenomenon, the reality, the part of the world of which it is the referent (Han & Kamber, 2001; Montes-y-Gomez et al., 2001).

To obtain the transformation of knowledge contained in a dataset, from tacit to explicit, TM follows a chain of operations: text refining (TR), natural language processing (NLP), information retrieval (IR), information extraction (IE), computational linguistics, clustering, categorization (CT), topic tracking, concept linkage and machine learning (ML).

Text Mining is a young, interdisciplinary field, borrowing techniques from the general field of Data Mining, and combining methodologies from various other areas (Stavrianou et al., 2007). TM's aim is about discovering unknown facts and hidden truths that may exist in the lexical, semantic or even statistical relations of text collections.

In this chapter we present Text Mining as an inherently Merged Method because its techniques are derived from different approaches. Its objectives differ from information retrieval because, according to Anna Stavrianou et al. (2007, p. 23):

- the objective of IR is to retrieve documents that partially match a query and select from these documents some of the best matched ones (van Rijesbergen, 1979);
- whereas the objective of TM is to discover hitherto unknown facts and hidden truths.

For us, the objective of TM is to make the knowledge contained in a dataset from tacit to explicit using merge-techniques (all joined together in a unique approach). So, our goal is to show how socialization, deconstruction, confirmation and construction of knowledge through Text Mining are possible. In this process, the researcher is guided by the theoretical framework of his/her work and the objectives it sets. Indeed, Text Mining techniques are useful to find and deal with various model variables. There are many factors that can affect data extraction, and these are not explicit and even hidden in many unstructured text collections. Text Mining is a suitable technique for finding these factors in text/documents. But the lantern of Diogenes is represented here by the theories that underlie any research work that seeks to use this method.

Definition

Several scholars have analysed and defined Text Mining, saying it is a variation on a field called Data Mining (Navathe & Ramez, 2000) that tries to find interesting patterns in large databases (Gupta & Lehal, 2009).

A common definition of Text Mining is that of Ah-Hwee Tan (1999), which tells us: Text Mining, also known as text data mining (Hearst, 2003) or knowledge discovery from textual databases (Feldman & Dagan, 1995), refers generally to the process of extracting interesting and non-trivial patterns or knowledge from unstructured text documents. Marti Hearst defines Text Mining as:

> the discovery by computer of new, previously unknown information, by automatically extracting information from different written resources. A key element is the linking together of the extracted information to form new facts or new hypotheses to be explored further by more conventional means of experimentation. (2003, p. 1).

Mining is required to extract knowledge, whether it is Text or Data Mining:

> The problem of Knowledge Discovery from Text (KDT) (Karanikas & Manchester, 2001) is to extract explicit and implicit concepts and semantic relations between concepts using Natural Language Processing (NLP) techniques. Its aim is to get insights into large quantities of text data. KDT, while deeply rooted in NLP, draws on methods from statistics, machine learning, reasoning, information extraction, knowledge management, and others for its discovery process. (Gupta & Lehal, 2009, p. 60)

But what kind of knowledge does Text Mining bring out? In Michael Polanyi's (1967) distinction between tacit and explicit knowledge, it would be explicit knowledge. However, it only becomes such after undergoing a process of conversion. According to Ikujiro Nonaka and Hirotaka Takeuchi (1995), there are four ways of converting knowledge: socialization, exteriorization, combination and interiorization. We can apply them to the process of deriving knowledge from TM.

Thus, the steps of the TM process require: the socialization of the texts collected in a *corpus*, the deconstruction of the texts, the construction of new fragments of text with meaning, and the validation of the text and its representation (see also, La Rocca, 2009).

Within this process of conversion and extraction of knowledge, we can also insert and rearrange the TM process described by Usama Fayyad et al. (1996), who, based on Ronald Brachman and Tej Anand (1996), emphasize the interactive nature of the process:

1. developing an understanding of the application domain, the relevant prior knowledge and the goals of the end-user;
2. creating a target dataset or subset;

3. data cleaning and processing, to remove noise or outliers, collect information to decide strategies for managing missing data;
4. data reduction and projection, finding characterizing elements for the representation of data according to the objectives;
5. choosing the Text Mining task, deciding the aim of the process of analysis, classification, clustering etc;
6. choosing the Text Mining algorithm(s) and the method to use to find the data pattern;
7. Text Mining, looking for interesting patterns in a particular form of representation: classification rules or trees etc. In this procedure, the researcher has a significant impact on the process due to the conduct of the previous steps;
8. interpreting mined patterns. In this step the researchers apply a quantitative hermeneutic approach to the text, by interpreting the data represented in words and reconstructing their history, finding wider meanings. Further, they study written language in relation to its social context with the purpose of extracting its meaning (such as in discourse analysis);
9. consolidating discovered knowledge. Knowledge is integrated into larger processes – in other words it is socialized again, just as Nonaka and Takeuchi (1995) argue in the spiral process;

The process of raising knowledge appears to have four stages here: understanding of the problem, refining of the text or *corpus*, mining and evaluation of the knowledge discovered (Table 9.1).

To develop these steps, a set of tools and knowledge are needed. Indeed, TM represents the evolution of other techniques that have already worked on texts and words to extract meaning from them. We can understand TM as an approach that brings out quantitative hermeneutics of textual data. The textual data, which are massive (for the mining of massive data check Leskovec et al., 2011), undergo a process of fragmentation and categorization, in order to become readable, analysable, interpretable by the researcher. The researcher relies on the numerical quantification of information to provide an interpretation of it.

Table 9.1 Four stages of knowledge creation within the TM process

	Tacit knowledge	Explicit knowledge
Tacit knowledge	Socialization Understanding	Deconstruction Refining
Explicit knowledge	Confirmation Mining	Validation/Representation Evaluation

Main procedures of TM

In the exploration of textual data – according to Ludovic Lebart et al. (1998, p. 11) there are four steps to follow: *problem – data – processing – interpretation*. By 'problem' we mean the identification of hypotheses or research questions which 'can give rise to an *a priori* formalization of a statistical or probabilistic model, or on the contrary can be tested in very general terms' (p. 11).

The *data* can be experimental, or they can arise from observation. They can follow a deductive or inductive path. The *processing* phase includes both the descriptive part of the statistics and the inferential part. Of no less importance is the moment of data *interpretation* in which the results and methods of analysis used are discussed. Currently in this sequence – given the evolution of the automatic and semi-automatic analysis tools and not forgetting machine learning – it is necessary to add the *meta-data* or *meta-information*, understood as that set of information on the data matrix that comes from, but does not appear directly from, reading the data. In short, it emerges from the analysis of the processes making tacit knowledge explicit.

This transformation of the text is pursued not only within linguistic statistics but also within Text Mining. The text in its basic form must be transformed in order to reveal the information it contains.

The first phase is text refining (TR), where the *corpus* (collection of texts) is loaded into software, then transformed into an intermediate form and worked to obtain knowledge. The application of different techniques enables very specific representations, which are determined by the researcher's goal. For example, NLP is the research field whose ultimate goal is to parse and understand language (Manning & Schütze, 1999). For this reason, we begin to fragment the text into small units of meaning represented first by the word, then by the sentence, and then again by the elementary context units. In all these moves, different approaches for the study of the text emerge. An overview of the analysis processes shows that these techniques follow each other (Manning & Schütze, 1999).

- Tokenization: is one of the first stages, dividing the text into units called tokens, each of which is either a word or something else, e.g., a number, a punctuation mark, a date. Punctuation is often considered – simply – as a delimiter, a borderline sign. However, it often contains relative information on the emphasis that words and phrases take on within the text.
- Stemming: is the process that extracts the root of a word, removing affixes and endings.

- Lemmatization: is the process that seeks the lemma – the word as it appears in the vocabulary –- starting from a word root. Compared to stemming, with lemmatization we proceed to the disambiguation between different basic forms which can correspond to a flexed form.

- Find collocations (Term Extraction): a collocation is an expression with meaning, which is made up of two or more words and corresponds to an idiomatic use, e.g., *strong* tea, *mass* communication etc. A characteristic of collocations is that their meaning can no longer be deduced from the meaning of the individual parts – they must be considered together.

- n-grams: is a generic sequence of *n* words. The most frequent n-grams are those for which n varies from 2 to 4. These are called: *bigram, trigram, four-gram*. The difference from collocations is that n-grams do not always correspond to idiomatic expressions; they can simply be formed by a 'preposition + article'.

- Word sense disambiguation: is an operation that consists in understanding which of its meanings an 'ambiguous' word employs in the text. Words, in fact, can have multiple meanings depending on whether they display polysemy or homonymy. These problems can be solved in two ways, using internal or external meta information. In the first case, lexical, dictionary-based resources are used; in the second case, learning-based methods are used, which can be implemented through categorization algorithms or through clustering algorithms.

- Anaphora Resolution: anaphora is a rhetorical figure which consists in the repetition (in the beginning of verse or propositions) of the word or expression with which the main verse or proposition begins. In this case, the task is to identify and resolve anaphoric relationships between the entities/sentences present within a text.

- Part of Speech (PoS) Tagging: through this operation a label/tag is attributed to each word of a sentence identifying what it corresponds to in the analysis of speech or grammatical analysis. By attributing a grammatical function to each word, tagging also works as a disambiguator, because if two words belong to two syntactic categories, it is able to determine which of these categories is the most plausible in the context in which the word is placed.

In these operations we find the importance of linguistics in extracting information from a text (see Figure 9.1). By applying these procedures, information extraction (IE) begins to be possible, with the aim of building a system that finds and links relevant information while ignoring extraneous and irrelevant information (Cowie & Lehnert, 1996). Carrying out these procedures allows you to extract information. It does not seem odd to say – at this point – that this is a Merged Method because different approaches merge

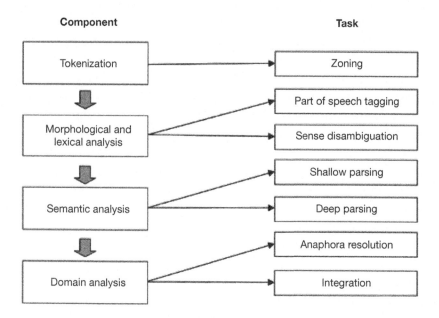

Figure 9.1 Major components and tasks of Text Mining.
(*Source*: Feldman & Sanger, 2007, p.105; quoted in Miner et al., 2012, p. 130)

in this technique. Of course, the way these technical steps are employed depends on the research goal and theoretical approach.

To extract and transform information contained in texts and then visualize it, it is necessary to query them. A query consists of index terms connected through the connectives: not, and, or; i.e., a conventional Boolean expression. Based on the similarity between a document and the query, the system predicts whether that document is relevant or not. For queries the following techniques are used.

- In the Vector Model, documents and queries are represented as vectors in a t-dimensional space, where 't' is the total number of distinct index terms in a set of texts. Within a set of index terms, not all terms are relevant for representing a document. For this reason, in the Vector Model, non-binary weights are assigned to index terms in document queries.

- As the name implies, the Probabilistic Model is based on the theory of probability; therefore, given a query, there is a set of documents that contains the relevant documents, for which a first probabilistic description is hypothesized, with which the system is initialized, and that is progressively improved through the iteration of the querying process.

- The Latent Semantic Indexing Model (LSIM) turns the analysis system upside down. It is based on the idea that in some cases the index terms are inadequate to represent the semantic content of a document. The basic idea is that information is often not contained so much in the linguistic representations of the texts but is instead contained in the concepts expressed and in the links between them. Working on the concepts, similarity is assessed on a semantic and not a lexical basis.

- Clustering and text categorization also play a key role in the search for information synthesis and information similarity. In clustering, the goal is the assignment of multivariate entities to a few categories (classes, groups) not defined *a priori*. The criterion is to group entities that are very similar to each other, rather than on their similarity to other groups.

- Text Categorization is based on categorization or classification that uses an opposite process to clustering. It is a procedure that refers to the task of automatically assigning one or multiple predefined category labels to free text documents (He et al., 2000). At this stage we return to deductive Content Analysis, where conceptual categories are created and then words are inserted into them. In categorization or classification, the terms must be attributed to one or more previously created classes/categories in a deductive way.

- Categorization can also be used with topic tracking 'to further specify the relevance of a document to a person seeking information on a topic' (Gupta & Lehal, 2009, p. 63). Topic tracking is very relevant today in understanding the tracking generated by users when viewing/searching documents online. It is the ensemble of these procedures that allows knowledge to become explicit (see Table 9.2).

Table 9.2 Discovering knowledge through TM

	Tacit knowledge	Explicit knowledge
Tacit knowledge	Socialization Understanding Linguistic analysis	Deconstruction Refining Content Analysis
Explicit knowledge	Confirmation Mining Discourse analysis	Validation/Representation Evaluation Text categorization/Clustering

Brief history of Text Mining

As we have already said, TM arises from the merging of different disciplines, approaches and techniques, which make it a merge method (see also 'Knowing and know-how' and 'The merging point' below).

First, let us consider how linguistic statistics provide the basis for this field. The field involves the same mix of disciplines that gave rise to linguistic statistics.

Textual statistics is influenced by different disciplines which, for various reasons and with different purposes, have approached the study of texts, such as: linguistics, Discourse analysis, Content Analysis, information retrieval, natural language processing and artificial intelligence. The combination of elements from linguistics, mathematics and information technology has given this Merged Method a multifaceted aspect and a variable range of action. In this way, statistics became an observation tool for linguistic phenomena, and are becoming an analysis tool for language.

But, if we go back in time, we find that the first applications of the extraction of information from documents or texts are linked to the activities of science libraries (see Figure 9.2). There, information retrieval and information summarization were used to index, to analyse abstracts and to group documents.

The first key date in the story of information extraction is 1987, the year in which the extraction of information from a large number of texts was applied to the Message Understanding Conference (MUC). That conference was initiated by the US Naval Ocean System Center (NOSC) and Defense Advance Research Project Agency (DARPA). These conferences reported the results of previous text analysis by various groups to fill

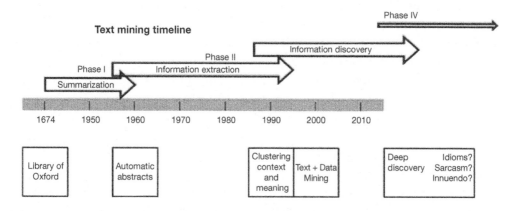

Figure 9.2 Timeline of phases of development in Text Mining.

(*Source*: Miner et al., 2012)

in templates provided in the form and exam. The submissions were evaluated against a test key' (Miner et al., 2012, p. 9). Other conferences that followed one another from 1989 to 1997 used the MUC's procedures to analyse issues other than naval matters, such as terrorism and microelectronics production. From these first applications comes the logical application architecture of Text Mining. The requirement was to: define the process of named entity recognition (phase syntactic analysis); formalize the test metrics and precision; disambiguate names and sentences; and to define: the importance of robustness of machine learning process; the importance of 'deep understanding' to minimize the danger of local pattern matching; the importance of resolving anaphoras.

The second key passage in the story of Text Mining is the encounter with the Web and its development. During the IEEE International Conference on *Tools with Artificial Intelligence* (ICTAI, 1997) the question was raised: 'Is there any benefit in applying Data Mining and AI to the World Wide Web?' (Cooley et al., 1997). The answer is obviously yes, and this is where the roots of modern Text Mining appear around the early 2000s. As the timeline shows, other issues are still ongoing or to be developed, such as algorithms' recognition of sarcasm in Sentiment Analysis.

A case study

A closely associated technique that also works with texts and words is *Sentiment Analysis*, which is one of the principal Big Data Text Mining applications currently in use.

Sentiment Analysis is a method that uses a range of digital tools to automate the detection of affective content in text (Thelwall, 2017). It is distinct from 'opinion mining', which involves software that extracts user opinions about products, services, or other topics from online text (Cambria and Schuller, 2013). Sentiment Analysis does that too but also involves software programs that extract sentiments from text to estimate the affective (emotional) state of the text's author.

A basic form of Sentiment Analysis is lexical Sentiment Analysis. Lexical approaches are broadly generic in that they work across different topics and types of text. A predefined lexical corpus (e.g., a list or network of words that indicate sentiment) is processed by algorithms. Beyond simple matching in a text there are algorithms that apply natural language processing techniques to get more information from the text. A basic lexical method could start with a list of positive and negative words, counting how often they occur or applying a formula, e.g., a weighted sum, to categorize the text as positive, negative, or neutral. Algorithms that go beyond this may include processing features to seek out negation or recognize symbols, e.g., emoticons. To perform lexical methods a human-coded lexicon is needed (Tong, 2001).

Beyond the lexical approach, Sentiment Analysis requires machine learning and has to be recalibrated for each different topic or text type. Outputs may be a summative polarity judgement for each text examined, measures of strength of positive or negative feeling, an assessment of how strongly the text expresses a given emotion, or a collation of the topics covered in the text and the sentiments associated with them.

As a case study we introduce a paper by Luca Giuliano and Gevisa La Rocca (2010) that works on this topic from the point of view of the validity and reliability of the positive–negative criterion when one uses techniques of automatic text classification. Their attention focuses also on marker categories because they have a different weight when addressing the positive or negative tones of speech. Their aim is: to hone the positive–negative category applying it to a specific corpus of articles which appeared in *The Guardian, The Independent,* the *Daily Telegraph* and *The Times* newspapers from 2003 to 2008 and with China as subject (corpus China–-UK). Sergio Bolasco and Francesca della Ratta-Rinaldi (2004), based on the outcomes of their study, suggest threshold points in their negative index (Occ. Neg/Pos*100) of 50% for large corpuses and 40% for smaller ones, from which on a text can be said to have a negative connotation. Bolasco and della Ratta-Rinaldi (2004) used the tools produced within the General Inquirer (GI) software (Stone et al., 1962), and for the evaluation of the text tone, following Marchand's example (1998), they chose adjectives as the category. Marchand, in fact, stresses the importance of adjectives to evaluate the rating of a text. With these references, Giuliano and La Rocca build a set of steps to classify the corpus in an automatic way according to the criterion positive–negative, and they created a specific sub-dictionary of the research subject.

The three steps are as follows.

1. *Ex ante:* they analysed the General Inquirer dictionary (Id) distinguishing and organizing the various categories it contains. The positive–-negative category inserted in the Inquirer dictionary came from the work of Charles Osgood et al. (1957) on the three different semantic dimensions, then adopted by Ole Holsti in the Stanford Political Dictionary of 1969. In this list of nouns structured in categories it is possible to find nouns present in more than one category, potentially making the attribution ambiguous. The ambiguity could be caused by certain polysemic words and, in particular, by bisemic words when referred to the negative–positive polarity: these are words which are positive or negative according to the context. The first thing to do – in this case – is therefore to examine and reduce the list of the Id, to a list of words exclusively classifiable in the positive–negative categories.

Table 9.3 Headwords of the Inquirer dictionary per semantic category

Headwords Id	Negative	Positive
Monosemic	1,989	1,621
Bisemic (Pos & Neg)	16	16
Polysemic	286	278
Total	2,291	1,915
Unique headwords	2,005	1,637

Source: Giuliano & La Rocca, 2010, p. 64

The list of the negative–positive words, examined from this point of view, gives rise to the following observations (see Table 9.3).

- In the list of the Id the identified polysemies (278 positive headwords and 286 negative ones) are not classifiable according to 'evaluative' semantics, but according to other meanings which are independent from it.
- Only 16 headwords are bisemic from the evaluative point of view. Their presence therefore has no influence in the overall attribution of tone to a corpus with a rather extended lexicon.
- The list reduced to the headwords with only one entry consisting of 1,637 positive headwords and 2,005 negative ones.

Later, they examine the list considering the marker categories, which seems more informative. The adjectives, which are certainly decisive in classifying the tone of speech as positive or negative, are present in the list with respectively 35.86 and 32.07% of the headwords. The presence of verbs and nouns is too significant to be neglected, but we must stress the different relevance verbs have inside each of the two semantic categories: 17.96% among the positive headwords and 21.79% among the negative ones. The choice to include or not the verbs in the list is decisive, as we will see, when classifying the tone of speech.

2. *In itinere:* they carried out an experimental control on the validity and reliability of the list of adjectives taken from the Id for the creation of a negativity index. This was carried out on a corpus of 4,216 articles from the four newspapers (see Table 9.4). The corpus has been normalized using the software TalTac 2.5 (Bolasco, 2000) and entered as a headword for the English language with TreeTagger.

Table 9.4 Lexico-statistic characteristics of the corpus*

Token words (N)	2,558,606
Type words (V)	69,981
Type/token ratio = (V/N)*100	2.73
% hapax	43.97
Mean = N/V	36.56

*Software used: TalTac 2.5 by Bolasco, Baiocchi & Morrone, 2006.
Source: Giuliano & La Rocca, 2010, p. 65

It is in this delicate moment that the negativity indicator is applied to the corpus and it becomes possible to see its strengths and weaknesses. The list of positive–negative headwords applied to the semantic tagging of the corpus China–UK allows us to observe how the negativity index (Occ. Neg/Pos*100) is very sensitive to the headwords used from the grammatical point of view (see Table 9.5). Using the complete vocabulary, they obtain a negativity index of 66.36, whereas with the list of adjectives only the index is less negative (59.75). The overall score of the negativity index is decisively influenced by the presence of the verbs which, by themselves, have a negativity index of 83.19.

The researchers found that the evaluation of the newspapers provided different results according to the composition of the indicator. The ADJ (adjectives) indicator reveals that *The Guardian* is the newspaper with the most negative tone towards China, while *The Independent* appears to be the least negative; the VERBS indicator indicates the *Daily Telegraph* as the most negative and *The Times* as the least negative; the NOUNS indicator reveals that *The Independent* is the most negative and that *The Times* is the least negative; finally, the ALL indicator presents *The Guardian* as the most negative

Table 9.5 Negativity index of the corpus China–UK

Grammatical category	Negative	Positive	N/P*100
Adjectives	20,319	34,085	59.61
Verbs	27,623	24,484	112.82
Nouns	63,362	67,055	94.49
Others	4,675	7,717	60.58
All categories	115,979	133,341	86.98

Source: Giuliano & La Rocca, 2010, p. 65

Table 9.6 Negativity index of the corpus China–UK based on ranges of frequency (F.R.)

Grammatical category	High F.R. N/P*100	Low F.R. N/P*100
Adjectives	48.19	78.00
Verbs	96.83	158.11
Nouns	82.12	128.74
Others	64.21	67.04
All categories	76.48	114.59

Source: Giuliano & La Rocca, 2010, p. 67

and *The Times* as the least negative. Evaluation based on years is stabler. In all the three main marker categories the year with the highest negativity index is 2003. A greater variability can be found instead in the lowest index: 2006 for the ADJ indicator; 2004 for the VERBS and NOUNS indicators; 2008 for the ALL indicator.

They also produce an evaluation considering the position (frequency range, divided into high, medium, low) that the terms occupy in their lists. In the medium–high frequency range (see Table 9.6) the negativity index of the adjectives reaches its lowest value, while the highest value is reached among the verbs belonging to the low frequency level. If, when calculating the negativity index, they consider only the adjectives, the importance of those with a positive valence in the medium–high frequency becomes decisive for the result.

The semantic tagging carried out on the corpus China–UK was necessary to calculate a negativity index for each printed article and to order them from the most to the least negative based on their general tone. In this classification list they calculated the distribution in quartiles and built a new evaluation variable with four modalities which were added to the previous variables of the corpus (Newspaper and Year):

- POS1= positive (first quartile of the articles with a negativity index from 0 to 40%)
- NEG2 = quite negative (second quartile with an index between 41% and 65%)
- NEG3 = negative (third quartile with an index between 66% and 100%)
- NEG4 = very negative (fourth quartile with an index over 100%).

3. *Ex post:* To the original corpus China–UK they applied the ASPAR (correspondence analysis of the table Word × Responses, carried out with Lebart's DTM software) procedure, where the responses represented by the newspaper articles and

the variables of the categories (Year, Newspaper and Evaluation) were used as explanatory variables. The hypothesis underpinning this analysis was that among the first factors extracted it was necessary to identify a dimension of negativity which made it possible to position in a linear way the negative and the positive words of the GI. Around this were gathered other words not included in the list and which were positioned along the same dimension. The results of the ASPAR procedure can be seen in Figures 9.3 (positive words) and 9.4 (negative words), which represent the factorial plane made up of axes 3 and 4. Along the third axis are positioned most of the words of the Id list. Its interpretation in terms of negativity–positivity is confirmed by the projection of the modalities of the variable Evaluation (see Figure 9.5). The fourth axis represents the time-dimension. In the semantic field strongly characterized by a negative tone, as results from the quadrants III and IV, there are words such as: accused, aggression, arrested, atrocities, boycotted, crimes. In quadrants I and II are positioned words less characterized by negativity or strongly positive such as: accommodation, admired, aesthetic, art, beautiful.

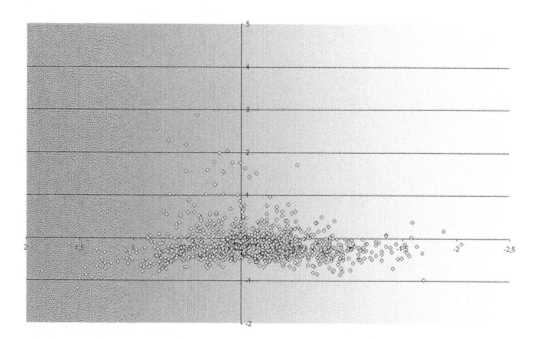

Figure 9.3   Correspondence analysis of Corpus UK: factorial plane of positive words (Axis 3) and time dimension (Axis 4).

(*Source*: Giuliano & La Rocca, 2010, p. 68)

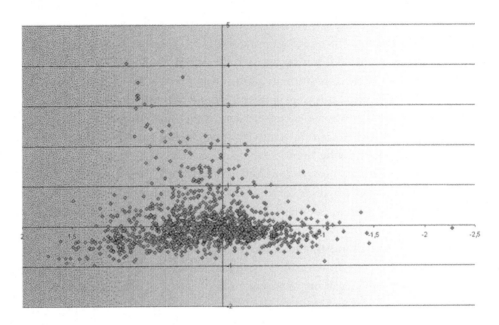

Figure 9.4 Correspondence analysis of Corpus UK: factorial plane of negative words (Axis 3) and time dimension (Axis 4).

(*Source*: Giuliano & La Rocca, 2010, p. 69)

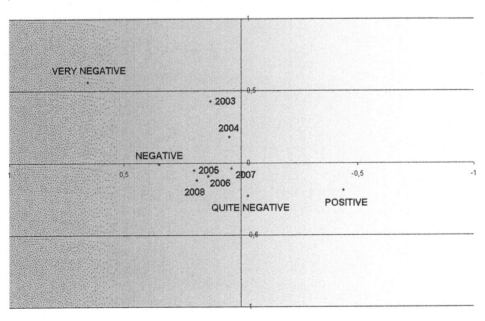

Figure 9.5 Correspondence analysis of Corpus UK: factorial plane of negative–positive (Axis 3) and time dimension (Axis 4).

(*Source*: Giuliano & La Rocca, 2010, p. 69)

China and Beijing are positioned in the negative semantic field, confirming the validity of the negativity indicator, especially in its overall composition which considers terms selected in all the marker categories. In the negative semantic field, we also find words such as bird flu, communist party, death penalty, Sars and virus which were not inserted in the list of the GI. The same can be said for Confucianism, evolution, glamour present in the positive semantic field. We must stress that some words which in other contexts would be considered positive, are considered negative in this corpus, such as Dalai Lama, democratic and human rights, since they recall and emphasize difficulties, conflicts and claims.

This case study shows that Sentiment Analysis is a hybrid method involving both quantitative and qualitative elements, but the qualitative data collected need to be designed from the outset such that they can be integrated with quantitative data and the principal qualitative analytical elements are confined to the initial development of categories to be built into the algorithm and the application of human reasoning when inspecting outputs for obnoxious associations arising from hidden bias in the algorithm and spurious interpretations arising from features like sarcasm or irony. It would, however, be unsafe to conclude that the qualitative aspect of Sentiment Analysis is insignificant. In terms of time expended in conducting a Sentiment Analysis, the identification and resolution of problematic associations and spurious interpretations may often be a greater call on a project's intellectual resources than the run-time for the quantitative component. Moreover, if such associations are missed the results can be highly consequential in the real world. Some of the most sophisticated Sentiment Analysis is conducted for profit, drawing on personal information without consent and without the means to validate or rebut resultant analyses. There are cases where particular interpretations of Sentiment Analysis output have been used to target advertising at particular socio-demographic groups. One study showed how companies could tailor their marketing to female consumers by exploiting their feelings about their appearance. It identified times of the week when women apparently felt worst about their looks, enabling advertisers to focus certain kinds of message on particular days of the week (Kramer et al., 2014). Sentiment Analysis can thus be used for market manipulation, and in this particular case the interpretation of Facebook data was undermined by systematic differences amongst sociodemographic groups in the propensity of women to post mood state information.

This study demonstrates how TM – in its various applications – is a merge method because quantitative techniques rely on qualitative ones and vice versa, in order to arrive at quantitative hermeneutics of the textual datum. This process of interpenetration of techniques and approaches continues throughout the work carried out within Text Mining, showing how the data are co-constructed. The researcher feeds the categories to be used, the algorithms extract the information from a large database, the researcher goes back over the quantitative data, interprets them, looks for techniques suitable for visualizing and synthesizing them, and finally places their meaning within broader theories.

Knowing and know-how

The use of a Text Mining approach to classifying the sentiment of a text has been widely discussed in the literature (e.g., Bollen et al., 2011; Liu, 2012; Balbi et al., 2018). Most methods are based on a top-down approach, where *a priori* coding procedure of terms, or text, is performed focusing on the manifest content of the word. Here we introduce Emotional Text Mining (ETM) (Greco, 2016a; Greco & Polli, 2020a), a Text Mining procedure that, employing bottom-up logic, allows for context-sensitive Text Mining approaches to unstructured data, which constitutes 95% of Big Data (Gandomi & Haider, 2015). ETM is an unsupervised Text Mining procedure, based on a socio-constructivist approach and a psychodynamic model (Greco, 2016b). According to this approach, sentiment is not only the expression of a mood but also the evidence of latent and social thinking processes that includes interactions, behaviour, attitudes, expectations and communication. Thus, according to the semiotic approach to analysis of textual data, ETM supports social profiling. This has been applied in different fields (Cordella et al., 2018a, 2018b; Laricchiuta et al., 2018; Greco et al., 2019; Greco & Polli, 2020b) and, particularly, in the analysis of political debate in order to profile social media users and to anticipate or explain their political choices (Greco et al., 2017, Greco et al., 2018a; Greco et al., 2018b; Greco et al., 2019; Greco & Polli, 2019). While human reasoning proceeds from the semiotic to the semantic level in generating text, the statistical procedure simulates the inverse process, moving from the semantic level to the semiotic. For this reason, ETM performs a sequence of synthesis procedures, from text pre-processing and the selection of keywords to multivariate analysis, to identify the semiotic level, starting from the semantic. We will use here the work of Giovanni Boccia Artieri, Francesca Greco and Gevisa La Rocca (2021) on COVID-19's representation in the first stage of the Italian contagion as expressed on Twitter.

Method and workflow

In their work the authors look for the answer to two research questions.

- What are the reactions of users on Twitter at the start of the coronavirus news? What kind of emotional reactions has this virus elicited in users?
- How do users' actions and reactions help redefine the meaning of the coronavirus hashtag?

All the messages in Italian containing the word 'coronavirus' and '#coronavirus' were collected from Twitter for four days, from 24 to 28 February 2020. Data extraction was carried out with the retweet package in R (v.0.7.0; Kearney, 2020) providing an interface to the Twitter web **API**.

All the messages were collected in a corpus and two lexical indicators were calculated: the type–token ratio (TTR) and the percentage of hapax (Hapax%; **hapax legomenon** or hapax is a word or an expression that occurs only once within a context) to check whether it was possible to statistically process data. They created a set of steps:

1. they cleaned and preprocessed data with the software T-Lab (v.2018, Lancia, 2018) and selected the documents that had at least nine words excluding the retweet;
2. in order to select the terms, they lemmatized and excluded the stopwords, 'coronavirus' and '#coronavirus' and the words with a low rank of frequencies (Bolasco, 1999);
3. on the document-term matrix, they performed a cluster analysis based on a bisecting k-means method based on cosine similarity (Savaresi & Boley, 2004; Steinbach et al., 2000, Steinbach et al., 2003), limited to 10 partitions, excluding all the tweets that did not have at least two co-occurring keywords. The bisecting k-means clustering algorithm combines k-means clustering with divisive hierarchy clustering. With bisecting k-means, you get not only the clusters but also the hierarchical structure of the clusters of data points. k-means algorithms can use cosine similarity or squared Euclidean distance (Tan et al., 2006);
4. to choose the optimal solution, they calculated the Calinski–Harabasz (Calinski & Harabasz, 1974), the Davies–Bouldin and the intraclass correlation coefficient (ρ) indices (Greco & Polli, 2020a);
5. they performed a correspondence analysis (Lebart & Salem, 1994) on the cluster-term matrix. To facilitate the correspondence analysis results interpretation, each term is considered only on the factor where its absolute contribution is highest compared to those of the other factors. In this way each factor has only exclusive terms;
6. they considered also the cluster partition in which each cluster was divided into two subclusters to identify two subtopics for each previously identified macro area (cluster);
7. finally, they measured the sentiment according to the number of messages classified in the subcluster and its interpretation.

Findings for the first research question

The sample of 436,925 tweets was collected during the media storm in online Italian newspapers. It consisted of 72.8% retweets and resulted in a large corpus of 11,324,811 tokens. On the basis of the large size of the corpus, both lexical indexes highlighted its richness (TTR = 0.008; Hapax% = 36.3) and indicated the possibility of proceeding with ETM. Text selection and preprocessing reduced the sample of tweets to 98,788 documents. The results of the cluster analysis show that 643 terms allowed for the classification of 89.3% of the documents. The clustering validation measures indicated that the first optimal solution was four clusters. Correspondence analysis detected three latent dimensions, and the explained inertia for each factor is reported in Table 9.7. In Figure 9.6, we can understand the emotional map of COVID-19 emerging from the Italian tweets. It shows how the clusters are placed in the factorial space produced by the three factors.

As shown in Table 9.7, ultimately, the Twitter users symbolize COVID-19 by means of three general dimensions: the *actor*, the *danger* and the *reaction*.

The first factor distinguishes the *actors* in *institutions* and *people*; the second factor reflects the double nature of the *danger*, the *contagion* and the *alarm*; and the third factor categorizes the *reaction* in terms of movement restriction (*control*) and *lockdown*. The location of the cluster in the factorial space has a specific configuration: they are located on the axes of the second and the third factors (see Figure 9.7). It implies that each cluster is almost always explained by only two factors: the first and the second factor for clusters 2 and 3 and the first and third factor for cluster 1 and 4.

This configuration of the factor space is found whenever the topic is symbolized by two opposite dimensions that cannot be integrated with each other (Greco, 2016b; Cordella et al., 2018b), which in this case are *institutions* and *people*. In the COVID-19 symbolization, the first factor distinguishes the actors into victims (people) and protectors (institutions). The danger (Factor 2) concerns only the victims, while the reaction (Factor 3) pertains to the protectors. This irreconcilable distinction suggests a conflict between the institution, which should protect, and people, who need protection, and, probably, a distrust of citizens towards institutions.

Table 9.7 Correspondence analysis results

Factor	Eigenvalues	%	Cum %	Label	Negative pole	Positive pole
1	0.303	39.0	39.0	Actor	Institution	People
2	0.269	34.5	73,5	Danger	Contagion	Alarm
3	0.206	26.5	100	Reaction	Control	Lockdown

Source: Boccia Artieri et al., 2021, p. 294

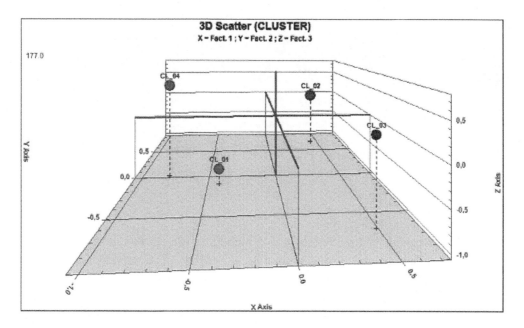

Figure 9.6   Factorial space.

(*Source*: Boccia Artieri et al., 2021:294)

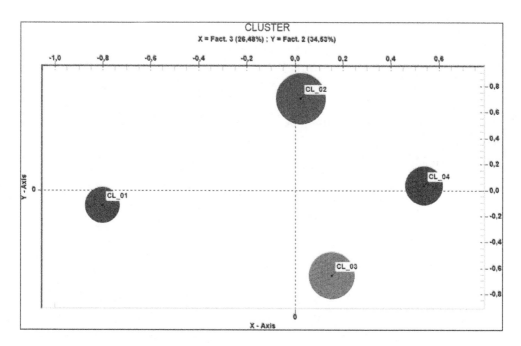

Figure 9.7   Factorial space.

(*Source*: Boccia Artieri et al., 2021:295)

Table 9.8 Cluster location in the symbolic space

Cluster	Tweet	Tweet	Label	Factor 1	Factor 2	Factor 3
		%		Actor	Danger	Reaction
1	17,902	20.30	The Damned North	Institution		Control
2	26,488	30.04	The Rising of the Flame	People	Alarm	
3	24,229	27.48	The Affordances of the Virus	People	Contagion	
4	19,553	22.18	The Hidden Dimension	Institution		Lockdown

Source: Boccia Artieri et al., 2021, p. 295

The interpretation of the factorial space highlights the emotional map by which people, in general, emotionally symbolize COVID-19, and supports the cluster interpretation according to location in the symbolic space (see Table 9.8).

Coronavirus is represented as an 'invisible enemy', which has the ability to limit people's rights and threaten their lives. Hence, the virus becoming a danger and calling into question citizens, public actors, institutions and new control policies. These aspects are the result of the analysis which distributes the clusters in the factorial space.

The four clusters are of different sizes (see Table 9.8) and reflect different COVID-19 representations. As the four clusters reflect four main macro-areas, they interpret also the eight-cluster partition in which each cluster was divided into two subclusters, highlighting the specificities of each macro-area (see 'Findings for the second research question' section).

These procedures answered the researchers' first research question. As news in the press levelled off, the flow of Twitter traffic grew. This communicative flow captured the reactions – made up of a multitude of feelings – of Italians.

Findings for the second research question

Within a few days the meaning of the word and the hashtag 'coronavirus' changed, through human use and interaction, and, above all, following social, political and pandemic events. Then coronavirus becomes an umbrella under which multiple meanings and emotions are collected. The work that takes place here gives us the opportunity to analyse – at a specific point in time – the evolution of its meanings. We can retrospectively reconstruct sensemaking (La Rocca, 2020a).

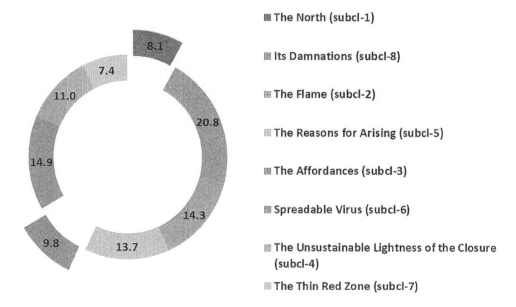

The North (subcl-1)

Its Damnations (subcl-8)

The Flame (subcl-2)

The Reasons for Arising (subcl-5)

The Affordances (subcl-3)

Spreadable Virus (subcl-6)

The Unsustainable Lightness of the Closure (subcl-4)

The Thin Red Zone (subcl-7)

Figure 9.8 The ranking of coronavirus nuances.
(*Source*: Boccia Artieri et al., 2021:298)

Exploring the tweets reveals the many meanings of coronavirus. These can be enclosed in interpretative categories. These categories come from below (inductively) because they collect the meanings that users have attributed to coronavirus. In the steps analysis they descend from the subclusters. They obtain eight interpretative categories of meaning, each with a symbolic weight, depending on the different use that users have made over the days – here analysed – in the meanings related to coronavirus (see Figure 9.8).

To identify the sentiment associated with the eight categories they created two opposite conceptual categories: surrender and resist. They chose this criterion because all the messages in the emergency period highlighted a negative sentiment, requiring them to consider the sentiment from a different perspective. The result is particularly interesting: a third of the representations (35.5% of texts) reflect the intention to surrender to the health threat while almost two-thirds (64.5%) highlight the intention to resist and face the emergency (see Figure 9.9). They have considered The North, The Flame and Affordances as representations highlighting a passive position in facing pandemic (Surrender). The health emergency was such an unexpected and frightening event that it left people astonished and in need of information and support. On the other hand, they considered Its Damnations, Reasons for Arising, Spreadable Virus, Unsustainable Lightness of the Closure and The Thin Red Zone as representations reflecting the intention to react to the pandemic by facing the emergency.

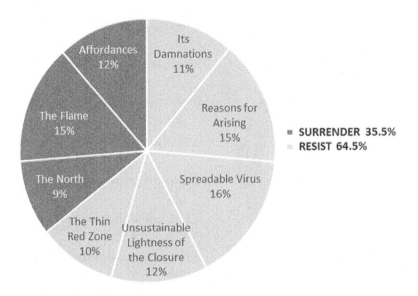

Figure 9.9   The sentiment on coronavirus.
(*Source*: Boccia Artieri et al., 2021:303)

The merging point

The coronavirus study offers us the opportunity to see firsthand where Text Mining becomes a Merged Method. Tweets are Big Data, traces, comments left by users; it is impossible to read them all manually. They thus become a collection of anonymous data from which information can be extracted. In the process of extracting information, textual data undergoes a set of processing techniques.

- The first phase is a lexical analysis, which recalls both linguistic statistics and natural processing language. In the process of converting knowledge from tacit to explicit, this is the stage of socialization.
- In the second phase, through local text analysis, information is extracted from the documents by analysing the individual sentences. This procedure resembles Content Analysis. This is the stage of deconstruction.
- In a third phase, through inference, elementary events are integrated into more complex ones or a new interpretation is created. All this happens thanks to Discourse analysis. This is the phase of confirmation.
- In a last phase, everything must be validated and summarized, i.e., it takes the form of a geometric output, capable of displaying the results of this long analysis

process. The software in this case resorts to text categorization or clustering, but in conclusion it responds to the needs of data visualization. The last phase is the one in which the inferential statistics exert their greatest pressure. In fact, given a set of texts (dataset/corpus), the question is how to quickly find information from them. In this sense, the corpus must be interrogated by query and displayed results. For queries the following are used: the Boolean Model, the Vector Model, the Probabilistic Model, the Latent Semantic Indexing Model and clustering and text categorization.

Step by step the data undergoes a process of transformation and reduction that allows knowledge to be extracted from them. In this process the data are co-constructed and become the fruit of the relationship between their literal meaning (descriptive level) and their figurative meaning (connotative level). An example of this transformation process is the creation of conceptual categories generated to reconstruct the nuances of meaning of the coronavirus hashtag, or those created *ad hoc* to interpret the reasons for negative sentiment. The analyst is able to identify categories because the data have undergone a process of transformation, reduction, re-elaboration (see Table 9.9).

Table 9.9 Identikit of Text Mining as a Merged Method

Characteristics of the researchers' work in the Merged Method	Identification in Text Mining
Data are co-constructed	Data are all textual data from interviews, observations, documents, newspaper articles, comments, posts, tweets, that are too extensive to treat manually
Data are relational and interactional outcomes	Written texts, their manifest and latent meaning, their decomposition and re-composition using quantitative techniques, the interpretation that the researcher provides of them
Methods predetermine the way the world is assembled	The Text Mining approach, the chosen processing techniques, determine the way of looking at the problem and social reality
Abandoning the concept of validity (true-value), and rediscovery of fidelity	Validity is represented by the number of documents and is entrusted at the beginning (first phase) to lexical indicators
The researcher's orientation is not to find an out-there truth but to create the best (social and relational) conditions for gathering information	Text Mining aims to identify meaning from existing documents by extracting it from them

(continued)

Table 9.9 (Continued)

Characteristics of the researchers' work in the Merged Method	Identification in Text Mining
Social actors under study are participants	All the documents that are selected are carriers of knowledge, opinions, feelings, emotions, and they are an expression of the social actors
The main aim is to guarantee participants' free expression	Freedom of expression is always guaranteed in the Text Mining approach, as well as anonymity
Researchers' active listening should be pursued	Researchers express their active listening in keeping attention on what the textual data say and what they don't say
Results/findings are interpretations	The findings result from the interpretations contained in the documents. Researchers look at them by moving on multiple dimensions: their statistical representativeness, semantic and semiotic content, their organization in clusters, the reduction into categories of viewable and shareable data

Advantages and disadvantages

There are many advantages and disadvantages associated with the different techniques used.

Advantages:

- the aim of TM is about discovering unknown events and hidden phenomena that may exist in the lexical, semantic or even statistical relations of text collections;
- allows you to work with a large amount of data, reducing complexity;
- Sentiment Analysis is much used in business research, where firms monitor social media for sentiment associated with products and brand names;
- you can find many resources online such as: SentiStrength (http://sentistrength. wlv.ac.uk), a lexical sentiment strength detection program (Thelwall et al., 2010).

Disadvantages:

- you need a computer with a lot of memory;
- requires software licence or knowing the syntax of open source software;
- you have to employ quantitative and qualitative data analysis;
- classifier systems rapidly produce good results where texts are focused on a specific topic (Thelwall, 2017 gives the example of movie reviews) but do not

perform well when applied more broadly. Behind the classification is the conversion of texts into 'feature vectors' (sets of relevant terms);

- another thing that can defeat an algorithm is sarcasm, where the intended meaning carries the opposite polarity to the literal meaning of the words (Thelwall's example is 'I am extremely happy to be injured');
- where pursuing policy-related research it is important to be aware that Sentiment Analysis is not foolproof and can produce flawed estimates of sentiment.

Practical tips

Text Mining uses algorithms, so you need to know that:

- the performance of algorithms is conventionally tested by comparison with results produced by human raters. This requires at least a thousand texts, and coders must be given precise and consistent instructions. The usual assessment is a statistic expressing the correlation between human and computer scores, which may then be compared with other algorithms, the one with the highest correlation being chosen. The algorithm is then seen as validated and is further referenced against human coding only if misleading results are observed;
- further, Text Mining work with online resources increasingly permits very large samples to be analysed qualitatively (while noting that in quantitative research, generalizability is not a simple function of sample size but of sample representativeness). Because very large amounts of text can be quickly processed, researchers can derive insights that might not be discernible with small amounts of data.

When you work with sentiment, remember that:

- in the contemporary environment it is hardly necessary to note the ethical, political and legal challenges that arise where sentiments are monitored in order to influence and manipulate target populations, with social media users unaware of Sentiment Analysis being applied to communications they wrote for other purposes and assumed were private (Kennedy, 2012). Sentiment Analysis can also refine other software which interacts with humans; it has, for instance, been incorporated into automatic chat systems.

There is another element to consider when applying Text Mining to the study of hashtags:

- it is necessary to keep in mind the very nature of the hashtag, which was born as a thematic aggregator and has become a multi-semantic umbrella that changes its meaning from post to post by sharing (La Rocca, 2020a, 2020b; La Rocca & Rinaldi, 2020).

Further reading

A handbook you can use to work with Text Mining is:

Feldman, R., & Sanger, J. (2007). *The text mining handbook: Advanced approaches in analyzing unstructured data*. New York: Cambridge University Press.

On Sentiment Analysis and emotional Text Mining you can use:

Liu, B. (2012). *Sentiment analysis: Mining opinions, sentiments, and emotions*. Williston, VT: Morgan & Claypool.

To start using R on Text Mining:

Silge, J., & Robinson, D. (2017). *Text mining with R: A tidy approach*. Newton. MA: O'Reilly & Associates Inc.

For textual data statistical analysis go to http://lexicometrica.univ-paris3.fr/jadt where you can access the proceedings of the Jadt International Conference on the Statistical Analysis of Textual Data.

10

THE SYMLOG METHOD: HOW TO ANALYSE BEHAVIOUR AND GROUP DYNAMICS

Contents

- Definition
- Brief history of the Symlog method
- A case study
- Knowing and know-how
- The merging point
- Advantages and disadvantages
- Practical tips
- Further reading

The method discussed in this chapter combines the focus on words of the Content Analysis and Text Mining methods with the focus of Chapters 5, 6 and 7 on researcher–participant interaction. The Symlog method, an acronym that stands for SYstematic Multiple Level Observation of Groups, was developed by Robert Freed Bales (1950, 1953, 1970; Bales & Cohen, 1979; Bales, 1999), with the aim of understanding group behaviours, and their interactions, in order to produce a codification of the latter. Various versions of the method are applied to particular purposes or to the context in which they are used, but all versions contain 26 very detailed adjective rating forms.

In its workflow Symlog uses several techniques, making it a Merged Method:

- non-participant observation (a type of ethnography) carried out by the researchers;
- a questionnaire based on the Symlog Adjective Rating Form, classically organized in three dimensions: upward–downward, positive–negative, forward–backward. Participants assign a score to each of 26 adjectives using a rating scale;
- Bales Report, where the 26 values are assigned into conceptual categories;
- Field Diagram Report, a two-dimensional projection of the results contained in the Bales Report;
- Symlog cube-space, which describes the direction of values, for the individual and organizational values identified in the Bales Report;
- the data collected through the Symlog questionnaire are analysed and synthesized using statistical procedures, like **ANOVA**, factor analysis.

Furthermore, 'the results of SYMLOG analyses can be combined with a group socio-gram, not only to provide a picture of who is interacting with whom in the group, but also to understand what kind of interaction is taking place' (Stangor, 2004, p. 35).

Observations are generally performed at fixed time intervals in order to verify/observe the presence of change in the attitudes; these observations/measurements are made by assessors, experts in group dynamics. The Symlog method can be applied to the study of verbal and non-verbal behaviour and for each of these aspects of behaviour it gathers both the participant's and the observer's point of view, ultimately providing an overall picture of group behaviour.

Definition

Symlog is a systematic observation technique, and it can therefore be defined as an observation and ranking procedure for interactive behaviour. It is based on 26 ratings (see Table 10.1) of certain aspects of group member behaviours, generally applied at the end of each session, at pre-established intervals, or at a time after the observation (interactive behaviour retrospective ranking).

As Richard Brian Polley claims (1991, p. 93): 'Only systematic observation, with valid and reliable instruments, provides a record of events themselves rather than the retrospective reconstruction of the event.' To track these systematic observations over time, researchers use the Bales Report and Field Diagram Report, tools that allow researchers to quantify the observations collected. Furthermore, with the Symlog method,

Table 10.1 Symlog Adjective Rating form

U	Active, dominant, talks a lot
UP	Extroverted, outgoing, positive
UPF	A purposeful democratic task leader
UF	An assertive business-like manager
UNF	Authoritarian, controlling, disapproving
UN	Domineering, tough-minded, powerful
UNB	Provocative, egocentric, show-off
UB	Jokes around, expressive, dramatic
UPB	Entertaining, sociable, smiling, warm
P	Friendly, equalitarian
PF	Works cooperatively with others
F	Analytical, task oriented, problem solving
NF	Legalistic, has to be right
N	Unfriendly, negativistic
NB	Irritable, cynical, won't cooperate
B	Shows feelings and emotions
PB	Affectionate, likeable, fun to be with
DP	Looks up to others, appreciative, trustful
DPF	Gentle, willing to accept responsibility
DF	Obedient, works submissively
DNF	Self-punishing, works too hard
DN	Depressed, sad, resentful
DNB	Alienated, quits, withdraws
DB	Afraid to try, doubts own ability
DPB	Quietly happy just to be with others
D	Passive, introverted, says little

Source: Bales & Cohen, 1979, quoted in Keyton & Wall, 1989, p. 551

academics have tried to incorporate the idea that interaction occurs in a wider context and that therefore, if the goal is analysis of group dynamics, it is also necessary to take into consideration the context in which the relationships developed.

In the study of small groups, Paul Hare (1985) identifies three main schools: *group dynamics* and *field theory*, with reference to the work of Kurt Lewin (1952), **sociometry** and the work of Jacob Levi Moreno (1953), and *small group research*, initially referring to the work of Bales (1950, 1985). According to Hare, Bales and his colleagues' SYMLOG 'brings together some of the insights from both Moreno and Lewin with a technology that holds much promise for future analyses' (Hare, 1985, p. 42). Proposed by Bales and Stephen Cohen in the ambit of *new field theory*, Symlog, in addition to being a method, or better, a set of methods for the measurement of interactive behaviour, 'is an integrated theory of personality and group dynamics' (Bales, 1988, p. 320). It can be defined as field theory, because Symlog takes effective account of the fact that every act of behaviour takes place in a larger context, an interactive field of influences. The approach assumes that one needs to understand the larger context – personal, interpersonal, group and situation – in order to understand patterns of behaviour and to influence them successfully. In Symlog, theory and method are tightly connected, so that the dimensions of what is called Symlog-space (see Figure 10.2) cannot be interpreted without understanding the psychological and socio-psychological theories underlying it.

Bales (1950, 1970; Bales et al., 1987) developed the Symlog method in one of his first studies, based on three main assumptions: '(a) people interact on three dimensions, (b) people use these dimensions intuitively when evaluating their own interaction and then interaction of others, and (c) people can make sense of and respond to descriptions of their own and of others' interaction' (Keyton & Wall, 1989, p. 545).

The three orthogonal dimensions (in point a) are applied to both verbal and non-verbal behaviours as follows: upward–downward (UD), which defines behavioural elements such as dominance or submissiveness; positive–negative (PN), which refers to friendly or unfriendly aspects of behaviour; forward–backward (FB), which refers to whether the participant takes on board the dominant person's agenda or challenges it. The different combinations of the three structural dimensions generate 26 values that flow into the Symlog questionnaire (see Table 10.1). Each of the 26 values on the Symlog rating form is designed to measure a specific vector direction out from the centre of the three-dimensional space and, assesses either one, two, or all three value dimensions simultaneously. Based on these dimensions, an individual or group of individuals are distributed in the Symlog space and projected on two dimensions called 'Field Diagrams' (see Figure 10.1).

According to Joann Keyton and Victor Wall (1989, p. 546), 'explanations of group behavior are based on the configuration of individuals or groups within Symlog space as presented in the Field Diagram'.

Figure 10.1 provides a two-dimensional depiction of the three-dimensional Symlog space comprising a field diagram. The horizontal axis represents the dimension values

VALUES ON ACCEPTING TASK-ORIENTATION OF ESTABLISHED AUTHORITY

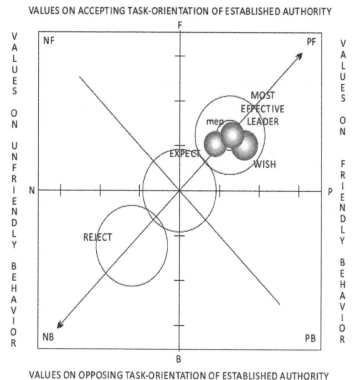

VALUES ON OPPOSING TASK-ORIENTATION OF ESTABLISHED AUTHORITY

© 2005 SYMLOG Consulting Group. Used with permission.

Figure 10.1 Symlog reference field diagram.

(*Source:* Copyright 2005. SYMLOG Consulting Group, San Diego, CA; quoted in Ford, 2014, p. 14)

on friendly behaviour, and the vertical axis represents the dimension from accepting the task orientation of established authority to opposing it. The third dimension, values on dominance vs values on submissiveness, is represented by the size of the small circle marking the location of an image on the other two dimensions. The figure displays the sample results of ratings made by group members about their group and relevant concepts. It shows the diversity represented in the group and illustrates the patterns of group interaction. The large circle in the upper right quadrant represents the reference circle, which contains images that share similar kinds of values and behaviours. In the upper right quadrant, we find – in addition – the **MEP** (Most Effective Profile), which is a universal standard MEP or 'gold standard' against which to measure multiple levels of interaction so as to have a reference point to systematically and simultaneously improve leadership, teamwork and organizational effectiveness. The opposition circle, in the lower left quadrant, contains those images which the group tends to reject in themselves and others.

Brief history of the Symlog method

The Symlog method begins with Arthur Couch's PhD thesis in 1960. Polley (1991) tells us how in this dissertation – in a pioneering way – a factorial analysis was applied to human behaviour and to social interaction. The six dimensions identified by Couch derive from a factorial analysis applied to data coming from 12 groups, each with five undergraduates, who answered a large battery of personality tests and which were the subject of participant observation in a wide variety of tasks across five meetings each.

> Although factor analysis is not independent of the original categories of measurement and observation, Couch's data set was so exhaustive as to deserve credence. Bales, Cohen and Stephen Williamson (1979) based their SYmlog (SYstematic Multiple Level Observation of Groups) explicitly on the results of Couch's dissertation. (Polley, 1991, p. 93).

This study is the basis on which Bales, Cohen and Williamson consolidated their three dimensions (as per 'Definition' section above). Bales dedicated more than 30 years of study to it in the Social Interaction Laboratory of the Department of Psychology and Social Relations at Harvard University. In the department – as Keyton and Wall (1989) note – Bales and his colleagues, including Talcott Parsons, Gordon W. Allport, Henry A. Murray and Clyde M. Kluckhohn, had been engaged in the analysis of social relations and human behaviour using established approaches. The Symlog method as a 'project ... really started with the vision of rapid computer-produced feedback to the group' (Bales & Cohen 1979, p. xiv). In concrete terms, this approach presented itself as the answer to the requirements of collecting observations about verbal and non-verbal behaviours and providing expeditiously a summary of the results observed.

In fact, Symlog also allows codification of the verbal content of interactions, even if the behaviour itself could be codified without using the verbal content; similarly, the verbal content can be codified without considering the behaviour. Each 'declaration' is first codified with a PRO code (for favourable sentences) and with a CON code (for unfavourable ones). The content of the declarations is then codified referring to the three categories. After these first codifications, the level of the value statements is codified; the levels begin with the Self and broaden: Self, Other, Group, Situation, Society and Fantasy (Polley, 1991, p. 94).

The method became 'a simple sentence in a simple language' (Bales & Cohen, 1979, p. xv); in fact, it was also used to analyse the messages' content, and in both uses it is able to describe: (1) the point of view of each participant, (2) the view of each observer, (3) an overall picture of the group's image.

In 1979, with the publication of Bales et al.'s book, the method was spread, even though it did not contain example studies and/or techniques to investigate the validity and reliability of the tools used. Instead, the book presents the structure of the multiple-level field theory, the real-time interaction scoring method used by the observers, a case study methodology and specific information on how to use the tools. Later on, other studies addressed these dimensions (Wish et al., 1980; Isenberg & Enni, 1981; Solomon, 1981).

An important change was introduced in Polley (1985), which modified the 26 Adjective Rating Form elaborated by Bales and Cohen, having studied their application in work behaviour. This opened Symlog to application in organizational settings, as a 'level midway between behavior and expressed values' (Polley, 1985, p. 276). Subsequently Polley (1986, 1987) returned to work on Bales and Cohen's dimensions to better adapt them to labour market and organizational contexts (see Table 10.2). Symlog thus became used in applied management and organizational studies to evaluate the effectiveness of small workgroups, working relationships between different employees and the influence of managers. The organization and individual values developed by Polley are still used within the SYMLOG Consulting Group, which has a patent and copyright of the Symlog method.

The dimensions identified by Polley can be represented in a field diagram and a Symlog cube-space (Figure 10.2), where physical directions are coordinated with names for describing the value directions for individual and organizational values.

> The large cube representing the social-psychological space is divided into 27 smaller cubes, each representing 1–3 of the vectors. The one in the centre of the cube is the average, not perceived to be high or low in any of the dimensions. To derive the measures of the dimensions, questionnaires or observations are used, with 26 statements or categories reflecting each one of the 26 smaller cubes. (Hillmer & Blubaugh, 1994, p. 9)

From the 1980s work based on this method spread, with contributions from all over the world (Polley et al., 1988; Orlik, 1989; Becker-Beck & Schneider, 1990; Fisch et al., 1991; Hare & Hare, 1996), but applications in professional settings outside the academic environment advanced much slower.

Simultaneously, the study of the method's synthetic analyses has proceeded using statistics and software. Polley (1984) also pioneered in this domain, developing a computer software package for quantitative data analysis and creating field diagrams. Raw data were entered into an IBM-PC, and scores from each individual were used to plot

Table 10.2 Symlog individual and organization values

Values on dominant behavior	
U	Individual financial success, personal prominence and power
UP	Popularity and social success, being liked and admired
UPF	Active teamwork toward common goals, organizational unity
UF	Efficiency, strong impartial management
UNF	Active reinforcement of authority, rules and regulations
UN	Tough-minded, self-oriented assertiveness
UNB	Rugged, self-oriented individualism, resistance to authority
UB	Having a good time, releasing tension, relaxing control
UPB	Protecting less able members, providing help when needed
Neither dominant nor submissive	
P	Equality, democratic participation in decision-making
PF	Responsible idealism, collaborative work
F	Conservative, established, 'correct' ways of doing things
NF	Restraining individual desires for organizational goals
N	Self-protection, self-interest first, self-sufficiency
NB	Rejection of established procedures, rejection of conformity
B	Change to new procedures, different values, creativity
PB	Friendship, mutual pleasure, recreation
Values on submissive behavior	
DP	Trust in the goodness of others
DPF	Dedication, faithfulness, loyalty to the organization
DF	Obedience to the chain of command, complying with authority
DNF	Self-sacrifice if necessary to reach organizational goals
DN	Passive rejection of popularity, going it alone
DNB	Admission of failure, withdrawal of effort
DB	Passive non-cooperation with authority
DPB	Quiet contentment, taking it easy
D	Giving up personal needs and desires, passivity

the location on each dimension in the field diagram. The average diagrams were used in comparing groups to one another and in analysing leader behaviour.

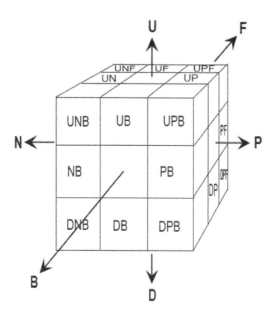

Figure 10.2 Symlog cube diagram.

(*Source:* Bales, 1983, p. 9)

A case study

To profile a study in which the Symlog method has been used we consider an exemplar from 1990, conducted by Joann Keyton and Jeff Springston on the redefinition of group effectiveness and cohesiveness. They based their work on careful analysis of the work of Lynne Kelly and Robert Duran (1985a, 1985b), because these previous studies aimed at investigating the relation between the perceptions of the group members regarding the group's interactions and their assessments of the group's effectiveness.

Kelly and Duran (1985a, 1985b) measured subjects' perceptions and performance in two consecutive group task projects. In these studies, the grades assigned for each project were used as a measure of group effectiveness. The Symlog Adjective Rating Form was used to measure the group members' perception of their interaction while preparing their project. The authors focus on two aspects: (1) group cohesion and (2) group leadership.

Group cohesion was defined as the extent to which perceptions of members' behaviour clustered together in three-dimensional Symlog-space (recall that the three dimensions are: dominant to submissive; friendly to unfriendly; instrumentally controlled to emotionally expressive). Group-average ratings that produced similar scores for all members were taken as an indication of group cohesion; those resulting in dissimilar scores indicated lack of cohesiveness (Keyton & Springston, 1990, p. 236). The level of cohesion has been calculated as the average Euclidean distance between member plotted scores on each of three dimensions. Whereas polarization is the degree to which group members perceive their interaction as similar on the three Symlog dimensions. So: 'A low polarization score indicates that group members perceive themselves as interacting in a similar fashion. A high polarization score indicates that group members perceive themselves as behaving differently in the interaction. Kelly and Duran believe that this score reflects the level of cohesiveness within the group' (Keyton & Springston, 1990, p. 236).

Regarding group leadership, they used the Symlog plotting locations by visually examining each group average field diagram for evidence of task leadership: 'Groups that were less effective appeared to be associated with the lack of a task leader and one of two patterns of cohesiveness. These groups have either a high degree of cohesiveness (polarization distance scores of 3.50 or under) or low cohesiveness (polarization distance scores of 6.0 or higher)' (1990, p. 236).

Taking into consideration these studies and their results, Keyton and Springston elaborate their hypotheses:

H1: Highly effective groups are characterized by the presence of an identifiable task leader and moderate SYMLOG polarization index (3.5 to 6.0).

H2: Ineffective groups are characterized in two ways: (a) strong cohesiveness with little variation of members on SYMLOG dimension (i.e., SYMLOG polarization index of less than 3.5) and no identifiable task leader or (b) strong coalition formation as described by SYMLOG polarization indexes greater than 6.0 and no identifiable task leader. (p. 236)

With the aim of testing and confirming the polarization index already identified as an index of group cohesion, the sample of groups was extended from N = 8 in their previous work to N = 47; furthermore, they used an additional formula for calculating polarization intensity, two additional measures of group cohesiveness, and an additional evaluation of group output as a measure of group effectiveness.

The 47 groups consisted of a number of participants varying between three and seven, for a total of 248 students; the groups formed spontaneously; the students were free to aggregate; the students' ages varied between 18 and 22; female presence was dominant in an approximate order of 2 to 1. The groups were assigned tasks aimed at delivering two presentations on group communication topics. To prepare them the students met in classroom 13 times. Groups met seven times in class before making the first presentation; they then had six months to prepare the second presentation. Only three of the 13 class meetings were used to collect data. The first data collection occurred during the second meeting; the second was during the meeting before the first presentation; the third and last was during the preparations for the second presentation. However, in the data analysis they considered only the assessments made during the second and third administration because they noticed that during the second meeting there was still considerable confusion and poor awareness of requirements among the participants.

The students completed the 26 Adjective Rating Form, using an assessment scale between two and zero, where zero means 'never or seldom', 1 'sometimes' and 2 'often or always'. The Symlog position was calculated for each group member, then the individual ratings were averaged within the group to produce a group index of perception about the interaction behaviour in the group. The Symlog position was used to calculate the Euclidean distance or polarization index of each group.

The same formula, representing a reconfiguration of Polley's original polarization formula (1985), had been used in previous studies. Table 10.3 shows the group polarization index range calculated by Keyton and Springston.

The polarization index was then reconfigured in a unification index (Polley, 1989) calculated for each group (see Table 10.4). The unification index is based on the dimensions PN and FB and is read in the opposite way to the polarization index – a high unification score indicates a highly cohesive group, whereas a low unification score indicates a highly diverse group.

Keyton and Springston then assessed the effectiveness of the cohesiveness index using other assessment tools administered during the same meetings – time 2 and time 3 – in which the data were collected with Symlog. The results obtained for cohesion using 20-item Group Attitude Scales (Evans & Jervis, 1986) and 18-item Wheeless

Table 10.3 Summary of polarization indexes (N = 47 groups)

	Mean	SD	Minimum	Maximum
Time 2	5.357	4.149	1.495	10.563
Time 3	5.257	4.600	1.663	11.594
Polarization categories				
	Low	Moderate	High	
Time 2	<3.282 (N = 6 groups)	3.282 to 7.432 (N = 34 groups)	>7.432 (N = 7 groups)	
Time 3	<2.957 (N = 5 groups)	2.957 to 7.557 (N = 37 groups)	>7.557 (N = 5 groups)	

Source: Keyton & Springston, 1990, p. 241

Table 10.4 Summary of unification indexes (N = 47 groups)

	Mean	SD	Minimum	Maximum
Time 2	93.515	8.102	69.038	100.00
Time 3	92.595	9.906	64.352	100.00

Source: Keyton & Springston, 1990, p. 242

Solidarity Scales (Wheeless et al., 1982) stressed how they are correlated, even where all of them emphasize different factors. For group effectiveness, the grades for the assessment of the group presentations required preparation of a specific grid based on the following criteria: (1) clarity of presentation, (2) usefulness, (3) creativity, (4) audience involvement. The assessment for the first three criteria was made by the course instructors. They used a scale of 10 items, where 10 corresponds to excellent and 0 to failure; students had already been informed of the assessment criteria. The specification for the audience involvement criterion required an external assessment variable attributed to the audience. In this case, the assessment scale was of seven items (see Table 10.5).

Four analysis phases were required to accommodate all the elements used in the various scales.

- This was useful in the first phase to identify how the 47 groups were positioned within the polarization index, divided into low, moderate and high, and to single out their levels of cohesiveness.
- It was useful also to generate a breakdown of polarization scores by categorizing the scores, with high polarization being greater than the mean polarization plus

Table 10.5 Summary of group variables (N = 47 groups)

Variable (Meeting)	Mean	SD	Minimum	Maximum
Group attitude (2)	111.541	10.206	88.600	131.250
Group attitude (3)	108.982	10.495	82.800	136.750
Solidarity (2)	63.104	8.491	42.167	76.200
Solidarity (3)	64.200	8.590	37.000	81.500
Grade (2)	6.532	1.600	2.000	10.000
Grade (3)	7.064	2.026	2.000	10.000
External evaluation (3)	47.681	13.650	21.000	77.000

Source: Keyton & Springston, 1990, p. 242

one-half standard deviation; moderate polarization being within a range one-half standard deviation above and below the mean; and low polarization being less the mean polarization minus one-half standard deviation. The polarization levels were used as categories and weighting factors, and a regression was then introduced inside the category levels to verify if the polarization scores were predictors of group effectiveness (group grade and external evaluation). Unfortunately, the results did not find significant relation levels. At this point, they decided to use other measures to evaluate group effectiveness.

- In the third phase, a unification index was used as predictor of group effectiveness. In this case there were again three levels: high-unified groups, those scored one-half standard deviation above the mean or higher; low-unified groups, those scored one-half standard deviation below the mean or lower; and moderately unified groups, those scoring between the parameters of the other two. A regression weighted by the number of members of the group was used to test the capacity of the unification index as a predictor of group effectiveness. But again, no significant results were obtained.

- In the fourth and final analysis phase, Keyton and Springston admitted becoming doubtful that there was a relationship between group effectiveness and group cohesiveness. Hence, they decided to explore the relation between the four operationalizations of cohesiveness: polarization, unification, group attitude and solidarity. They then introduced some regressions to understand the ability of the polarization score to predict group attitude and solidarity. With the same spirit, they made regressions on all the indexes. The results led them to deduce that 'measures of cohesiveness – polarization, unification, group attitude and solidarity – do in fact measure group cohesiveness, at least as operationalized by one other' (Keyton & Springston, 1990, p. 250).

- It seems that to regard cohesiveness as a predictor of group effectiveness is premature, and maybe even unfounded. Keyton and Springston offer various reasons for not finding a relationship, ranging from the composition of the groups to their characteristics; the fact that these were student groups; and that the goal of the assigned task differed from those faced by work groups in organizational contexts. Workers also face 'political' issues inside and outside the group and in such cases the inter-dependence between the competent group members increases. However, in terms of Symlog's utility, the study found that findings from the tools used were tightly correlated with one another.

Knowing and know-how

In order to understand how to develop a study that uses the Symlog method, we consider the work published by George Whaley and David Ford in 2012 and titled 'Examining collegiality and social justice in academia and the private sector: an exploratory SYMLOG analysis'.

The authors carried out their study to compare the perceptions of private sector, high-technology employees to the perceptions of university faculty members regarding organizational culture, social justice and collegiality. Symlog was used to record the perceptions of respondents to four different concepts of organizational culture, two different aspects of social justice and two measures of collegiality. Comparative findings of gender differences across the eight concepts raised key organizational culture, legal, measurement, governance and social policy issues for academia and high-tech organizations.

Identification of research questions

Whaley and Ford's study provides the opportunity to point out two other important concepts of the Symlog method: (1) MEP and (2) image.

- In Symlog research the MEP represents the location of the value position, derived from thousands of ratings by subjects interviewed or observed; for example, in research on leadership or corporate culture these may be managers. 'MEP' represents a balance between an emphasis on accepting the task-orientation of established authority and emphasis on friendly behaviour. Indeed, according to Bales (1999) and Koenigs (1993), MEP's location in the field diagram represents the empirical solution to the dynamic puzzle of leadership (see 'Analysis' section).
- People may also have images of individual members of the category, for instance media figures or people they know, but also of concepts, symbols, places. These images, known as *exemplars* (Bodenhausen et al., 1995), may also be brought to mind when the individual thinks about members of the social category, the values and concepts. Thus Symlog – through the 26 adjective ratings – brings out the image that a certain group has of the corporate culture, of the place where they work and so on.

Whaley and Ford developed seven targeted research questions (see Table 10.6) intended to discover the images of the participants in relation to their eight concepts.

Table 10.6 Four of the research questions used by Whaley and Ford

R1	Do significant differences exist among the final field locations of the Collaboration (COL), Competence (COM), Cultivation (CUL) and Control (CON) images on the SYMLOG Field Diagram?
R2	Will Competence (COM) and Collaboration (COL) be rated closer to the Most Effective Profile (MEP) image on the PN dimension than Cultivation (CUL) and Control (CON) in that order?
R3	Is the Most Collegial Person (MCP) image closer to MEP on the PN dimension than any other concept rated?
R4	Is the Least Collegial Person (LCP) image the furthest from the MEP image on the PN dimension and also closer to Reject (REJ) than any other concept rated?

Source: Whaley & Ford, 2012, p. 21. Licensee NMIMS

The research question, in contrast to a hypothesis (used in the 'Case study' section is less generalizable and applicable outside the research context in which it originated because it already includes the causal links that the researcher plans to investigate.

Data collection

Whaley and Ford defined their study as explorative, using Symlog to measure eight different concepts derived from theoretical approaches developed in organizational analysis and studies of organizational culture. The four core organizational culture concepts – collaboration (COL), competence (COM), cultivation (CUL) and control (CON) – were individually rated. These concepts were followed by: the perceptions of respondents concerning the 'most collegial' (MCP) and 'least collegial' person (LCP) in their organization and the perceptions of 'distributive = fair results' (FAR) and 'procedural = fair procedures' (FAP) social justice concepts.

Each of the eight concepts was assessed using the same 26 Symlog items rated as: Often (O), Sometimes (S) or Rarely (R) (Whaley & Ford, 2012, p. 22). To compare individual, group and organizational evaluations two tools were used: the Bales Report and the Field Diagram Report. The data collected with the SYMLOG Individual and Organizational Values questionnaire of 26 values were subsequently integrated into the categories represented by the four core organizational culture concepts. This operation defines what is called the Bales Report. The results contained therein are represented in the Field Diagram Report (see Figure 10.3).

These two reports permit comparison of data and provide a basis for analysis of concept similarities, differences and relations. The measuring tool becomes the summary point of the methodological merge which takes place in this approach.

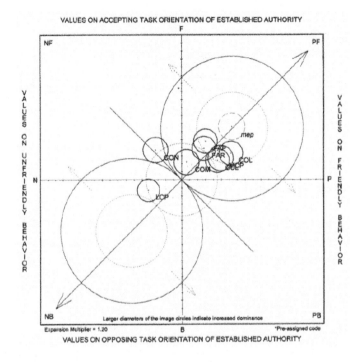

VALUES ON ACCEPTING TASK ORIENTATION OF ESTABLISHED AUTHORITY

VALUES ON OPPOSING TASK ORIENTATION OF ESTABLISHED AUTHORITY

Figure 10.3   Field diagram of final image locations for aggregate data.
(*Source:* Whaley & Ford, 2012, p. 25. Licensee NMIMS)

Sample

The survey was carried out on two different groups: (1) a group of 22 academics (5 women, 17 men); (2) a group of 100 private interviewees coming from the high-tech industry sector (50 women, 50 men) who were also enrolled as students (N = 70) in a graduate management course at the University of California; another part of the latter group was engaged full-time and could not therefore attend university courses (N = 30). The total of participants was 122 but one was not considered valid after questionnaire analysis, so the final sample was 121.

Analysis

The analyses consider personalized evaluations of conceptual issues, namely of organizational culture, social justice and collegiality. The evaluation of the perceptions aimed to compare the results according to (1) type of organization, (2) gender of the respondent,

(3) work of the respondent and (4) location perspective. Two types of analysis were performed: the first based on the proximity of each image to the Symlog consensus MEP outcome location; the second on ANOVAs, used to investigate the independence of each image.

The authors chose Symlog assessment for its ability to provide a research-based universal standard (MEP) against which to measure multiple levels of interaction so as to systematically and simultaneously improve leadership, teamwork and organizational effectiveness. Thus, the Symlog MEP was used as the outcome measure against which to compare organizational culture, social justice and collegiality perceptions.

In the field diagram, the images of the circles reflect the perception, or rather the evaluation, that is attributed to the dimensions by means of the 26 adjectives. During the first phase, the 'proximity of each one of the eight measures of perception to the "reference" image, MEP, along the P/N dimension' was examined. 'If the image was more proximate to the MEP, the outcome was assumed to have perceived values that were consistent with effective organizational functioning' (Whaley & Ford, 2012, p. 23). They used a 'rule of thumb' described by Kelly and Duran (1985a, 1985b, see the Case study above), where the optimal level of cohesiveness is where groups display an average of interpersonal Euclidean distances varying between 3.5 and 5.9 on the Symlog unit scale. It is assumed that images with distances greater than or equal to 6.0 Euclidean distance scale units have significantly different locations in Symlog space. Images with distances less than 6.0 scale units can be considered to be close enough in their locations to be similar in meaning (Whaley & Ford, 2012, p. 23).

The different positions along the PN dimension were calculated using One-Way ANOVA.

The second part of the analysis worked with the image the Symlog analysis produced for the group and the organized subgroups according to gender compared to the eight conceptual categories of interest. For reasons of simplicity, we here show only the results of the field diagram deriving from the analysis of the entire group (see Figure 10.3) and not the subgroups.

Besides the MEP, the analysis was accompanied by Symlog dimension correlations (Table 10.7), together with Cronbach Alpha values. Cronbach's Alpha was calculated – in turn – for each of the collegiality images evaluated according to Symlog scales (Table 10.8).

Table 10.7 attends to reliability. Encouragingly, the values for each of the three Symlog dimensions (UD, PN, FB) were close to the suggested .70 minimum threshold value in most cases.

Differences among the images on the PN dimension were assessed using SPSS One-Way ANOVA computations incorporating a Tukey post hoc test of mean differences. Since the largest differences within settings were gender-based, the results of these analyses were arrayed along a continuum representing the interpersonal relations-oriented

Table 10.7 Symlog dimensions intercorrelations

	UD	PN	FB
UD	(.65)	.01	.16*
PN		(.66)	.22**
FB			(.70)

*$p < .05$; ** $p < .01$; Total sample reliability coefficients appear in parentheses on diagonal.

Source: Whaley & Ford, 2012, p. 27. Licensee NMIMS

Table 10.8 Collegiality image reliabilities*

Image	UD	PN	FB
Collaboration	.63	.58	.65
Competence	.68	.69	.71
Cultivation	.66	.65	.68
Control	.63	.62	.65
Most Collegial Person	.68	.66	.70
Least Collegial Person	.65	.68	.70
Fair Procedures	.61	.62	.62
Fair Results	.62	.64	.66

Note (in original): The Cronbach Alpha values shown were computed in the traditional sense. Most fall short of the recommended minimum value of .70. However, it should be recalled that many of the Symlog values load on more than one dimension. Therefore, use of 'traditional' reliability metrics is really inappropriate.

Source: Whaley & Ford, 2012, p. 28. Licensee NMIMS

positive–negative (PN) Symlog dimension (see Table 10.2) and divided by gender, but also by types of group selected (Figure 10.4).

The ANOVA results, used to obtain the positive–negative *continuum* of Figure 10.4, show that in both the groups selected there were gender differences. Furthermore, from this exploratory research we obtain the indication that 'collegiality' is used in two different perspectives according to whether it is observed within a university environment or the private sector.

The merging point

Symlog is a multilevel and multimethod system for internal assessment of group function made by members of the group. To do this it uses various data collection and

Symlog findings for Faculty*				Symlog findings for Private Sector*			
Negative	Male	Female		Negative	Male	Female	
↑	LCP^a	LCP^a		↑	LCP^a	CON^a	
	CON^a	CON^{ab}			CON^a	LCP^a	
	COM^b	COM^{abc}			COM^{ab}	COM^{ab}	
	FAR^{bc}	FAR^{abc}			FAP^{bc}	FAP^{bc}	
	FAP^{cd}	FAP^{abc}			FAR^{be}	FAR^{bcd}	
	COL^{cd}	COL^{abc}			CUL^{cd}	MCP^{cd}	
	CUL^{cd}	CUL^{abc}			MCP^{cd}	CUL^{cd}	
	MCP^{cd}	MCP^{bc}			COL^{de}	COL^{de}	
↓	mep^d	mep^c		↓	mep^e	mep^e	
Positive				Positive			

*Note: Images with the same superscript letter are not significantly different from one another; images with superscripts that differ are significantly different from one another at p < .05 on the PN dimension.

*Note: Images with the same superscript letter are not significantly different from one another; images with superscripts that differ are significantly different from one another at p < .05 on the PN dimension.

Figure 10.4 Symlog findings for Faculty and Private Sector.

(*Source*: Whaley & Ford, 2012, p. 24. Licensee NMIMS)

analysis techniques. In addition, data collection occurs in several rounds. Along with verbal behaviour, values and images and also nonverbal behaviour can be coded within three dimensions (as described above). In addition, these data may be obtained by act-to-act observations or scoring, or by retrospective ratings on an adjective checklist. The scoring method can be complex and requires training for reliable results, while the ratings can be used with little instruction (Rywick, 1987). The ratings combine both verbal and nonverbal behaviour into one global assessment of behaviour or values. The use of statistical techniques, such as the calculation of ANOVA and factor analysis, allows us to validate, group and synthesize the data (Table 10.9).

Advantages and disadvantages

The main advantages of this method are represented by:

- triangulation of analysis, involving participant self-analysis (we refer to this as internal analysis) and observer (we use the term external analysis);
- the possibility of evaluating verbal and non-verbal behaviour together;
- the combination of quantitative and qualitative analysis in forms of multimethod;

Table 10.9 Identikit of the Symlog method as a Merged Method

Characteristics of the researchers' work in the Merged Method	Identification in the Symlog method
Data are co-constructed	Data are verbal and non-verbal behaviour, continuously constructed and co-constructed through the rounds
Data are relational and interactional outcomes	Data are the result of the relationships between the observations collected by the participating observers, the evaluations coming from the questionnaire with 26 adjective ratings, sometimes also from sociograms or from additional questionnaires
Methods predetermine the way the world is assembled	The Symlog method determines the way to assess the small groups, the organizational contexts, the image that groups build of themselves and their environment
Abandoning the concept of validity (true-value), and rediscovery of fidelity	Validity is represented for the participants by the face validity of the rating system, because it is easy to use and does not require familiarity with the theoretical foundations
The researcher's orientation is not to find an out-there truth but to create the best (social and relational) conditions for gathering information	The Symlog method was conceived as a means to provide observation and ranking procedures for interactive behaviour
Social actors under study are participants	The subjects/participants are individuals behaving within their context
The main aim is to guarantee participants' free expression	Freedom of expression is guaranteed by anonymity
Researchers' active listening should be pursued	Researchers express their active listening in considering the ratings expressed by the participants
Results/findings are interpretations	The results are the result of the interpretations provided by the participants. Researchers look at them cumulatively, comparing them with the MEP, and identifying the prevailing image

- the presence and use of the MEP;
- the possibility of combining the set of techniques of this method with other systems, as made by Endre Sjøvold (2007) with the new application based on the Symlog method, the SPGR (Systematizing Person-Group Relations) method, which combines perspectives from Bales (1985, 1999) on social interaction systems, from Wilfred Bion (1987) on group emotionality, from Talcott Parsons et al. (1953a, 1953b) on group functions, and from Mills (1984) on group development;
- the presence of the SYMLOG Consulting Group, which organizes training courses.

The main disadvantages consist of:

- the possibility of interpreting behaviours and their signals in a variety of ways with the possibility of misinterpretation, although a degree of experience and knowledge improves the accuracy of the method;
- the matter of intrusion and potentially creating hostility in the group under analysis towards those who are studying it;
- the need to resort to software for data analysis, which makes the operation some-what cumbersome and limits the applicability of the approach in 'real time' as a method that groups can apply (via a facilitator or in self-analysis) in order to assess their functioning and provide guidance for improvement;
- SYMLOG Consulting Group has a patent and copyright of the Symlog method, which makes the application of this method expensive in financial terms.

Also, there are advantages and disadvantages deriving from the scales that this method tightly connects to its evaluation tool. Assessment scales have among their advantages the ease of use, a lower training requirement for the observers, the possibility of being used not only by the observers but by group members, and the possibility of using a wider number of categories (Weick, 1985). Amongst disadvantages, they are exposed to the subjective interventions of the observer, and are, therefore, potentially less reliable. Summary evaluation scales are more susceptible to an observer's systematic errors, such as the well-known 'halo effect', errors of leniency, errors of severity and the error of central tendency (Carter et al., 1951; Kerlinger, 1966).

Practical tips

To conduct research with the Symlog method it is essential to understand some rudiments of social and organization psychology. The first practical suggestion is not to proceed without having at one's disposal manuals on group interaction.

Equally important is the knowledge of assessment scales as measurement tools.

It is useful to arrange for data collection at different points in the observation process in order to have data to compare and contrast.

The Symlog website is useful, not least because it offers demos illustrating various tool applications. For certified Symlog trainers the Interactive Display Tool is a useful Internet-based resource specifically designed to simplify and greatly enhance professional presentations, allowing users to quickly elaborate and present data.

Further reading

As a first step, visit the Symlog website (www.symlog.com). It is highly specialized and provides both basic information and details of the products available. One section is dedicated to the method, another compares Symlog to other models, yet another details training courses, and more.

The second step is engaging with Bales' texts, among which the manual written with Cohen is indispensable:

Bales, R. F., & Cohen, S. P., with Williamson, S. A. (1979). *SYMLOG: A system for the multiple level observation of groups*. New York: Free Press.

To use Symlog, you need to have some grasp of social psychology and of group interactions, whether you are studying work groups, sports teams or something else. You may find useful the manual by Stangor:

Stangor, C. (2004). *Social groups in action and interaction*. New York: Psychology Press.

To strengthen your knowledge or for guidance on data interpretation, consult:

Pampel, F. C. (2000). *Logistic regression*. London: Sage.
Tacq, J. (1998). *Multivariate analysis techniques in social science research*. London: Sage.

11

CONCLUSION: THE WAYS AHEAD

Merged Methods, of which this text represents a first systematic exposition, present themselves as a methodological innovation in the field of social sciences. While in continuity with the direction pointed to by Mixed Methods (see Chapter 1), therefore in sympathy with them, Merged Methods represent an attempt to fill some of the epistemological (see Chapter 2), methodological (see Chapter 3) and design-oriented (see Chapter 4) gaps in Mixed Methods. In particular, Merged Methods address the ambiguity of the term 'qualitative', which has come to encompass almost everything – even approaches considered positivistic in the 1950s; the uncritical acceptance of the measurement approach, where the terms 'measures' and 'measurement' (and their neo-positivistic imprinting and use) are treated as unproblematic; the naïve pragmatism and related 'bricolage methodology', which put together (with a relatively unconvincing methodological rationale) neo-positivist methods (such as the questionnaire with forced choices and close-ended answers) and interpretative methods (like the discursive interview and focus group) in a methodological fruit salad.

Merged Methods propose to truly found an independent epistemology and methodology, a genuine third way compared to neo-positivist and interpretative methods, grasping what is good in their epistemologies and methodologies, and merging it not only on a theoretical level but also practical and technical levels. Furthermore, by paying close attention to building research methods tailored to the subjectivity of the participants, their cultures and communities, Merged Methods are particularly sensitive to purifying both the quantitative (Gobo, 2011b) and qualitative (Gobo, 2018) methods of their subtle colonial mindsets.

In that context, it is heartening to note the advances being made in the field of Indigenous Knowledge and Indigenous Research (Fielding, 2016), a field that is increasingly informed by the idea of 'mixing', as in Goodyear-Smith and 'Ofanoa's (2021, p. 1) advocacy of research frameworks 'whereby different perspectives are woven together to create new knowledge'. Goodyear-Smith and 'Ofanoa's frameworks have emerged specifically from collaborations between researchers from different non-Western cultural traditions in Samoa, but whose wider cultural context is the Pacific philosophy of connnectiveness and a collective holistic approach. It is clear in the frameworks offered by these scholars that the mixing that the frameworks encourage is, at heart, a long move in the direction of Merged Methods. To name but one thread, these are frameworks that dismantle binaries such as qualitative–quantitative, and researcher–participant. In the specific exemplar presented by Goodyear-Smith and 'Ofanoa (2021, p. 2), interactive dialogue (*'a'a talanoa'*) and maintaining relationship (*'teu le va'*) in a house (*'fale'*), or in a village, underpins holistic discussion of issues around health resources, with the outcome of that discussion being 'woven (*'tui'*) to provide resolutions for the betterment of individuals and communities'. At the heart of this process is the researcher, encouraging critical reflection and dialogue. Goodyear and 'Ofanoa demonstrate how these procedures and principles can be used in the co-construction of a research design that is, in all but name, a Merged Method, albeit one that, like the systematic review, we might regard as a meta-method. In similar vein, Martel et al. (2021) discuss the ideas behind a bi-cultural (Maori and New Zealand European) research design for a project that melded distinct worldviews by incorporating quantitative and interpretivist methods as equals in an integrated workable whole, drawing on the Maori concept of the 'braided river'. The empirical referent of the work was development of a mental health and lifestyle screening tool for use by young people, predominantly adolescent Maori people in Northland, New Zealand. Like the national protocol in use in Canada for research involving First Nations Peoples (Beaton et al., 2017), the collaboration benefited – indeed, was only possible – because of an overarching Treaty that is now binding on research conducted with Maori communities and Maori researchers in collaboration with non-Maori researchers.

Merged Methods have this clear potential to 'humanize' social research through the explicit attention they pay to the dependency between structural, societal influences (at macro or meso level) and interpretative, individual experiences (at micro level). Moreover, decolonizing research methods means including hard-to-reach populations, like those living in complex, under-researched circumstances. The necessary interdisciplinary, adaptive stance and context-sensitive design that flow from this view are inherent features of a Merged Methods approach. These characteristics enable researchers to absorb unforeseen intricacies, like unknown cultural customs and values. An example is provided by an Event History Calendar study into a resettlement community in the Philippines that was built for households evicted involuntarily due to natural disasters and devastating infrastructure projects (Quetulio-Navarra et al., 2015). The poor, low-literacy participants were clearly unfamiliar with the phenomenon called social research (and its subject of social capital). Given their group culture – as well as complex living circumstances – an intensive involvement of bystanders – household members, neighbours, or friends – was spontaneous and inevitable. This led to the adoption of an interviewing strategy in a 'natural experiment' allowing partly for 'third party co-construction' of the data (with cheerful examples of participants and 'helpers' enthusiastically doing a 'high five' when providing their joint outcome). Quality indicators in this study showed that data quality was not worsened by 'third party help' but mostly enhanced. Thus, by adapting to such vulnerable populations Merged Methods may provide valid and credible understandings that voice multilevel influences on 'social capital', the topic of study. In the end, the complexity of the phenomenon is captured by the concrete and tailor-made data construction procedure.

Full integration

Hence, beyond epistemological and methodological integration, Merged Methods also attempt to fully integrate qualitative and quantitative approaches *in a single instrument*, blending the advantages of both *in a single technique*. This has the benefit of increasing consistency at all levels: from research design to data construction, from data organization to data analysis. In this way, research findings can be better grounded and valid, while also lowering research costs, both in economic and time terms (see Table 11.1). Hence, Merged Methods research is conducted with one method only (instead of two or more, as in Mixed Methods or Multi-Methods Research).

In Part Two of the book several (of those that we, in retrospect, consider) Merged Methods have been explicated. Some of them have a long history; others are a recent invention. Some are completely emancipated from the neo-positivist mindset; others less so. Finally, some have a systematic and tested methodological apparatus; others are still in development. However, they all feature a single, compact, coherent instrument.

Obviously Merged Methods, as a concept and proposal, does not have behind it the centuries-old tradition of Mixed Methods, considered as a whole in its two lives or

Table 11.1   Identikit of the methods shown as a Merged Method

Characteristics of the researchers' work in the Merged Method	Identification in the Delphi Method (Chapter 5)	Identification in the Event History Calendar (EHC) and the Intervey (Chapter 6)	Identification in Q-Methodology (Chapter 7)	Identification in Multimodal Content Analysis (Chapter 8)	Identification in Text Mining (Chapter 9)	Identification in the Symlog method (Chapter 10)
Data are co-constructed	Data are expert opinions, continuously constructed and co-constructed through the rounds	Data are verbal or written responses of participants, expressed as reply to prompts and probes offered by the researcher/tool/interviewer	Data are the viewpoints of the participants, collected in the Q-sorts; data are the notes that the researcher takes during and at the end of each construction of the Q-sorts	Data are texts, images, graphic signs left by users such as comments, articles and other forms of expression. They are successively organized into categories by the researcher	Data are all textual data from interviews, observations, documents, newspaper articles, comments, posts, tweets, that are too extensive to treat manually	Data are verbal and non-verbal behaviour, continuously constructed and co-constructed through the rounds
Data are relational and interactional outcomes	Data are the result of the relationships between: the opinions of each expert, the researcher's analyses, the interaction between the panel participants (the latter guaranteed by the feedbacks)	Data are the result of conversational interactions between the participant and the researcher/interviewer, and the relationships between autobiographical themes, life events and the participant's perceptions	Data are the result of the relationships between: the opinions of each participant, the categories constructed by the researcher, the choice of sentences to be included in the categories, the notes of the researcher	The data are words, images, emojis, hashtags used in digital environments to exchange information, opinions, feelings and build a glossary of meanings	Written texts, their manifest and latent meaning, their decomposition and re-composition using quantitative techniques, the interpretation that the researcher provides of them	Data are the result of the relationships between the observations collected by the participating observers, the evaluations coming from the questionnaire with 26 adjective ratings, sometimes also from sociograms or from additional questionnaires

Methods predetermine the way the world is assembled	The Delphi	The EHC and Intervey	Q-Methodology	Multimodal Content Analysis	The Text Mining	The Symlog method
Methods predetermine the way the world is assembled	The Delphi approach chosen determines the way of looking at the problem and social reality	The EHC and Intervey procedures determine the way of looking at the problem and social reality, in terms of contexts, meanings, relationships with external influences	Q-Methodology allows the communicability of subjective points of view regarding controversial issues	Multimodal Content Analysis determines the way of looking at the problem and social reality, in terms of contexts, meanings, relationships	The Text Mining approach, the chosen processing techniques, determine the way of looking at the problem and social reality	The Symlog method determines the way to assess the small groups, the organizational contexts, the image that groups build of themselves and their environment
Abandoning the concept of validity (true-value), and rediscovery of fidelity	Validity is represented by the correct way of carrying out the interactions (Delphi per Delphi, round per round)	Validity is represented by the credibility of the participants' judgements in relation to contextual information, by the correct way of interacting during data collection, and the fidelity of interpretative data construction given the deductive categories employed	The validity of Q study is evaluated by content, face and Q-sorting validity	Validity is represented by the correct method of coding and decoding the texts, the data collected, which must be faithful to the interpretative categories whether they are produced from top-down or emerge from the bottom-up process	Validity is represented by the number of documents and is entrusted at the beginning (first phase) to lexical indicators	Validity is represented for the participants by the face validity of the rating system, because it is easy to use and does not require familiarity with the theoretical foundations

247

Characteristics of the researchers' work in the Merged Method	Identification in the Delphi Method (Chapter 5)	Identification in the Event History Calendar (EHC) and the Intervy (Chapter 6)	Identification in Q-Methodology (Chapter 7)	Identification in Multimodal Content Analysis (Chapter 8)	Identification in Text Mining (Chapter 9)	Identification in the Symlog method (Chapter 10)
The researcher's orientation is not to find an out-there truth but to create the best (social and relational) conditions for gathering information	The intent with which the Delphi Method is already born is to identify opinions that are the result of knowledge, skimming between speculations and opinions that are the fruit of value judgements	The EHC and Intervy procedures provide contextual information and interactive procedures that facilitate data construction by the participants	The intent with which Q-Methodology is conceived is to identify points of view that are the result of the way of looking at the world of the participants	The intent with which Multimodal Content Analysis is conceived is to identify and categorize all manifestations of polysemic digital communication, whether they are manifest or latent	Text mining aims to identify meaning from existing documents by extracting it from them	The Symlog method was conceived as a means to provide observation and ranking procedures for interactive behaviour
Social actors under study are participants	Panel participants are holders of expert knowledge and information	The actors/participants reconstruct in context their own attitudes, behaviour, decisions, evaluations, life events	Participants are holders of their own points of view	The work object of Multimodal Content Analysis are the traces left by any social actor in digital environments	All the documents that are selected are carriers of knowledge, opinions, feelings, emotions, and they are an expression of the social actors	The subjects/participants are individuals behaving within their context
The main aim is to guarantee participants' free expression	Freedom of expression is essential to the Delphi Method and is guaranteed by anonymity	To guarantee a communicative climate which enables freedom of expression is crucial to validity and fidelity of the data construction and is ensured by anonymity	Freedom of expression is crucial to Q-Methodology and is guaranteed by anonymity	Freedom of expression is already guaranteed by digital environments in which polysemic digital communication develops itself. The researcher collects the traces of conversation after their expression	Freedom of expression is always guaranteed in the Text Mining approach, as well as anonymity	Freedom of expression is guaranteed by anonymity

Researchers' active listening should be pursued	Researchers express their active listening in considering the opinions expressed by the experts and by re-modulating – consequently – the content of the questionnaire	Researchers perform their active listening in considering the opinions expressed by the participant and providing facilitating prompts and probes	Researchers express active listening in considering the points of view of the participants (during filling out and at the end of filling out) and consequently building the content of the categories starting from them	Researchers express their active listening in considering all the elements of the conversation, and interpreting them in the most faithful way to their original meaning	Researchers express their active listening in keeping attention on what the textual data say and what they don't say	Researchers express their active listening in considering the ratings expressed by the participants
Results/findings are interpretations	The results arise from the interpretations provided by the experts. Researchers look at them cumulatively, distinguishing the orientation of the majority and minority. They return their analyses through feedback-reports or one-day group meetings	The results arise from the participants' contextual and interactional interpretations that in the end of the data construction procedure are categorized by the researcher/interviewer	The results arise from the interpretations provided by the participants. Researchers look at them cumulatively, using the Q-sorts. They return the interpretation of the Q-sorts through factor analysis and the interpretation and rotation of factors	The results are the fruit of the expression of free comments, posts and other elements of communication. Researchers look at them a posteriori, in search of categories of meaning, aimed at guaranteeing a mapping of the manifest and latent elements of communication. The researchers work to produce a categorization of all the elements present in the collected data	The findings result from the interpretations contained in the documents. Researchers look at them by moving on multiple dimensions: their statistical representativeness, semantic and semiotic content, their organization in clusters, the reduction into categories of viewable and shareable data	The results follow from the interpretations provided by the participants. Researchers look at them cumulatively, comparing them with the MEP, and identifying the prevailing image

'waves' (see Chapter 1). Hence, Merged Methods cannot be compared or put at the same level of development as Mixed Methods, which has attained a large community of practices, ideas, books, articles and researchers, organized in associations, institutions, conferences and journals.

However, this kind of gap is normal and very common in science. For example, in the physical and natural sciences new theories must necessarily face the severe criticisms of the theories already widely established. At that point the gap is uneven because the tools and procedures of the new theories still have to be refined, improved and perfected. Thus, the new theories cannot be judged according to the parameters of a mature and paradigmatic theory such as that of 'normal science' (Kuhn, 1962). A child (even if they have good reasons) cannot measure herself or himself with the cognitive and communicative competence of an adult. Therefore, Merged Methods cannot be asked to solve all the problems that other approaches display. However, a process has begun and many perplexities, weaknesses and gaps in Merged Methods can be improved and overcome with the contribution of those who employ and study them. The seed was sown. Will they take root in the soil of social science methodology?

GLOSSARY

Agent-based modelling Computational models for simulating the actions and interactions of autonomous agents.

Aided recall Procedures in survey or interviewing studies that aim to improve the completeness of retrospective accounts by providing respondents with memory cues.

ANOVA Analysis of Variance.

API Application programming interface, which is a software intermediary that allows two applications to talk to each other.

Big Data Online data marked by volume, velocity and variety.

Bounding procedures Procedures in survey or interviewing studies that aim to enhance the dating of past events and behaviour by clearly demarcating the recall period.

Bricolage methodology A Mixed Method process, transdisciplinary practices and multitextual communication employed by bricoleur researchers.

Centroid Central point within a mapped area of interest.

Classification A term used both about the process to classify (distinguishing and distribution kinds of 'things' into different groups) and about the resulting set of classes, as well as the assignment of elements to pre-established classes.

Classifying See Classification.

Closed-ended questions A survey item that allows respondents to choose an option of answer already entered in the survey.

Compatibility thesis The argument that quantitative–positivist and qualitative–interpretative methods can be combined irrespective of their different ontological and epistemological origins.

Complexity science The study of complexity as a single natural phenomenon discoverable using the tools of mathematics, computer science and physics.

Conversational interviewing Survey interviewing technique that allows interviewers to provide unscripted clarifications to standardized questions while containing the meaning of the question.

Counting The process of determining the number of elements of a finite set of objects. This process is (somehow) 'natural' (because to enumerate a researcher does not need special training or a particular instrument).

Decolonizing research Undoing the privileging of dominant Euro-centred cultural values and beliefs in research and knowledge production.

Di-graph (social science) A graph whose nodes represent a chronology of states of a social domain and whose arcs represent human (inter)actions.

Emoji Graphical icon used to convey expressive feeling.

Emoticon A computer icon designed to display a writer's mood or emotion.

Estimate-talk-Estimate (ETE) Or Mini-Delphi is the technique in which the meetings between the participants take place face-to-face.

Factor analysis Is a technique that is used to reduce a large number of variables into fewer numbers of factors.

Fuzzy logic A mathematical means to accommodate the fact that much human decision-making is based on imprecise and non-numerical information.

Hapax legomenon Word or phrase that appears only once in a text.

Indigenous Research Research engaged with Indigenous peoples and communities that is characterized by relational axioms, rooted in a holistic, localized worldview.

Intercorrelations Correlation between the members of a group of variables and especially between independent variables.

Interpretative dimensions/features Reflective meanings and interpretations of phenomena as understood by the persons involved in the study, as agents who act with others in a social and cultural context.

Intervey A Merged Method which puts together two characteristics: 'int' indicates the conversational component drawn from the (qualitative) in-depth interview; 'vey' transfers this dialogic component into the (quantitative) survey. The neologism is used to revitalize both Likert's practice and Galtung's interview method.

KDD/KDT Knowledge Discovery from Text/Data.

Landmark events Salient events from people's lives that are utilized in survey or interviewing studies to facilitate recall of other events and particularly the dates of these events.

Measuring The process by which the magnitude of a property X (owned by an object A) is compared with the magnitude of the same property owned by the instrument-unit, chosen conventionally to measure the property X (unit of measure). Measuring is not natural but 'conventional': in order to measure, the researcher needs an operational convention and a special instrument.

MEP Most effective profile.

Merged epistemology It merges the main or essential principles of the two epistemologies traditionally linked to qualitative (phenomenology, interactionism, constructivism, enactivism) and quantitative (transcendental or critical realism, moderate realism, agential realism, dialectical realism, internal realism) approaches.

Merged Method A fully integrated technique or method, which hybrids qualitative and quantitative approaches *in a single instrument*, blending the advantages of both *in a single technique*.

Mixed Method The combination of at least one qualitative method (designed to collect words) and at least one quantitative component (designed to collect numbers) in a single research project, study or programme of inquiry.

Multidimensional scaling (MDS) Is a means of visualizing the level of similarity of individual cases of a dataset.

Multimodal Research design combining several different modes of communication.

Naïve pragmatism The mixing of epistemologically different techniques (as standardized interview and the discursive interview), used as simple tools and within a post-positivistic attitude, without taking into account their nature and intrinsic limits.

NLP Natural language processing. A research field whose ultimate goal is to parse and understand language.

Open-ended question A survey item that allows respondents to use their own words.

Performativity of the method Its capacity for partially constructing data, having an inner force.

Phenomenological experiences Conscious sensory, affective, contextual and vivid experiences and memories as produced through autobiographical recall.

Quantitative techniques Usually defined as those techniques based on quantitative data and use of descriptive and inferential statistical analysis.

R A free software environment for statistical computing and graphics.

RAND Corporation Research institute with its headquarters in Santa Monica, California.

Relational systems analysis The study of multiple, interacting social mechanisms influencing human behaviour.

Scaling A set of procedures designed to detect concepts that are complex and not directly observable. These procedures share a number of basic assumptions: psychic properties (attitudes) are continuous properties, and an attitude can be reduced to several dimensions, each of which can be detected by means of specific indicators.

Sentiment Analysis A suite of methods for understanding the current attitudes and intentions of a subject population, including both lexical and machine learning approaches, whose main tasks include polarity detection, sentiment strength detection and fine-grained emotion detection.

Sociometry Is a quantitative method for measuring social relationships.

SPSS Statistical Package for the Social Sciences.

Stata Is statistical software for data science.

Structural dimensions/features Characteristics and elements of phenomena that are historically, societally and/ or socially determined and function as conditions or constraints to persons involved in the study.

Structuration theory Social theory regarding the synthesis of societal structure effects and individual agency effects on human behaviour, acknowledging the interaction of meaning, standards and values, and power.

Survey facesheet Front page of a survey questionnaire soliciting demographic information, e.g., age.

Symlog Acronym for SYstematic Multiple Level Observation of Groups.

Systemic approach An approach based on systems thinking and complexity theory, in which the characteristics or the parts are viewed with respect to the whole to which they belong.

Triangulation Combining methods in pursuit of convergent validation or integrating complementarity perspectives.

Trigonometrical view A strong version of the complementary concept of triangulation in which a combination of methods is necessary to establish a valid result.

Unobserved phenomena Social constructs that refer to descriptive and/or causal structures and mechanisms in reality but are not directly observable and identifiable.

Visual stimuli A stimulus normally in the form of a picture or colour shown on screen or paper.

REFERENCES

Abell, P. (2009). A case for cases: Comparative narratives in sociological explanation. *Sociological Methods and Research*, *38*(1), 38–70.

Adcock, R., & Collier, D. (2001). Measurement validity: A shared standard for qualitative and quantitative research. *American Political Science Review*, *95*, 529–546.

Adler, M., & Ziglio, E. (Eds) (1995). *Gazing into the oracle: The Delphi method and its application to social policy and public health*. Bristol, PA: Jessica Kingsley.

Agar, M. H. (1986). *Speaking of ethnography*. London: Sage.

Akhtar-Danesh, N., Baumann, A., & Cordingley, L. (2008). Q-methodology in nursing research: A promising method for the study of subjectivity. *Western Journal of Nursing Research*, *30*(6), 759–773.

Androutsopoulos, J. (2010). Localising the global on the participatory web: Vernacular spectacles as local responses to global media flows. In N. Coupland (Ed.), *Handbook of language and globalization* (pp. 203–231). Oxford: Wiley–Blackwell.

Androutsopoulos, J. (2011). From variation to heteroglossia in the study of computer-mediated discourse. In C. Thurlow & K. Mroczek (Eds), *Digital discourse: language in the new media* (pp. 277–298). London: Oxford University Press.

Archibald, M. M., Radil, A. I., Zhang, X., & Hanson, W. E., (2015). Current mixed methods practices in qualitative research: A content analysis of leading journals. *International Journal of Qualitative Methods*, *14*(2), 5–33.

Aspers, P., & Corte, U. (2019) What is Qualitative in qualitative research, *Qualitative Sociology*, *42*, 139–160.

Atkinson, P. (2013). Ethnographic writing: The avant-garde and a failure of nerve. *International Review of Qualitative Research*, *6*(1), 19–36.

Atkinson, P., & Silverman, D. (1997). Kundera's immorality: The interview society and the invention of the self. *Qualitative Inquiry*, *3*(3), 304–325.

Austin, J. L. (1962) *How to do things with words*. Oxford: Clarendon Press.

Bailey, K. D. (1978). *Methods in social research*. New York: Free Press.

Balán, J., Browning, H. L., Jelin, E., & Litzler, L. (1969). A computerized approach to the processing and analysis of life histories obtained in sample surveys. *Behavioral Science*, *14*(2), 105–120.

Balbi, S., Misuraca, M., & Scepi, G. (2018). Combining different evaluation systems on social media for measuring user satisfaction. *Information Processing and Management*, *54*(4), 674–685.

Bales, R. F. (1950). *Interaction process analysis: A method for the study of small groups*. Cambridge, MA: Addison–Wesley.

Bales, R. F. (1953). The equilibrium problem in small groups. In T. Parsons, R. F. Bales & E. A. Shils (Eds), *Working papers in the theory of action* (pp. 111–161). New York: Free Press.

Bales, R. F. (1970). *Personality and interpersonal behavior*. New York: Holt, Rinehart & Winston.

Bales, R. F. (1983). *Overview of the SYMLOG system: measuring and changing behavior in groups*. San Diego: SYMLOG Consulting Group.

Bales, R. F. (1985). The new field theory in social psychology. *International Journal of Small Group Research*, 1(1), 1–18.

Bales, R. F. (1988). A new overview of the SYmlog system: Measuring and changing behavior in groups. In R. B. Polley, A. P. Hare & P. J. Stone (Eds), *The Symlog practitioner. applications of small group research* (pp. 319–344). New York: Praeger.

Bales, R. F. (1999). *Social interaction systems*. New Brunswick, NJ: Transaction.

Bales, R. F., & Cohen, S. P., with Williamson, S. A. (1979). *SYMLOG: a system for the multiple level observation of groups*. New York: Free Press.

Bales, R. F., Koenigs, R. J., & Roman, P. D. (1987). Criteria for adaptation of SYMLOG rating items to particular populations and cultural contexts. *International Journal of Small Group Research*, 3(2), 161–179.

Barad, K. (2007). *Meeting the universe halfway*. Durham, NC: Duke University Press.

Barsalou, L. W. (1988). The content and organization of autobiographical memories. In U. Neisser & E. Winograd (Eds), *Remembering reconsidered: Ecological and traditional approaches to the study of memory* (pp. 193–243). New York: Cambridge University Press.

Baur, N. (2017). Process-oriented micro-macro-analysis. Methodological reflections on Elias and Bourdieu. *Historical Social Research*, 42(4), 43–74.

Bazeley, P. (1999). The *bricoleur* with a computer. *Qualitative Health Research*, 9(2), 279–287.

Bazeley, P. (2002). The evaluation of a project involving an integrated analysis of structured qualitative and quantitative data. *International Journal of Social Research Methods*, 5(3), 229–243.

Bazeley, P. (2006). The contribution of computer software to integrating qualitative and quantitative data and analyses. *Research in the Schools*, 13(1), 64–74.

Bazeley, P. (2010). Computer-assisted integration of mixed method data sources and analyses. In A. Tashakkori and C. Teddlie (Eds), *The Sage handbook of mixed methods in social and behavioral research* (2nd ed., pp. 431–467). Thousand Oaks, CA: Sage.

Bazeley, P. (2015a). Mixed methods in management research. *The Electronic Journal of Business Research Methods*, 13(1), 27–36.

Bazeley, P. (2015b) Writing up multimethod and mixed methods research for diverse audiences. In S. Hesse-Biber & R. Burke Johnson (Eds), *The Oxford handbook of multi-method and mixed methods research inquiry* (pp. 296–313). Oxford: Oxford University Press.

Bazeley, P. (2016). Mixed or merged? Integration as the real challenge for mixed methods. *Qualitative Research in Organizations and Management, 11*(3), 189–194.

Bazeley, P. (2018a). *Integrating analyses in mixed methods research.* London: Sage.

Bazeley, P. (2018b). 'Mixed methods in my bones': transcending the qualitative/ quantitative divide. *International Journal of Multiple Research Approaches, 10*(1), 334–341.

Beaton, B., Perley, D., George, C., & O'Donnell, S. (2017). Engaging remote marginalized communities using appropriate online research methods. In N. Fielding, G. Blank & R. Lee (Eds), *The Sage handbook of online research methods.* London: Sage.

Beatty, P. (1995). Understanding the standardized/non-standardized interviewing controversy. *Journal of Official Statistics, 11*(2), 147–160.

Becker, H. S. (1970). *Sociological work: Method and substance.* New Brunswick, NJ: Transaction Books.

Becker, H. S. (2017). *Evidence.* Chicago, IL: University of Chicago Press.

Becker, H. S., & Geer, B. (1957). Participant observation and interviewing: A comparison. *Human Organization, 16*(3), 28–32.

Becker, S., & Diop-Sidibe, N. (2003). Does use of the calendar in surveys reduce heaping? *Studies in Family Planning, 34*(2), 127–132.

Becker-Beck, U., & Schneider, J. F. (1990). Kleingruppenforschung im deutschsprachigen Raum [Small group research in German-speaking parts of the world]. *Zeitschrift für Sozialpsychologie, 21,* 274–297.

Belli, R. F. (1998). The structure of autobiographical memory and the Event History Calendar: Potential improvements in the quality of retrospective reports in surveys. *Memory, 6*(4), 383–406.

Belli, R. F., & Al Baghal, T. (2016). Parallel associations and the structure of autobiographical knowledge. *Journal of Applied Research in Memory and Cognition, 5,* 150–157.

Belli, R. F., Bilgen, I., & Al Baghal, T. (2013). Memory, communication, and data quality in calendar interviews. *Public Opinion Quarterly, 77*(1), 194–219.

Belli, R. F., & Callegaro, M. (2009). The emergence of calendar interviewing. In R. F. Belli, R. P. Stafford, & D. F. Alwin (Eds), *Calendar and time diary methods in life course research* (pp. 31–54). Thousand Oaks, CA: Sage.

Belli, R. F., Lee, E. H., Stafford, F., & Chou, C.-H. (2004). Calendar and question-list survey methods: Association between interviewer behaviors and data quality. *Journal of Official Statistics, 20*(1), 185–218.

Belli, R. F., Shay, W., & Stafford, F. (2001). Event History Calendars and question list surveys: A direct comparison of interviewing methods. *Public Opinion Quarterly, 65,* 45–74.

Belli, R. F., Smith, L., Andreski, P., & Agrawal, S. (2007). Methodological comparisons between CATI event history calendar and conventional questionnaire instruments. *Public Opinion Quarterly*, *71*, 603–622.

Belli, R. F., Stafford, R. P., & Alwin, D. F. (2009). *Calendar and time diary methods in life course research*. Thousand Oaks, CA: Sage.

Benzécri, J. P. (1964). *Sur l'analyse factorielle des proximités*. Publication of the Institute of Statistics, University of Paris, vol. XIII, 235–282.

Berelson, B. (1952). *Content analysis in communication research*. Glencoe, IL: Free Press.

Berger, P. (2002). Whatever happened to sociology. *First Things*, 126, 27–29.

Bergman, M. (2008). The straw men of research and their influence on mixed methods research. In M. Bergman (Ed.), *Advances in mixed methods research* (pp. 11–21). London: Sage.

Biesta, G. (2010). Pragmatism and the philosophical foundations of mixed methods research. In A. Tashakkori & C. Teddlie (Eds), *Handbook of mixed methods research for the social and behavioral sciences* (2nd ed., pp. 95–118). Thousand Oaks, CA: Sage.

Bilgen, I., & Belli, R. F. (2010). Comparison of verbal behaviors between calendar and standardized conventional questionnaires. *Journal of Official Statistics*, *26*, 481–505.

Bion, W. R. (1987). *Experiences in groups*. London: Tavistock Publications.

Blaikie, N. W. H. (1991). A critique of the use of triangulation in social research. *Quality and Quantity*, *25*(2), 115–136.

Blank, G. (2017) 'Online research methods and social theory', in N. Fielding, R. Lee and G. Blank (Eds) *The SAGE handbook of online research methods*, second edition (pp. 628–641). London: Sage.

Blei, D., Ng, A., & Jordan, M. (2003). Latent Dirichlet allocation. *Journal of Machine Learning Research*, 3, 993–1012.

Blossfeld, H-P., & Rohwer, G. (1995). *Techniques of event history modelling*. Mahwah, NJ: Lawrence Erlbaum Associates.

Blum, Z. D., Karweit, N. L., & Sørensen, A. B. (1969). *A method for the collection and analysis of retrospective life histories*. Baltimore, MD: Johns Hopkins University.

Blumer, H. (1956). Sociological analysis and the 'variable'. *American Sociological Review*, *21*, 633–660.

Boccia Artieri, G., & La Rocca, G. (2019). The election day of Pope Francis: between sentiment and emotions online. *SAT 2019. Socio-Affective Technologies: An interdisciplinary approach CEUR-WS.org*, 2474, 7–12.

Boccia Artieri G., Greco F., & La Rocca G. (2021). The construction of the meanings of #coronavirus on Twitter: An analysis of the initial reactions of the Italian people. *International Review of Sociology*, *31*(2), 287–309.

Bodenhausen, G. V., Schwarz, N., Bless, H., & Wanke, M. (1995). Effects of atypical exemplars on racial beliefs: Enlightened racism or generalized appraisals? *Journal of Experimental Social Psychology, 31*, 48–63.

Bolasco, S. (1999). *Analisi multidimensionale dei dati*. Rome: Carocci.

Bolasco S. (2000). TALTAC: un environnement pour l'exploitation de ressources statistiques et linguistiques dans l'analyse textuelle. Un exemple d'application au discours politique. *JADT*, pp. 342–353.

Bolasco, S., & della Ratta-Rinaldi, F. (2004). Experiments on semantic categorisation of texts: Analysis of positive and negative dimension. *JADT*, pp. 202–210.

Bolasco, S., Baiocchi, F. & Morrone, A. (2006). TaLTaC2, Trattamento Automatico Lessicale e Testuale per l'Analisi del Contenuto di un Corpus (ver. 2.0.1). Roma: CISU.

Bollen, J., Mao, H., & Zeng, X. (2011). Twitter mood predicts the stock market. *Journal of Computational Science, 2*(1), 1–8.

Bourdieu, P., Chamboredon, J. C., & Passeron, J. C. (1968). *Le métier de sociologue: Problèmes épistémologiques*. Paris: Mounton.

boyd, d. (2010). Social network sites as networked publics: Affordances, dynamics, and implications. In Z. Papacharissi (Ed.), *A networked self: Identity, community, and culture on social network sites* (pp. 39–58). New York: Routledge.

boyd, d., & Crawford, K. (2012). Critical questions for Big Data. *Information, Communication & Society, 15*(5), 662–679.

Brachman, R., & Anand, T. (1996). The process of knowledge discovery in databases: A human-centered approach. In U. Fayyad, G. Piatetsky-Shapiro, P. Smyth & R. Uthurusamy (Eds), *Advances in knowledge discovery and data mining* (pp. 37–58). Menlo Park, CA: AAAI Press.

Bradburn, N. M. (1983). Response effects. In P. H. Rossi, J. D. Wright & A. B. Anderson (Eds), *Handbook of survey research* (pp. xx–xx). New York: Academic Press.

Bradburn, N. M., Sudman, S., & Blair. E. (1979). *Improving interviewing method and questionnaire design*. San Francisco, CA: Jossey-Bass.

Brannen, J. (1992). *Mixing methods: Qualitative and quantitative research*. London: Gower.

Brier, A., De Giorgi, E., & Hopp, B. (2016). *Strategies in computer-assisted text analysis*. Southampton: National Center for Research Methods Working Papers, 3/16.

Briggs, C. L. (1984). Learning how to ask: Native metacommunicative competence and the incompetence of the fieldworkers. *Language and Society*, 13, 1–28.

Brouwer, M. (1999). Q is accounting for tastes. *Journal of Advertising Research, 39*(2), 35–39.

Brown, N. R. (2005). On the prevalence of event clusters in autobiographical memory. *Social Cognition, 23*(1), 35–69.

Brown, S. R. (1980). *Political subjectivity: Applications of Q methodology in political science.* New Haven, CT: Yale University Press.

Brown, S. R. (1986). Q technique and method: Principles and procedures. In W. D. Berry & M. S. Lewis-Beck (Eds), *New tools for social scientists: Advances and applications in research methods* (pp. 57–76). Beverly Hills, CA: Sage.

Brown, S. R. (1993). A primer on Q methodology. *Operant Subjectivity, 16*(3/4), 91–138.

Brückner, E., & Mayer, K. U. (1998). Collecting life history data: Experiences from the German life history study. In J. Z. Giele & G. H. Elder (Eds), *Methods of life course research: Qualitative and quantitative approaches* (pp. 152–181). Thousand Oaks, CA: Sage.

Bryman, A. (2006). Integrating quantitative and qualitative research. *Qualitative Research, 6*(1), 97–113.

Bryman, A. (2007). Barriers to integrating quantitative and qualitative research. *Journal of Mixed Methods Research, 1*(1), 8–22.

Burt, C. (1972). The reciprocity principle. In S. R. Brown & D. J. Brenner (Eds), *Science, psychology, and communication: Essays honoring William Stephenson* (pp. 39–56). New York: Teachers College Press.

Burt, C. and Stephenson, W. (1939). Alternative views on correlations between persons. *Psychometrika, 4*, 269–281.

Burt, C. D. B., Kemp, S., & Conway, M. A. (2003). Themes, events, and episodes in autobiographical memory. *Memory & Cognition, 32*, 317–325.

Burt, C. D. B., Kemp, S., & Conway, M. (2008). Ordering the components of autobiographical events. *Acta Psychologica, 127*(1), 36–45.Burzan, N. (2016). *Methodenplurale Forschung.* Weinheim: Beltz.

Calinski, T., & Harabasz, J. (1974). A dendrite method for cluster analysis. *Communications in Statistics, 3*, 1–27.

Cambria, E. and Schuller, B. (2013). New avenues in opinion mining and sentiment analysis, *Intelligent Systems, 28* (2), 15–21.

Campbell, D. (1987). Guidelines for monitoring the scientific competence of preventive intervention research centres. *Knowledge: Creation, Diffusion, Utilisation, 8*(3), 389–430.

Campbell, D., & Fiske, D. (1959). Convergent and discriminant validation by the multitrait-multimethod matrix. *Psychological Bulletin, 56*(2), 81–105.

Caracelli, J. & Greene, J. (1993) Data analysis strategies for mixed-method evaluation designs, *Educational Evaluation and Policy Analysis, 15* (2), 195–207.

Caracelli, V., & Greene, J. (1997). Crafting mixed-method evaluation designs. In J. Greene & V. Caracelli (Eds), *Advances in mixed-method evaluation* (pp. 19–32). San Francisco, CA: Jossey-Bass.

Carter, L., Haytorn, W., Meirowitz, B., & Lanzetta, J. (1951). The relation of categorizations and ratings in the observation of group behavour. *Human Relations, 4*, 239–254.

Cartwright, N. (1989). *Nature's capacities and their measurement.* Oxford: Clarendon Press.

Charmaz, K. (2014). *Constructing grounded theory.* London: Sage.

Chilisa, B. (2011) *Indigenous Research Methodologies.* London: Sage.

Cicourel, A. V. (1964). *Method and measurement in sociology.* New York: Free Press.

Cicourel, A. V. (1996). Ecological validity and white room effects. *Pragmatic and Cognition, 4*(2).

Cisneros-Puebla, C., & Fielding, N. (2009). CAQDAS-GIS convergence: Towards a new integrated mixed method research practice? *Journal of Mixed Methods Research, 3*(4), 349–370.

Coleman, J. S. (1986). Social theory, social research, and a theory of action. *American Journal of Sociology, 91*(6), 1309–1335.

Colleoni, E. (2013). Beyond the differences: The use of empty signifiers as organizing device in the #occupy movement. Workshop Material Participation: Technology, the Environment and Everyday Publics, University of Milan.

Collier, D., & Elman, C. (2008). Qualitative and multi-method research: Organization, publication, and reflections on integration. In Janet M. Box-Steffensmeier, Henry E. Brady, & David Collier (Eds), *The Oxford handbook of political methodology* (ch. 4). Oxford: Oxford University Press.

Collins, K. M. T., Onwuegbuzie, A. J., & Jiao, Q. G. (2007). A mixed methods investigation of mixed methods sampling designs in social and health science research. *Journal of Mixed Methods Research, 1*(3), 267–294.

Collins, R. (1988). *Theoretical sociology.* San Diego, CA: Harcourt Brace Jovanovich.

Colt, J. S., Engel, L., Keifer, M., Thompson, M. L., & Zahm, S. (2001). Comparability of data obtained from migrant farmworkers and their spouses on occupational history. *American Journal of Industrial Medicine, 40*, 523–530.

Conrad, F. G., & Schober, M. F. (2005). Promoting uniform question understanding in today's and tomorrow's surveys. *Journal of Official Statistics, 21*, 215–231.

Converse, P. E. (1964). *The nature of belief system in mass-publics.* In E. A. David (Ed.), *Ideology and discontent* (pp. 202–261). Glencoe, IL: Free Press.

Converse, J. M. (1987). *Survey research in the United States: Roots and emergence 1890–1960.* Berkeley, CA: University of California Press.

Converse, P. E. (1970). Attitudes and non attitudes: continuation of a dialogue. In E. R. Tufte (Ed.), *The quantitative analysis of social problems*. Reading, MA: Addison–Wesley.

Conway, M. A. (1996). Autobiographical knowledge and autobiographical memories. In D. Rubin (Ed.), *Remembering our past: Studies in autobiographical memory* (pp. 67–93). Cambridge: Cambridge University Press.

Conway, M. A., & Pleydell-Pearce, C. W. (2000). The construction of autobiographical memories in the self-memory system. *Psychological Review, 107*, 261–288.

Coogan, J., & Herrington, N. (2011). Q methodology: an overview. *Research in Secondary Teacher Education, 1*(2), 24–28.

Cooley, R., Srivastava, J. & Mobasher, B. (1997). Web mining: Information and pattern discovery on the World Wide Web. In Proceeding of the 9th IEEE International Conference on Tools With Artificial Intelligence (ACTAI, 1997).

Cordella, B., Greco, F., Carlini, K., Greco, A., & Tambelli, R. (2018a). Infertilita e procreazione assistita: evoluzione legislativa e culturale in Italia. *Rassegna di Psicologia, 35*(3), 45–56.

Cordella, B., Greco, F., Meoli, P., Palermo, V., & Grasso, M. (2018b). Is the educational culture in Italian universities effective? A case study. In D. F. Iezzi, L. Celardo & M. Misuraca (Eds), *JADT '18: Proceedings of the 14th International Conference on Statistical Analysis of Textual Data* (pp. 157–164). Rome: Universitalia.

Cordingley, L. (1999). Health, social support, independence and marital status in older women: A study using the SF-36 and Q methodology. (Unpublished doctoral dissertation). University of Manchester, Manchester, UK.

Cordingley, L., Webb, C., & Hillier, V. (1997). Q methodology. *Nurse Researcher, 3*(3): 3–45.

Couch, A. S. (1960). Psychological determinants of interpersonal behaviour. (Unpublished doctoral dissertation). Harvard University, Cambridge, MA.

Cowie, J., & Lehnert, W. (1996). Information extraction. *Communications of the ACM, 39*(1), 80–91.

Coxon, A. P. M. (1982). *The user's guide to multidimensional scaling*. London: Heinemann Educational Books.

Craig, W. J., Harris, T. M., & Weiner, D. (Eds) (2002). *Community participation and geographic information systems*. London: Taylor and Francis.

Creswell, J.W. (1997). *Qualitative inquiry and research design: Choosing among five approaches*. Thousand Oaks, CA: Sage.

Creswell, J. W. (2009). *Research design: Qualitative, quantitative and mixed methods approaches* (2nd ed.). Thousand Oaks, CA: Sage.

Creswell, J. W. (2011a). *Designing and conducting mixed methods research*. London: Sage.

Creswell, J. W. (2011b). Controversies in mixed methods research. In N. K. Denzin & Y. S. Lincoln (Eds), *The Sage handbook of qualitative research* (4th ed., pp. 269–283). London: Sage.

Creswell, J. W., & Plano Clark, V. (2007). *Designing and Conducting mixed methods research*. Thousand Oaks, CA: Sage.

Creswell, J. W., & Plano Clark, V. (2011). *Designing and conducting mixed methods research* (2nd ed.). Thousand Oaks, CA: Sage.

Creswell, J. W., & Plano Clark, V. (2018). *Designing and conducting mixed methods research* (3rd ed.). Thousand Oaks, CA: Sage.

Cronbach, L. J. (1975). Beyond the two disciplines of scientific psychology. *American Psychologist, 30*(2), 116–127.

Cronbach, L. J., & Meehl, P. E. (1955). Construct validity in psychological tests. *Psychological Bulletin, 52*(4), 281–302.

Daigneault, P. M., & Jacob, S. (2014). Unexpected but most welcome: Mixed methods for the validation and revision of the participatory evaluation measurement instrument. *Journal of Mixed Methods Research, 8*(1), 6–24.

Dalkey, N. C. (1968). *Predicting the future. P-3948*. Santa Monica, CA: The RAND Corporation.

Dalkey, N. C. (1969). *The Delphi Method: An experimental study of group opinion*. RM-5888PM. Santa Monica, CA: The RAND Corporation. Available at: www.rand.org/content/dam/rand/pubs/research_memoranda/2005/RM5888.pdf

Dalkey, N. C., & Helmer, O. (1963). An experimental application of the Delphi method to the use of experts. *Management Science, 9*(3), 458–467.

Davis, H. C., & Michelle, C. (2011). Q methodology in audience research: Bridging the qualitative/quantitative 'divide'? *Participations. Journal of Audience & Receptions Studies, 8*(2), 527–561.

De Groot, M. H. (1974). Reaching a consensus. *Journal of the American Statistical Association, 69*(345), 118–121.

Della Porta, D., & Keating, M. (Eds) (2008). *Approaches and methodologies in the social sciences: A pluralist perspective*. Cambridge: Cambridge University Press.

Dellinger, A. B., & Leech, N. L. (2007). Toward a unified validation framework in mixed methods research. *Journal of Mixed Methods Research, 1*(4), 309–332.

Dennis, K. E. (1986). Q-methodology – relevance and application to nursing research. *Advances in Nursing Science, 8*, 6–17.

Dennis, K. E. (1992). Commentary: Looking at reliability and validity through Q-colored glasses. *Operant Subjectivity, 16*, 37–44.

Dennis, K. E., & Goldberg, A. P. (1996). Weight control self-efficacy types and transitions affect weight-loss outcomes in obese women. *Addictive Behaviors, 21,* 103–116.

Denzin, N. K. (1969). Symbolic interactionism and ethnomethodology: A proposed synthesis. *American Sociological Review, 34*(6), 922–934.

Denzin, N. (1970). *The research act.* New York: McGraw Hill.

Denzin, N. K., & Lincoln, Y. S. (2005). Introduction: the discipline and practice of qualitative research. In N. K. Denzin & Y. S. Lincoln (Eds), *The Sage handbook of qualitative research* (pp. 1–32). Thousand Oaks, CA: Sage.

Deutscher, I. (1973). *What we say/What we do.* Glenview, IL: Scott, Foresman.

Dewey, J. (1938). *Logic, the theory of inquiry.* New York: Henry Holt and Co.

Dex, S. (1995). The reliability of recall data: a literature review. *Bulletin de Méthodologie Sociologique, N. 49,* Dec, 58–89.

Di Zio S., & Pacinelli, A. (2011). Opinion convergence in location: A spatial version of the Delphi method. *Technological Forecasting and Social Change, 78*(9), 1565–1578.

Diesing, P. R. (1971). *Patterns of discovery in the social sciences.* Chicago, IL: Aldine-Atherton.

Dijkstra, W., Smit, J. H., & Ongena, Y. P. (2009). An evaluation study of the event history calendar. In R. F. Belli, R. P. Stafford & D. F. Alwin (Eds), *Calendar and time diary methods in life course research* (pp. 257–275). Thousand Oaks, CA: Sage.

Drasch, K., & Matthes, B. (2013). Improving retrospective life course data by combining modularized self-reports and event history calendars: Experiences from a large scale survey. *Quality and Quantity, 47*(2), 817–838.

Driscoll, D. L., Appiah-Yeboah, A., Salib, P., & Rupert, D. J. (2007). Merging qualitative and quantitative data in mixed methods research: How to and why not. *Ecological and Environmental Anthropology, 3*(1), 19–28.

Eden, S., Donaldson, A., & Walker, G. (2005). Structuring subjectivities? Using Q methodology in human geography. *Area, 37*(4), 413–422.

Eisenhower, D., Mathiowetz, N. A., & Morganstein, D. (1991). *Recall error: Sources and bias reduction techniques.* In P. P. Biemer, R. M. Groves, L. E. Lyberg, N. A. Mathiowetz & S. Sudman (Eds), *Measurement errors in surveys* (pp. 127–144). New York: John Wiley.

Ellingsen, I. T., Thorsen, A. A., & Størksen, I. (2014). Revealing children's experiences and emotions through Q methodology. *Child Development Research, 9,* 1–9.

Elliott, J. (2005). *Using narrative in social research.* Beverly Hills, CA: Sage.

Engel, L., Keifer, M., & Zahm, S. (2001). Comparison of a traditional questionnaire with an icon/calendar-based questionnaire to assess occupational history. *American Journal of Industrial Medicine, 40,* 502–511.

Erickson, F. (2007, May). *Specifying 'usually' and 'some': Using simple descriptive statistics in qualitative inquiry*. Presented at the 2007 Congress of Qualitative Inquiry, Urbana, IL.

Erzberger, C., & Kelle, U. (2003). Making inferences in mixed methods. In A. Tashakkori & C. Teddlie (Eds), *Handbook of mixed methods in social and behavioral research*. Thousand Oaks, CA: Sage.

Evans, N. J., & Jarvis, P. A. (1986). The group attitude scale: A measure of attraction to group. *Small Group Behavior, 17*(2), 203–216.

Fakis, A., Hilliam, R., Stoneley, H., & Townend, M. (2014). Quantitative analysis of qualitative information from interviews: A systematic literature review. *Journal of Mixed Methods Research, 8*(2), 139–161.

Fayyad, U., Piatetsky-Shapiro, G., & Smyth, P. (1996). From data mining to knowledge discovery: An overview. In U. Fayyad, G. Piatetsky-Shapiro, P. Smyth & R. Uthurusamy (Eds), *Advances in knowledge discovery and data mining* (pp. 1–36). Cambridge, MA: MIT Press.

Feldman, R., & Dagan, I. (1995). Knowledge discovery in textual databases (KDT). In Proceedings of the First International Conference on Knowledge Discovery and Data Mining (KDD-95), Montreal, Canada, 20–21 August (pp. 112–117). AAAI Press.

Feldman, R., & Hirshi, H. (1996). Mining association in text in the presence of background knowledge. In Proceedings of the 2nd International Conference on Knowledge Discovery in Databases and Data Mining (KDD'96), Portland, Oregon (pp. 343–346).

Feldman, R., & Sanger, J. (2007). *The text mining handbook: Advanced approaches in analyzing unstructured data*. New York: Cambridge University Press.

Feltham-King, T., & Macleod, C. (2016). How content analysis may complement and extend the insights of discourse analysis. *International Journal of Qualitative Methods, 1*(9), 1–9. doi:10.1177/1609406915624575.

Ferrazzi, P., Tagalik, S., Christie, P., Karetak, J., Baker, K., & Angalik, L. (2019). Aajiiqatigiingniq: An Inuit consensus methodology in qualitative health research. *International Journal of Qualitative Methods, 18*, 1–9. doi:10.1177/1609406919894796.

Fielding, J., & Fielding, N. (2013). Integrating information from multiple methods into the analysis of perceived risk of crime: The role of georeferenced field data and mobile methods. *Journal of Criminology*, Article ID 284259. doi:10.1155/2013/284259.

Fielding, N. (2009). Going out on a limb: postmodernism and multiple method research. *Current Sociology, 57*(3), 427–447.

Fielding, N. (2012). Triangulation and mixed methods designs. *Journal of Mixed Methods Research, 6*(2), 124–136.

Fielding, N. (2014). Qualitative research and our digital futures. *Qualitative Inquiry, 20*(9), 1064–1073.

Fielding, N. (2016). Qualitative research in a glocalizing world. In N. Denzin & M. Giardina (Eds), *Global dimensions of qualitative inquiry* (pp. 47–62). Walnut Creek, CA: Left Coast Press.

Fielding, N. (forthcoming). The role of the qualitative researcher in a politics of rèsistance. *Qualitative Inquiry.*

Fielding, J. and Fielding, N. (1986). *Linking data.* Los Angeles: Sage

Fielding, N., & Lee, R. (1991). Computing for qualitative research: Options, problems and potential. In N. Fielding & R. Lee (Eds), *Using computers in qualitative research* (pp. 1–13). London: Sage.

Fielding, N., & Schreier, M. (2001). On the compatibility between qualitative and quantitative research methods. *Forum: Qualitative Social Research, 2*(1), Article 4.

Fisch, R., Daniel, H. D., & Beck, D. (1991). Kleingruppenforschung – Schwerpunkt und Forschungstrends [Small group research: The center of gravity and trends in research]. *Gruppendynamik, 21,* 237–261.

Flick, U. (1992). Triangulation revisited: Strategy of validation or alternative? *Journal for the Theory of Social Behavior, 22*(2), 175–197.

Flick, U. (2008). *Designing Qualitative Research.* London: Sage.

Flick, U. (2011). Mixing methods, triangulation and integrated research – challenges for qualitative research in a world of crisis. In N. Denzin and M. Giardina (Eds), *Qualitative inquiry and global crisis* (pp. 132–152). Walnut Creek, CA: Left Coast Press.

Forbes, A., Ritchie, S., Walker, J., & Young, N. (2020). Applications of two-eyed seeing in primary research focused on indigenous health: A scoping review. *International Journal of Qualitative Methods, 19,* 1–18. doi:10.1177/1609406920929110.

Ford, D. J. (2014). Do race and gender matter within the context of organizational culture change? An American case study of assessing identity group consensus in organizational culture perceptions. *NMIMS Management Review, XXIV,* April–May, 11–29.

Fowler, F. J., Jr., & Mangione, T. W. (1990). *Standardized survey interviewing: Minimizing interviewer-related error.* London: Sage.

Franzosi, R., Doyle, S., McClelland, L. E., Putnam Rankin, C., & Vicari, S. (2013). Quantitative narrative analysis software options compared. *Quality & Quantity, 47*(6), 3219–3247.

Freedman, D., Thornton, A., Camburn, D., Alwin, D., & Young DeMarcco, L. (1988). The life history calendar: A technique for collecting retrospective data. *Sociological Methodology, 18,* 37–68.

Fryer, D. (1992). Introduction to Marienthal and beyond. *Journal of Occupational and Organizational Psychology, 65,* 257–268.

Fulop, L, Maréchal, G., & Rifkin, W. (2009). Management knowledge and learning. In S. Linstead, L. Fulop & S. Liley (Eds), *Management and organization: A critical text* (pp. 32–88). Basingstoke: Palgrave.

Fung, H. H. (2013). Aging in culture. *Gerontologist, 53* (3), 369–377.

Gallagher, K., & Porock, D. (2010). The use of interviews in Q methodology. *Nursing Research, 59*(4), 295–300.

Galtung, J. (1967). *Theory and method of social research.* Oslo: Universitets Forlaget.

Gandomi, A., & Haider, M. (2015). Beyond the hype: Big Data concepts, methods, and analytics. *International Journal of Information Management, 35*(2), 137–144.

Gee, J. P. (1991). A linguistic approach to narrative. *Journal of Narrative and Life History, 1,* 15–39.

Geertz, C. (1972). Deep play: Notes on the Balinese cockfight. *Dedalus, 101,* 1–37.

Georgakopoulou, A. (2000). Analytical positioning vis-à-vis narrative positioning. *Narrative Inquiry, 10*(1), 185–190.

Gerlach, A. (2018). Thinking and researching relationally: Enacting decolonizing methodologies with an indigenous Early Childhood Program in Canada. *International Journal of Qualitative Methods, 17,* 1–8. doi:10.1177/1609406918776075.

Gibson, J. (1979) *The Ecological Approach to Visual Perception,* New York, N.Y.: Psychology Press.

Giddings, L. S. (2006). Mixed-methods research: Positivism dressed in drag. *Journal of Research in Nursing, 11*(3), 195–203.

Giuliano, L., & La Rocca, G. (2010). Validity and reliability of the automatic classification of texts according to the negative–positive criterion. Statistical Analysis of Textual Data. Proceedings of 10th International Conference *JADT: Journées d'Analyse statistique des Données Textuelles* (pp. 62–71). Rome: Led.

Glaser, B. G., & Strauss, A. L. (1967). *The discovery of grounded theory.* Chicago, IL: Aldine.

Glaser, J., & Laudel, G. (2013). Life with and without coding. *Forum: Qualitative Social Research, 14*(2), Article 5.

Glasner, T. J., &. Van der Vaart, W. (2009). Applications of calendar instruments in social surveys: A review. *Quality and Quantity, 43,* 333–349.

Glasner, T. J., Van der Vaart, W., & Dijkstra, W. (2015). Calendar instruments in retrospective web surveys. *Field Methods, 27*(3), 265–283.

Glynos, J., Howarth, D., Norval, A., & Speed, E. (2009). Discourse analysis: Varieties and methods. Retrieved from http://eprints.ncrm.ac.uk/796.

Gobo, G. (2004). *Sampling, representativeness and generalizability.* In C. Seale, G. Gobo, J. F. Gubrium, D. Silverman, (a cura di), *Qualitative Research Practice* (pp. 435–56). London: Sage.

Gobo, G. (2006). Set them free: Improving data quality by broadening the interviewer's task. *International Journal of Social Research Methodology, 9*(4), 279–301.

Gobo, G. (2008a). *Doing ethnography.* London: Sage.

Gobo, G. (2008b). *Re-conceptualizing generalization: Old issues in a new frame.* In P. Alasuutari, J. Brannen & L. Bickman (Eds), *The Sage handbook of social research methods* (pp. 193–213). London: Sage.

Gobo, G. (2011a). Back to Likert: Towards a conversational survey. In M. Williams & P. Vogt (Eds), *The Sage handbook of innovation in social research methods* (pp. 228–248). London: Sage.

Gobo, G. (2011b). Glocalizing methodology? The encounter between local methodologies. *International Journal of Social Research Methodology, 14*(6), 417–437.

Gobo, G. (2016). Why 'merged' methods realize a higher integration than 'mixed' methods. A reply, in *Qualitative Research in Organizations and Management: An International Journal, 11*(3): 199–208.

Gobo, G. (2018). Qualitative research across boundaries: Indigenousation, glocalization or creolization? In C. Cassell, A. Cunliffe and G. Gandy (Eds), *The Sage handbook of qualitative business and management research methods* (pp. 495–514). London: Sage.

Gobo, G., & Mauceri, S. (2014). *Constructing survey data: An interactional approach.* London: Sage.

Goldman, N., Moreno, L., & Westoff, C. F. (1989). Collection of survey data on contraception: An evaluation of an experiment in Peru. *Studies in Family Planning, 20*(3), 147–157.

Gomm, R., Hammersley, M., & Foster, P. (Eds) (2000). *Case study method.* London: Sage.

Good, J. M. M., & Brown, S. (2008). The relationship of Q methodology to quantitative, qualitative, and mixed methods. *International Society for the Scientific Study of Subjectivity*, Hamilton, Ontario, Canada.

Goodman, C. M. (1987). The Delphi technique: A critique. *Journal of Advanced Nursing, 12*(6), 729–734.

Goodyear-Smith, F., & 'Ofanoa, M. (2021). Fa'afaletui: A Pacific research framework. *Journal of Mixed Methods Research.* doi.org/10.1177/1558689820985948.

Gorard, S. (2010). Research design, as independent of methods. In A. Tashakkori & C. Teddlie (Eds), *Handbook of mixed methods in social and behavioral research* (2nd ed., pp. 237–251). Thousand Oaks, CA: Sage.

Gordon, T. J., & Helmer, O. (1964). *Report on a long-range forecasting study. P-2982.* Santa Monica, CA: The RAND Corporation. https://www.rand.org/pubs/papers/P2982.html

Gordon, T. J., & Pease, A. (2006). RT Delphi: An efficient, 'round-less', almost real time Delphi method. *Technological Forecasting and Social Change, 73*(4), 321–333.

Gostkowski, Z. (1974). Toward empirical humanization of mass survey. *Quality and Quantity*, 8(1), 11–26.

Graffigna G., & Gambetti R.C. (2015). Getting insights or getting lost? An integrated mixed-method approach to social media discourses and its impact on marketing decision-making, *International Journal of Internet Marketing and Advertising*, 9(2), 103–120.

Greco, F. (2016a). *Integrare la disabilità. Una metodologia interdisciplinare per leggere il cambiamento culturale*. Milan: Franco Angeli.

Greco, F. (2016b). *Les lois et le changement culturel: Le handicap en Italie et en France*. Rome: Sapienza Università Editrice.

Greco, F. (2019). Il dibattito sulla migrazione in campagna elettorale: Confronto trail caso francese e italiano. *Culture e Studi nel Sociale*, 4(2), 205–213.

Greco, F., & Polli, A. (2019). Vaccines in Italy: The emotional text mining of social media. *Rivista Italiana di Economia Demografia e Statistica*, 73(1), 89–98.

Greco, F., & Polli, A. (2020a). Emotional text mining: Customer profiling in brand management. *International Journal of Information Management*, 51, 101934. doi:10.1016/j.ijinfomgt.2019.04.007.

Greco, F., & Polli, A. (2020b). Security perception and people well-being. *Social Indicator Research*, 1–18.

Greco, F., Alaimo, L., & Celardo, L. (2018a). Brexit and Twitter: The voice of people. In D. F. Iezzi, L. Celardo & M. Misuraca (Eds), *JADT '18: Proceedings of the 14th International Conference on Statistical Analysis of Textual Data* (pp. 327–334). Rome: Universitalia.

Greco, F., Celardo, L., & Alaimo, L. M. (2018b). Brexit in Italy: Text mining of social media. In A. Abbruzzo, D. Piacentino, M. Chiodi & E. Brentari (Eds), *Book of short papers SIS 2018* (pp. 767–772). Milan: Pearson.

Greco, F., Maschietti, D., & Polli, A. (2017). Emotional text mining of social networks: The French pre-electoral sentiment on migration. *RIEDS*, 71(2), 125–136.

Greco F., S. Monaco, M. Di Trani, B. Cordella (2019). Emotional text mining and health psychology: the culture of organ donation in Spain. In M. Carpita, and L. Fabbris (Eds), *ASA Conference 2019 - Book od Short Papers Statistics for Health and Well-being, University of Brescia, September 25–27*, (pp. 125–129). Padova: CLEUP.

Greene, J. C. (2007). *Mixed methods in social inquiry*. San Francisco, CA: Jossey-Bass.

Greene, J. (2008). Is mixed methods social inquiry a distinctive methodology? *Journal of Mixed Methods Research*, 2, 7–22.

Greene, J. C., Caracelli, V. J., & Graham, W. F. (1989). Toward a conceptual framework for mixed method evaluation designs. *Educational Evaluation and Policy Analysis*, 11(3), 255–274.

Grémy J.P. (2007). Les 'défaillances de la mémoire' dans les enquêtes de victimation. *Bulletin de Méthodologie Sociologique, 94*, 39–56.

Grimmer, J., & Stewart, B. M. (2013). Text as data: The promise and pitfalls of automatic content analysis methods for political texts. *Political Analysis, 21*(3), 267–297.

Groves, Robert M., Fultz, Nancy, H., & Martin, E. (1992). Direct questioning about comprehension in a survey setting. In J. M. Tanur, *Questions about questions: Inquiries into the cognitive bases of surveys* (pp. 49–61). New York: Russell Sage Foundation.

Guest, G. (2013). Describing mixed methods research: An alternative to typologies. *Journal of Mixed Methods Research, 7*(2), 141–151.

Gupta, V., & Lehal, G. S. (2009). A survey of text mining techniques and applications. *Journal of Emerging Technologies in Web Intelligence, 1*(1), 60–76.

Hacking, I. (1983). *Representing and intervening: Introductory topics in the philosophy of natural science*. Cambridge: Cambridge University Press.

Haitana, T., Pitama, S., Cormack, D., Clarke, M., & Lacey, C. (2020). The transformative potential of Kaupapa Māori research and Indigenous methodologies: Positioning Māori patient experiences of mental health services. *International Journal of Qualitative Methods, 19*, 1–12.

Hall, B., & Howard, K. (2008). A synergistic approach conducting mixed methods research with typological and systemic design considerations. *Journal of Mixed Methods Research, 2*(3), 248–269.

Hall, J. (2013). Pragmatism, evidence, and mixed methods evaluation (Special Issue: Mixed methods and credibility of evidence in evaluation). *New Directions for Evaluation, 138*, 15–26.

Hammersley, M. (1987). Some notes on the terms 'validity' and 'reliability'. *British Educational Research Journal, 13*(1), 73–81.

Hammersley, M. (1992). *What's wrong with ethnography? Methodological explorations*. London: Routledge.

Hammersley, M. (2008). Troubles with triangulation. In M. Bergman (Ed.), *Advances in mixed methods research* (pp. 22–36). London: Sage.

Hammersley, M. (2010). Is social measurement possible, and is it necessary? In G. Walford, E. Tucker & M. Viswanathan (Eds), *The Sage handbook of measurement*. London: Sage.

Hammersley, M. (2018). Commentary on the 'indistinguishability' thesis, *Journal of Mixed Methods Research, 12*(3), 256–261.

Hammersley, M., & Atkinson, P. (1983). *Ethnography: Principles in practice*. London: Tavistock.

Han, J., & Kamber, M. (2001). *Data mining: concepts and techniques* (Morgan-Kaufman Series of Data Management Systems). San Diego: Academic Press.

Hansen, A. (1995). Using information technology to analyze newspaper content. In R. M. Lee (Ed.) *Information technology for the social scientist.* London: UCL Press.

Hardey, M., & Burrows, R. (2008). New cartographies of 'knowing capitalism' and the changing jurisdictions of empirical sociology. In N. Fielding, R. Lee & G. Blank (Eds), *The Sage handbook of online research methods* (pp. 507–518). London: Sage.

Hare, A. P. (1985). The significance of SYMLOG in the study of group dynamics. *International Journal of Small Group Research, 1*(1), 38–50.

Hare, S. E., & Hare, A. P. (1996). *SYMLOG field theory.* Westport, CT: Praeger.

Harkness, J. A., Braun, M., Edwards, B., Johnson, T. P., Lyberg, L. E., Mohler, P. Ph., Pennell, B. E., & Smith, T. W (Eds) (2010). *Survey methods in multicultural, multinational, and multiregional contexts.* Oxford: Wiley.

Harris, D. A., & Parisi, D. (2007). Adapting life history calendars for qualitative research on welfare transitions. *Field Methods, 19,* 40–58.

Hayashi, C. (1956). Theory and examples of quantification (II). *Proceedings of the Institute of Statistics and Mathematics, 4*(2), 19–30.

He, J., Tan, A. H., & Tan, C. L. (2000). A comparative study on Chinese text categorization methods. In PRICAI2000 Workshop on Text and Web Mining, Melbourne, pp. 24–35.

Hearst, M. (2003). What is text mining? Available at: https://people.ischool.berkeley.edu/~hearst/text-mining.html

Heise, D. R. (1969). Problems in path analysis and causal inference. In E. Borgatta (Ed.), *Sociological methodology.* San Francisco, CA: Jossey-Bass

Held, M. B. E. (2019). Decolonizing research paradigms. The context of settler colonialism: an unsettling, mutual, and collaborative effort. *International Journal of Qualitative Methods, 18,* 1–16. doi:10.1177/1609406918821574.

Helmer, O. (1963). *The Systematic Use of Expert Judgment in Operations Research. P-2795.* Santa Monica (CA): The RAND Corporation.

Helmer, O. (1964). *Convergence of expert consensus through feedback. P-2973.* Santa Monica, CA: The RAND Corporation.

Helmer, O. (1966). *The use of the Delphi Technique in problems of educational innovation. P-3499.* Santa Monica, CA: The RAND Corporation.

Helmer, O. (1967a). *Systematic use of expert opinions. P-3721.* Santa Monica, CA: The RAND Corporation.

Helmer, O. (1967b). *Analysis of the future: The Delphi method. P-3558.* Santa Monica, CA: The RAND Corporation.

Helmer, O. (1967c). *The future of science. P-3607.* Santa Monica, CA: The RAND Corporation.

Helmer, O. (1972). Cross-impact gaming. *Futures, 4,* 149–167.

Helmer, O., & Rescher, N. (1959). On the epistemology of the inexact sciences. *Management Science, 6*(1), 25–52.

Hesse-Biber, S. (2010a). Qualitative approaches to mixed methods practice. *Qualitative Inquiry, 16*(6), 455–468.

Hesse-Biber, S. (2010b). Emerging methodologies and methods practices in the field of mixed methods research, *Qualitative Inquiry, 16*(6), 415–418.

Hesse-Biber, S. (2015). Mixed methods research: The 'thing-ness' problem. *Qualitative Health Research, 25*(6), 775–788.

Hillmer, B. H., & Blubaugh, J. A. (1994). SYMLOG in the communication classroom: Applications for small group communication behavior awareness. Paper presented at the Annual Meeting of the Speech Communication Association (80th, New Orleans, LA, 19–22 November 1994).

Hogenraad, R., Mckenzie, D., & Peladeau, N. (2003). Force and influence in content analysis: The production of new social knowledge. *Quality and Quantity, 37*(3), 221–238.

Holstein, J. A., & Gubrium, J. F. (1995). *The active interview*. Thousand Oaks, CA: Sage.

Holstein, J. A., & Gubrium, J. F. (1999). What is family? Further thoughts on a social constructionist approach. *Marriage & Family Review, 28*(3–4), 3–20.

Holsti, O. R. (1969). *Content Analysis for the Social Sciences and Humanities*. Reading, MA: Addison-Wesley.

Hoppin, J., Tolbert, P., Flagg, E., Blair, A., & Zahm, S. (1998). Use of a life events calendar approach to elicit occupational history from farmers. *American Journal of Industrial Medicine, 34*, 470–476.

Houtkoop-Steenstra, H. (2000). *Interaction and the standardized survey interview: The living questionnaire*. Cambridge: Cambridge University Press.

Howe, K. R. (1988). Against the quantitative–qualitative incompatibility thesis or dogmas die hard. *Educational Researcher, 17*, 10–16.

Howe, K. R. (2004). A critique of experimentalism. *Qualitative Inquiry, 10*(4), 42–61.

Howell Smith, M. C., Babchuk, W. A., Stevens, J., Garrett, A. L., Wang, S. C., & Guetterman, T. C. (2020). Modeling the use of mixed methods – grounded theory: Developing scales for a new measurement model. *Journal of Mixed Methods Research, 14*(2), 184–206.

Hoxtell, A. (2019). Automation of qualitative content analysis. *Forum: Qualitative Social Research, 20*(3), Article 15.

Hsieh, H. F., & Shannon, S. E. (2005). Three approaches to qualitative content analysis. *Qualitative Health Research, 15*(9), 1277–1288.

Hyden, L. C. (1995). Illness, time and narrative. In D. Trakas (Ed.), *Issues in research perspectives and methodology from the behavioural sciences*. Athens: Institute of Child Health.

Hymes, D. H. (1978). *What is ethnography? Working paper in sociolinguistics*, 45. Austin, TX: Southwest Educational Development.

International Conference on Tools with Artificial Intelligence (9th), ICTAI '97, Newport Beach, CA, USA, November 3–8, 1997. IEEE Computer Society 1997.

Isenberg, D. J., & Ennis, J. G. (1981). Perceiving group members: A comparison of derived and imposed dimensions. *Journal of Personality and Social Psychology, 41*, 293–305.

Ivankova, N. V. (2014). Implementing quality criteria in designing and conducting a sequential QUAN ! QUAL mixed methods study of student engagement with learning applied research methods online. *Journal of Mixed Methods Research, 8*(1), 25–51.

Ivankova, N. V. (2015). *Mixed methods applications in action research: From methods to community action*. Thousand Oaks, CA: Sage.

Ivankova, N., & Kawamura, Y. (2010). Emerging trends in the utilization of integration designs in the social, behavioural and health sciences. In A. Tashakkori & C. Teddlie (Eds), *The Sage handbook of mixed methods in social and behavioral research* (2nd ed., pp. 581–611). Thousand Oaks, CA: Sage.

Jacobs, T., & Tschötschel, R. (2019). Topic models meet discourse analysis: A quantitative tool for a qualitative approach. *International Journal of Social Research Methodology, 22*(5), 469–485.

James, L. E., & Burke, D. M. (2000). Phonological priming effects on word retrieval and tip-of-the-tongue experiences in young and older adults. *Journal of Experimental Psychology: Learning, Memory, and Cognition, 26*(6), 1378–1391.

Jaworska, S., & Nanda, A. (2016). Doing well by talking good. *Applied Linguistics, 14*, 1–28.

Jellison, S., Roberts, R., Bowers, A., Combs, T., Beaman, J., Wayant, C., & Vassar, M. (2019). Evaluation of spin in abstracts of papers in psychiatry and psychology journals. *BMJ Evidence-Based Medicine*, doi 10.1136/bmjebm-2019–111176.

Jewitt, C. (2014). *The Routledge handbook of multimodal analysis*. London: Routledge.

Jick, T. D. (1979). Mixing qualitative and quantitative methods: Triangulation in action. *Administrative Science Quarterly, 24*(4), 602–611.

Jillson, I. (1975). Developing guidelines for the Delphi method. *Technological Forecasting and Social Change, 7*, 221–222.

Johnson, B., & Onwuegbuzie, A. (2004). Mixed methods research: A research paradigm whose time has come. *Educational Researcher, 33*(7), 14–26.

Johnson, R. B., Onwuegbuzie, A. J., & Turner, L. A. (2007). Toward a definition of mixed methods research. *Journal of Mixed Methods Research, 1*(2), 112–133.

Jung, J-K. (2009). Computer-aided qualitative GIS: A software-level integration of qualitative research and GIS. In M. Cope & S. Elwood (Eds), *Qualitative GIS: A new approach* (pp. 115–135). London: Sage.

Jung, J.-K., & Elwood, S. (2010). Extending the qualitative capabilities of GIS. *Transactions in GIS, 14*(1), 63–87.

Karanikas, H., & Manchester, B. T. (2001). *Knowledge discovery in text and text mining software*. Centre for Research in Information Management, UK.

Karasz, A., & Singelis, T. M. (2009). Qualitative and mixed methods research in cross-cultural psychology. *Journal of Cross-Cultural Psychology, 40*(6), 909–916.

Kearney, M. W. (2020). rtweet. R package version 0.7.6. https://CRAN.R-project.org/package=rtweet.

Keeney, S., Hasson, F., & McKenna, H. (2006). Consulting the oracle: Ten lessons from using the Delphi technique in nursing research. *Journal of Advanced Nursing, 53*(2), 205–212.

Kelle, U. (1997). Theory building in qualitative research and computer programs for the management of textual data. *Sociological Research Online, 2*(2).

Kelle, U. (2001). Sociological explanations between micro and macro and the integration of qualitative and quantitative methods. *Forum: Qualitative Social Research, 2*(1), online. https://doaj.org/article/88b7a0c54b7342e8ade7a8113e63a0fa.

Kelly, L., & Duran, R. L. (1985a). Interaction and performance in small groups: A descriptive report. *International Journal of Small Group Research, 1*(2), 182–192.

Kelly, L., & Duran, R. L. (1985b). *The SYMLOG approach: A descriptive of small group performance*. Paper presented at the annual conference of the Speech Communication Association, Chicago.

Kennedy, H. (2012). Perspectives on sentiment analysis. *Journal of Broadcasting & Electronic Media, 56*(4), 435–450.

Kerlinger, F. N. (1966). *Foundations of behavioral research*. New York: Holt, Rinehart and Winston.

Kerlinger, F. N. (1986). *Foundations of behavioral research* (3rd ed.). New York: Holt, Rinehart and Winston.

Keyton, J., & Springston, J. (1990). Redefining cohesiveness in groups. *Small Group Research, 21*(2), 234–254.

Keyton, J., & Wall, V. D. (1989). Theory and method for measuring group and organizational communication. *Management Communication Quarterly, 2*(4), 544–567.

Knigge, L., & Cope, M. (2006). Grounded visualization: Integrating the analysis of qualitative and quantitative data through grounded theory and visualization. *Environmental Planning A, 38*, 2021–2037.

Knoblauch, H., & Schnettler, B. (2012). Videography: analysing video data as a 'focused' ethnographic and hermeneutical exercise. *Qualitative Research, 12*(3), 334–356.

Knoblauch, H., & Tuma, R. (2011). Videography: an interpretive approach to video-recorded micro-social interaction. In E. Margolis & L. Pauwels (Eds), *The SAGE handbook of visual methods* (pp. 414–430). Thousand Oaks, CA: Sage.

Koenigs, R. (1993). A cross-cultural view of leadership and teamwork: Attractors for affectiveness. Paper presented at the SYMLOG Cross-Cultural research Conference, Milan, Italy, September 3–5.

Korzybski, Alfred H. S. (1933). *Science and sanity: an introduction to non-Aristotelian systems and general semantics*. Chicago, IL: International Non-Aristotelian Library, Institute of General Semantics.

Kracauer, K. (1952). The challenge of qualitative content analysis. *Public Opinion Quarterly, 16*(4), 631–642.

Kramer, A., Guillory, J., & Hancock, J. (2014). Experimental evidence of massive-scale emotional contagion. *Proceedings of the United States National Academy of Sciences, 111*, 8788–8790.

Kress, G., & van Leeuwen, T. J. (2001). *Multimodal discourse: The modes and media of contemporary communication*. London: Arnold.

Krippendorff, K. (1980). *Content analysis: An introduction to its methodology*. London: Sage.

Krippendorff, K. (2004) Reliability in content analysis, *Human Communication Research, 30* (3), 411–433.

Krippendorff, K. (2018). *Content analysis: An introduction to its methodology* (4th ed.). London: Sage.

Krontoft, A., Fuglsang, L., & Kronborg, H. (2018). Innovation activity among nurses: The translation and preliminary validation of the Bricolage measure – a mixed-method study. *Nordic Journal of Nursing Research, 38*(3), 151–159.

Kuckartz, U. (2019). Qualitative content analysis: From Kracauer's beginnings to today's challenges. *Forum: Qualitative Social Research, 20*(3), Article 12.

Kuhn, T. (1962). *The structure of scientific revolutions*. Chicago, IL: University of Chicago Press.

Kvale, S. (2006). Dominance through interviews and dialogues. *Qualitative Inquiry, 12*(3), 480–500.

La Rocca, G. (2007). Tecniche di analisi qualitativa online. Software, media testi. Roma: Edizioni Kappa.

La Rocca, G. (2009). Organizzare l'informazione etnografica. Il ruolo dei CAQDAS. Rassegna Italiana di Sociologia, 1, 133–160.

La Rocca, G. (2018a). *Against Big Data? Using multimodal content analysis to reconstruct a semantic of hashtags*. Paper presented at the International Conference on Unspoken, Unseen, Unheard of Unexplored Realities in Qualitative Research, St. Gallen, Switzerland.

La Rocca, G. (2018b). *Nuove forme di comunicazione sociale. Antifragilità, communication voice, studio di caso*. Rome: Carocci.

La Rocca, G. (2019). *Mediatization of emotions*. Keynote lecture at the Ceecom 2019 – 12th Central and Eastern European Communication and Media Conference, Sofia, Bulgaria.

La Rocca, G. (2020a). Possible selves of a hashtag: Moving from the theory of speech acts to cultural objects to interpret hashtags. *International Journal of Sociology and Anthropology*, 12(1), 1–9.

La Rocca, G. (2020b). La fuerza de un signo. Perspectivas teóricas para el análisis de los hashtags #. *Barataria*, 27, 46–61.

La Rocca, G., & Rinaldi, C. (2020). LGBTQI+ icons between resistance and normalization: Looking for mediatization of emotions in hashtags. *Revue Internationale de Sociologie*, 30(1), 26–45.

Labov, W. (1982). Speech actions and reactions in personal narrative. In D. Tannen (Ed.), *Analyzing Discourse: Text and Talk* (pp. 219–247). Washington, DC: Georgetown University Press.

Labov, W. (2006). *Variation theory and the utility of linguistics*. Paper presented to Faire Signe, a colloquium in honor of Pierre Encrevé, Paris, October 18.

Lancia, F. (2018). *User's manual: Tools for text analysis*. T-Lab version Plus 2018.

Langenwalter, S. (1967). History of a questionnaire. New York: Columbia University Bureau of Applied Social Research, mimeo.

Laricchiuta, D., Greco, F., Piras, F., Cordella, B., Cutuli, D., Picerni E., et al. (2018). 'The grief that doesn't speak': Text mining and brain structure. In D. F. Iezzi, L. Celardo & M. Misuraca (Eds), JADT '18: Proceedings of the 14th International Conference on Statistical Analysis of Textual Data (pp. 419–427). Rome: Universitalia.

Law, J. (Ed.) (1986). *Power, action, and belief: A new sociology of knowledge?* London: Routledge and Kegan Paul.

Lazarsfeld, P. F. (1958). Evidence and inference in social research. *Daedalus, 87*(4), 99–130.

Lazarsfeld, P., & Oberschall, A. (1965). Max Weber and empirical social research. *American Sociological Review, 30*(2), 185–199.

Lebart, L., & Salem, A. (1994). *Statistique textuelle*. Paris: Dunod.

Lebart, L., Salem, A., & Berry, L. (1998). *Exploring textual data*. New York: Springer.

Lee, B. (2017). The fundamentals of Q methodology. *Journal of Research Methodology, 2*(2), 57–95.

Lee, S., Song, J., & Kim, Y. (2010). An empirical comparison of four text mining methods. *Journal of Computer Information Systems, 51*(1), 1–10.

Lee, V., Coombe, L., Mahoney, R., Allen, C., & Robinson, P. (2018). Incorporating Indigenous and non-Indigenous worldviews through innovative text analysis: An evaluation of Indigenous public health curricula. *International Journal of Qualitative Methods, 17*, 1–11.

Leskovec, J., Rajaraman, A., & Ullman, J. (2011). *Mining of massive datasets*. Cambridge: Cambridge University Press.

Levy, K., & Franklin, M. (2014). Driving regulation: using topic models to examine political contention. *Social Science Computer Review, 32*(2), 182–194.

Lewin, K. (1952). *Field theory in social science*. New York: Harper & Row.

Liamputtong, P. (2010). *Performing qualitative cross-cultural research*. Cambridge, UK: Cambridge University Press.

Lieber, E. (2009). Mixing qualitative and quantitative methods: Insights into design and analysis issues. *Journal of Ethnographical & Qualitative Research, 3*, 218–227.

Likert, R. (1932). A technique for the measurement of attitudes. *Archives of Psychology, 22*(140), 1–55.

Lincoln, Y. S., & Guba, E. G. (1985). *Naturalistic inquiry*. Beverly Hills, CA: Sage.

Linstone H. A., & Turoff M. (Eds) (1975). *The Delphi Method: Techniques and applications*. Reading, MA: Addison-Wesley Publ. Co.

Liu, B. (2012). *Sentiment analysis: Mining opinions, sentiments, and emotions*. San Rafael, CA: Morgan & Claypool.

Loftus, E. F., & Marburger, W. (1983). Since the eruption of Mt. St. Helens, did anyone beat you up? Improving the accuracy of retrospective reports with landmark events. *Memory & Cognition, 2*, 114–120.

Louah, L., & Visser, M. (2016). Q methodology, a useful tool to foster multi-actor innovation networks performance. In *IFSA Symposium 2016*. Newport, UK: International Farming Systems Association.

Luyt, R. (2012). A framework for mixing methods in quantitative measurement development, validation, and revision: A case study. *Journal of Mixed Methods Research, 6*(4), 294–316.

Lyman, S., & Scott, M. (1970). *A sociology of the absurd.* Pacific Palisades, CA: Goodyear.

Madge, J. (1962). *The origins of scientific sociology.* New York: Free Press.

Manning, C. D., & Schütze, H. (1999). *Foundation of Statistical Natural Language Processing.* Cambridge: MIT Press.

Manning, P., & Cullum-Swan, E. (1994). Narrative, content and semiotic analysis. In N. Denzin & Y. Lincoln (Eds), *Handbook of qualitative research* (pp. 436–477). Thousand Oaks, CA: Sage.

Marchand, P. (1998). *L'Analyse du discours assistèe par ordinateur: Concepts, méthods, outils.* Paris: Colin.

Mark, G., & Boulton, A. (2017). Indigenising photovoice: Putting Māori cultural values into a research method. *Forum: Qualitative Social Research, 18*(3), Art. 19. Online. https://doi.org/10.17169/fqs-18.3.2827.

Marradi, A. (1981). Misurazione e scale: qualche riflessione e una proposta. *Quaderni di Sociologia, 29*(4), 595–639.

Marradi, A. (1984). *Concetti e metodo per la ricerca sociale.* Florence: La Giuntina.

Marradi, A. (1985). Unità di misura e unità di conto. *Rassegna Italiana di Sociologia, 24*(2), 229–238.

Martel, R., Shepherd, M., & Goodyear-Smith, F. (2021). He awa whiria – a 'braided river': An Indigenous Māori approach to mixed methods research. *Journal of Mixed Methods Research.* doi.org/10.1177/1558689820984028.

Martyn, K. K. (2009). Adolescent health research and clinical assessment: Using self-administered event history calendar. In R. F. Belli, R. P. Stafford & D. F. Alwin (Eds), *Calendar and time diary methods in life course research* (pp. 69–86). Thousand Oaks, CA: Sage.

Mason, J. (1996). *Qualitative Researching.* Thousand Oaks, CA: Sage.

Mason, J. (2006). Mixing methods in a qualitatively-driven way. *Qualitative Research, 6*(1), 9–25.

Mason, W., Morris, K., Webb, C., et al. (2019). Towards full integration of quantitative and qualitative methods in case study research, *Journal of Mixed Methods Research,* https://doi.org/10.1177%2F1558689819857972.

Maxcy, S. (2003). Pragmatic threads in mixed methods research in the social sciences: The search for multiple modes of inquiry and the end of the philosophy of formalism. In A. Tashakkori & C. Teddlie (Eds), *The Sage handbook of mixed methods in social and behavioral research* (pp. 51–90). Thousand Oaks, CA: Sage.

Maxwell, J. A. (2010). Using numbers in qualitative research. *Qualitative Inquiry,* *20*(10), 1–8.

Maxwell, J. A. (2012). The importance of qualitative research for causal explanation in education. *Qualitative Inquiry, 18*(8), 655–661.

Maxwell, J. A (2013). *Qualitative research design: An interactive approach* (3rd ed.). London: Sage.

Maxwell, J. A. (2016). Expanding the history and range of mixed methods research. *Journal of Mixed Methods Research, 10*(1), 12–27.

Maxwell, J., & Loomis, D. (2003). Mixed methods design: An alternative approach. In A. Tashakkori & C. Teddlie (Eds), *The Sage handbook of mixed methods in social and behavioral research* (pp. 241–272. Thousand Oaks, CA: Sage.

Maynard, D. W., Houtkoop-Steenstra, H., Schaeffer, N. C., & Van der Zouwen, J. (Eds) (2002). *Standardization and tacit knowledge: Interaction and practice in the survey interview.* New York: Wiley.

Mayring, P. (1983). *Qualitative Inhaltsanalyse.* Weinheim: Beltz.

Mayring, P. (2000). Qualitative content analysis. *Forum Qualitative Social Research, 1*(2), Article 20.

Mayring, P. (2012). Qualitative Inhaltsanalyse – ein Beispiel für Mixed Methods. In M. Glazer-Zikuda et al. (Eds), *Mixed Methods in der empirischen Bildungsforschung* (pp. 27–36). Munster: Waxmann.

McKenna, H. P. (1994). The Delphi technique: A worthwhile research approach for nursing? *Journal of Advanced Nursing,* 19, 1221–1225.

McKeown, B., & Thomas, D. (1988). *Q methodology* (2nd ed. 2013). Newbury Park, CA: Sage.

Mead, D., & Moseley, L. (2001). The use of Delphi as a research approach. *Nurse Researcher, 8*(4), 4–23.

Mertens, D. M. (2003). Mixed methods and the politics of human research: the transformative-emancipatory perspective. In A. Tashakkori & C. Teddlie (Eds), *The Sage handbook of mixed methods in social and behavioral research* (pp. 135–164). Thousand Oaks, CA: Sage.

Mertens, D. M., & Hesse-Biber, S. (2013). Mixed methods and credibility of evidence in research. *New Directions for Evaluation, 138*, 5–13.

Mertens, D., Bazeley, P., Bowleg, L., Fielding, N., Maxwell, J., Molina-Azerin, J., & Niglas, K. (2016). Expanding thinking through a kaleidoscopic look into the future. *Journal of Mixed Methods Research, 10*(3), 221–227.

Miles, M. B., & Huberman, M. A. (1984). *Qualitative data analysis: A sourcebook of new methods.* Beverly Hills, CA: Sage.

Mills, T. M. (1984). *The sociology of small groups.* Englewood Cliffs, NJ: Prentice Hall.

Miner, G., Elder, J., Fast, A., Hill, T., Nisbet, R., & Delen, D. (2012). *Practical text mining and statistical analysis for non-structured text data applications*. Cambridge: Academic Press.

Mishler, E. G. (1986). *Research interviewing: Context and narrative*. Cambridge, MA: Harvard University Press.

Moerman, G. A. (2010). *Probing behaviour in open interviews: A field experiment on the effects of probing tactics on quality and content of the received information*. Amsterdam: VU University Amsterdam.

Mohr, J., & Bogdanov, P. (2013). Introduction – topic models: what they are and why they matter. *Poetics*, 41, 545–569.

Montes-y-Gomez, M., Gelbukh, A. F., & Lòpez-Lòpez, A. (2001). Discovering ephemeral associations among new topics. In Proceedings of the 13th International Joint Conferences on Artificial Intelligence, Inc. (IJCAI2001). Seattle, WA.

Morehouse, R. E. (2011). *Beginning interpretative inquiry. A step by step approach to research and evaluation*. London: Routledge.

Moreno, J. L. (1953). *Who shall survive?* New York: Beacon House.

Morgan, D. L. (2007). Paradigms lost and pragmatism regained: Methodological implications of combining qualitative and quantitative methods. *Journal of Mixed Methods Research*, 1, 48–76.

Morgan, D. L. (2014). Pragmatism as a paradigm for social research. *Qualitative Inquiry*, 20, 1045–1053.

Morgan, D. L. (2018). Living within blurry boundaries. *Journal of Mixed Methods Research*, 12(3), 268–279.

Morgan, D. L. (2019). Commentary: After triangulation, what next? *Journal of Mixed Methods Research*, 13(1), 6–14.

Morse, J. M. (2005). Evolving trends in qualitative research: Advances in mixed methods designs. *Qualitative Health Research*, 15(5), 583–585.

Morse, J.M., & Niehaus, L. (2009). *Mixed method design*. London: Eurospan.Moss, L., & Goldstein, H. (Eds) (1979). *The recall method in social surveys*. Windsor: NFER.

Murry, J. W. J., & Hammons, J. O. (1995). Delphi: A versatile methodology for conducting qualitative research. *The Review of Higher Education*, 18(4), 423–436.

Nastasi, B. K., Hitchcock, J. C., & Brown, L. M. (2010). An inclusive framework for conceptualizing mixed methods design typologies: Moving toward fully integrated synergistic research models. In A. Tashakkori & C. Teddlie (Eds), *The Sage handbook of mixed methods in social and behavioral research* (2nd ed., pp. 305–337). Thousand Oaks, CA: Sage.

Navathe, S. B., & Elmasri, R. (2000). *Fundamentals of Database Systems*. Singapore: Pearson Education, Inc.

Nelson, I. A. (2010). From quantitative to qualitative: Adapting the life history calendar method. *Field Methods, 22*(4), 413–428.

Nico, M., & Van der Vaart, W. (2012). Between an 'undoable science' and a 'new kind of research': Life course methods to study turning points and landmarks. In H. Kunneman (Ed.), *Good work: The ethics of craftsmanship* (p. 170–182). Amsterdam: Humanistics University Press.

Niglas, K. (2010). The multidimensional model of research methodology. In A. Tashakkori & C. Teddlie (Eds), *The Sage handbook of mixed methods in social and behavioral research* (2nd ed., pp. 215–235). Thousand Oaks, CA: Sage.

Nilsen, A., & Brannen, J. (2010). The use of mixed methods in biographical research. In Tashakkori, A., & Teddlie, C. (Eds), *The Sage handbook of mixed methods in social and behavioral research* (2nd ed., pp. 677–696). Thousand Oaks, CA: Sage.

Noelle-Neumann, E. (1970). Wanted: Rules for wording structured questionnaires. *Public Opinion Quarterly, 33*(2), 191–201.

Nonaka, I., & Takeuchi, H. (1995). *The knowledge-creating company: How Japanese companies create the dynamics of innovation*. Oxford: Oxford University Press.

Norman, D., & Helmer, O. (1963). An Experimental Application of the Delphi Method to the Use of Experts. *Management Science, 9*(3), 458–467.

Nuckols, R. (1953). A note on pre-testing public opinion questions. *Journal of Applied Psychology, 37*(2), 119–120.

O'Cathain, A. (2010). Assessing the quality of mixed methods research. In A. Tashakkori & C. Teddlie (Eds), *The Sage handbook of mixed methods in social and behavioral research* (2nd ed., pp. 531–555). Thousand Oaks, CA: Sage.

O'Cathain, A., Murphy, E., & Nicholl, J. (2007). Integration and publications as indicators of 'yield' from mixed methods studies. *Journal of Mixed Methods Research, 1*(2), 147–153.

O'Halloran, H. L. (2008). Systemic functional-multimodal discourse analysis (SF-MDA): constructing ideational meaning using language and visual imagery. *Visual Communication, 7*(4), 443–475.

O'Halloran, K. L. (2011). Multimodal discourse analysis. In K. Hyland & B. Paltridge (Eds), *Companion to discourse* (pp. 120–137). London: Continuum.

Onwuegbuzie, A. J., & Collins, K. M. (2007). A typology of mixed methods sampling designs in social science research. *The Qualitative Report, 12*(2), 281–316.

Onwuegbuzie, A. J., & Johnson, R. B. (2006). The validity issue in mixed research. *Research in the Schools, 13*(1), 48–63.

Onwuegbuzie, A. J., & Leech, N. L. (2005). On becoming a pragmatic researcher: The importance of combining quantitative and qualitative research methodologies. *International Journal of Social Research Methodology, 8*(5), 375–387.

Oppenheim, A. N. (1966). *Questionnaire design and attitude measurement.* New York: Basic Books.

Orlik, P. (1989). SYMLOG – wieder ein 'New Look', der in die Jahre kommt? [SYMLOG: Another 'new look' in the coming year?]. *Gruppendynamik, 19*, 221–241.

Osgood, C. E., Suci, G. J., & Tannenbaum, H. P. (1957). *The measurement of meaning.* Urbana, IL: University of Illinois Press.

Papacharissi, Z. (2015). Affective publics and structures of storytelling: Sentiment, events and mediality. *Information, Communication & Society,* 1–18.

Parsons, T., Bales, R. F., & Shils, E. A. (1953a). Phase movement in relation to motivation, symbol formation, and role structure. In T. Parsons, R. F. Bales & E. A. Shils (Eds), *Working papers in the theory of action* (pp. 163–269). New York: Free Press.

Parsons, T., Bales, R. F., & Shils, E. A. (Eds). (1953b). *Working papers in the theory of action.* New York: Free Press.

Pawson, R., & Tilley, N. (1997). *Realistic evaluation.* London: Sage.

Payne, G., & Williams, M. (2005). Generalization in qualitative research. *Sociology, 39*(2), 295–314.

Pearce, D. (2012). Mixed methods inquiry in sociology. *American Behavioral Scientist, 56*, 829–848.

Peltier, C. (2018). An application of two-eyed seeing: Indigenous research methods with participatory action research. *International Journal of Qualitative Methods, 17*, 1–12.

Pitrone, M. C. (1984). *Il sondaggio.* Milan: Angeli.

Plano Clark, V. (2010). Applying three strategies for integrating quantitative and qualitative databases. *Field Methods, 22*(2), 154–174.

Plano Clark, V. L., Anderson, N., Wertz, J. A., Zhou, Y., Schumacher, K., & Miaskowski, C. (2015). Conceptualizing longitudinal mixed methods designs: A methodological review of health sciences research. *Journal of Mixed Methods Research, 9*(4), 297–319.

Platt, J. (1996) *The history of research methods in America 1920–1960,* Cambridge: Cambridge University Press.

Polanyi, M. (1967). *The tacit dimension.* Chicago, IL: University of Chicago Press.

Polit, D. F., & Beck, C. T. (2008). *Nursing research: Generating and assessing evidence for nursing practice* (8th ed.). Philadelphia: Lippincott Williams & Wilkins.

Polley, R. B. (1984). *SYMLOG* [Computer program]. Portland, OR: Author.

Polley, R. B. (1985). The diagnosis of intact work groups. *Consultation, 4*(4), 273–283.

Polley, R. B. (1986). Rethinking the third dimension. *International Journal of Small Group Research, 2*(2), 134–142.

Polley, R. B. (1987). Dimensions of social interaction: A method for the improvement of rating scales. *Social Psychology Quarterly, 50*(1), 72–82.

Polley, R. B. (1991). Group process as diagnostic: an introduction. *Small Group Research, 22*(1), 92–98.

Polley, R.B. (1989). *GFD: Group field dinamics* [Computer program]. Portland, OR: Author.

Polley, R. B., Hare, A. P., & Stone, P. J. (1988). *The SYMLOG practitioner: Applications of small group research.* New York: Praeger.

Popper, K. (1935). *Logik der Forschung.* Vienna: Julius Springer. English trans. (1959) *The logic of scientific discovery.* London: Hutchison.

Popping, R. (2012). Qualitative decisions in quantitative text analysis research. *Sociological Methodology, 42*, 88–90.

Popping, R., & Roberts, C. W. (2009). Coding issues in semantic text analysis. *Field Methods, 21*(3), 244–264.

Poth, C. N. (2018). *Innovation in mixed methods research: A practical guide to integrative thinking with complexity.* London: Sage.

Powell, C. (2003). The Delphi technique: myths and realities. *Methodological Issues in Nursing Research, 41*, 376–382.

Psathas, G. (1995). *Conversation analysis: The study of talk-in-interaction.* London: Sage.

Quetulio-Navarra, M., Van der Vaart, W., & Niehof, A. (2015). Can 'third-party help' improve data quality in research interviews? A natural experiment in a hard to study population. *Field Methods, 27*(4), 426–440.

Raadgever, G. T., Mostert, E., & van de Giesen, N. C. (2008). Measuring perspectives on future flood management on the Rhine: Application and discussion of Q methodology. *Hydrology and Earth System Sciences Discussions, 5*, 437–474.

Ragin, C. (1987). *The comparative method: Moving beyond qualitative and quantitative strategies.* Berkeley, CA: University of California Press.

Ragin, C. (1995). Using qualitative comparative analysis to study configurations. In U. Kelle (Ed.), *Computer-aided qualitative data analysis* (pp. 177–189). Thousand Oaks, CA: Sage.

Ragin, C. (2000). *Fuzzy-set social science.* Chicago, IL: University of Chicago Press.

Rathnayake, C., & Suthers, D. D. (2018). Twitter issue response hashtags as affordances for momentary connectedness. *Social Media + Society*, 1–14. doi:10.1177/2056305118784780.

Rauch, W. (1979). The Decision Delphi. *Technological Forecasting and Social Change, 15*(3), 159–69.

Régnier, F. (1986). Un outil de décision pour l'entreprise. *Cpe Bulletin, 27*(May), 89–100.

Reichertz, J. (2007). Qualitative Sozialforschung. *Erwägen-Wissen-Ethik*, *18*(2), 195–208.

Reid, B. (2020). Positionality and research: 'Two-eyed seeing' with a rural Ktaqmkuk Mi'kmaw community. *International Journal of Qualitative Methods*, *19*, 1–12. doi:10.1177/1609406920910841.

Reimer, M., & Matthes, B. (2007). Collecting event histories with TrueTales: Techniques to improve autobiographical recall problems in standardized interviews. *Quality and Quantity*, *41*(5), 711–735.

Rickert, H. (1926). *Kulturwissenschaft und Naturwissenschaft*. Tübingen: Verlag von J. C. B. Mohr (Paul Siebeck).

Riesman, D. (1958). Some observations on the interviewing in the teacher apprehension study. In P. F. Lazarsfeld & T. Wagner Jr., *The academic mind* (pp. 266–370). Glencoe, IL: Free Press.

Riessman, C. K. (1993). *Narrative analysis*. Newbury Park, CA: Sage.

Risdon, A., Eccleston, C., Crombez, G., & McCracken, L. (2003). How can we learn to live with pain? A Q-methodological analysis of the diverse understandings of acceptance of chronic pain. *Social Science & Medicine*, *56*, 375–386.

Roberts, J., & Mulvey, E. P. (2009). Reports of life events by individuals at high risk for violence. In R. F. Belli, R. P. Stafford & D. F. Alwin (Eds), *Calendar and time diary methods in life course research* (pp. 191–206). Thousand Oaks, CA: Sage.

Roberts, M., Stewart, B., Tingley, D., et al. (2014), Structural topic models for open-ended survey responses, *American Journal of Political Science*, 58 (4), 1064–1082.

Robinson, W. S. (1950). Ecological correlations and the behavior of individuals. *American Sociological Review*, *15*(3), 351–357.

Robson, C. (2011). *Real world research*. Oxford: Wiley.

Rogers C., & Dymond, R. (Eds) (1954). *Psychotherapy and personality change*. Chicago, IL: University of Chicago Press.

Rorty, R. (1979). *Philosophy and the mirror of nature*. Princeton, NJ: Princeton University Press.

Roth, J. (1963). *Timetables: Structuring the passage of time in hospital*. Indianapolis, IN: Bobbs-Merrill.

Rowe, G., Wright, G., & Bolger, F. (1991). Delphi: A reevaluation of research and theory. *Technological Forecasting and Social Change*, *39*(3), 235–251.

Rowe, G., Wright, G., & McColl, A. (2005). Judgment change during Delphi-like procedures: The role of majority influence, expertise, and confidence. *Technological Forecasting and Social Change*, *72*, 377–399.

Rucks-Ahidiana, Z., & Bierbaum, A. H. (2015). Qualitative spaces: Integrating spatial analysis for a mixed methods approach. *International Journal of Qualitative Methods, 14*(2), 92–103.

Ryen, A, & Gobo, G. (2011). Managing the decline of globalized methodology. *International Journal of Social Research Methodology, 14*(6), 411–415.

Rywick, T. (1987). SYMLOG rating form reliability. *International Journal of Small Group Research, 3*(1), 119–125.

Sackman, H. (1975). *Delphi-critique: Expert opinion, forecasting and group process.* Lexington, MA: Lexington Books.

Saetra, H. (2016). Exploring the use of agent-based modelling in mixed methods research (Unpublished dissertation). Ostfold University College, Halden, Norway.

Sandelowski, M. (2014). Unmixing mixed methods. *Research in Nursing and Health, 37*, 3–8.

Sandelowski, M., Voils, C. I., & Knafl, G. (2009). On quantitizing. *Journal of Mixed Methods Research, 3*(3), 208–222.

Sartori, G. (1970). Concept misformation in comparative politics. *American Political Science Review, 64*(4), 1033–1053.

Savaresi, S. M., & Boley, D. L. (2004). A comparative analysis on the bisecting K-means and the PDDP clustering algorithms. *Intelligent Data Analysis, 8*(4), 345–362.

Sayles, H., Belli, R. F., & Serrano, E. (2010). Interviewer variance between event history calendar and conventional questionnaire interviews. *Public Opinion Quarterly, 74*(1), 140–153.

Schaeffer, N. C. (1995). A decade of questions. *Journal of Official Statistics, 11*(1), 79–92.

Schatzman, L., & Strauss, A. L. (1973). *Field research.* Englewood Cliffs, NJ: Prentice Hall.

Schiebinger, L. (1993). Why mammals are called mammals: Gender politics in eighteenth-century natural history. *The American Historical Review, 98*(2), 382–411.

Schmolck, P. (2002). PQMethod (Version 2.11) [Computer software]. Neubiberg: University of the Bundeswehr Munich. Retrieved from http://schmolck.org/qmethod

Schober, M. F., & Conrad, F. G. (1997). Does conversational interviewing reduce survey measurement error? *Public Opinion Quarterly, 61*(4), 576–602.

Schober, M. F., & Conrad, F. (2002). A collaborative view of standardized survey interviews. In D. W. Maynard, H. Houtkoop-Streenstra, J. der Zouwen & N. C. Schaeffer (Eds), *Standardization and tacit knowledge* (pp. 67–94). New York: Wiley.

Schreier, M. (2012). *Qualitative content analysis in practice.* London: Sage.

Schreier, M. (2016). Kategorien – Codes – Kodieren. Keynote lecture, Conference 'Qualitative Inhaltsanayse – and beyond?'. Weingarten, Germany, 5 October.

Schreier M., Stamann, C., Janssen, M., Dahl, T., & Whittal, A. (2019). Qualitative content analysis: Conceptualizations and challenges in research practice. *Forum Qualitative Sozialforschung/Forum: Qualitative Social Research, 20*(3), Article 38.

Schuman, H., & Presser, S. (1979). The open and closed question. *American Sociological Review, 64*(5), 692–712.

Schuman, H., & Presser, S. (2000). *Questions and answers in attitude surveys: Experiments on question form, wording, and context.* Thousand Oaks, CA: Sage.

Schutz, A. (1953). Common-sense and scientific interpretation of human action. *Philosophy and Phenomenological Research, 14,* 1–38.

Schwarz, N., & Sudman, S. (Eds) (1994). *Autobiographical memory and the validity of retrospective reports.* New York: Springer-Verlag.

Sedoglavich, V., Akoorie, M. E. M., & Pavlovich, K. (2015). Measuring absorptive capacity in high-tech companies: Mixing qualitative and quantitative methods. *Journal of Mixed Methods Research, 9*(3), 252–272.

Sell, D. K., & Brown, S. R. (1984). Q methodology as a bridge between qualitative and quantitative research: Application to the analysis of attitude change in foreign study program participants. In J. L. Vacca & H. A. Johnson (Eds), *Qualitative research in education* (pp. 79–87). Kent, OH: Kent State University.

Selltiz, C., & Jahoda, M. (Eds) (1963). *Research methods in social relations.* New York: Holt & Rinehart.

Serafini, F., & Reid, S. F. (2019). Multimodal content analysis: Expanding analytical approaches to content analysis. *Visual Communication,* 1–27.

Sharp, H. (2019). Bricolage research in history education as a scholarly mixed-methods design. *History Education Research Journal, 16*(1), 50–62.

Shinebourne, P., & Adams, M. (2007). Q-methodology as a phenomenological research method. *Existential Analysis, 18*(1), 103–116.

Sieber, S. D. (1973). The integration of fieldwork and survey methods. *American Journal of Sociology, 78*(6), 1335–1359.

Silver, C., & Lewins, A. (2014). *Using software in qualitative research.* London: Sage.

Silverman, D. (1993). *Interpreting qualitative data: Methods for analysing talk, text and interaction.* London: Sage.

Silverman, D. (2000). *Doing qualitative research: A practical guide.* London: Sage.

Silverman, D. (2005). Instances or sequences? Improving the state of the art of qualitative research. *Forum Qualitative Sozialforschung/Forum: Qualitative Social Research, 6*(3), Art. 30, http://nbn-resolving.de/urn:nbn:de:0114-fqs0503301.

Silverman, D. (2017). How was it for you? The Interview Society and the irresistible rise of the (poorly analysed) interview. *Qualitative Research, 17*(2), 144–158.

Sjøvold, E. (2007). Systematizing person-group relations (SPGR). A field theory of social interaction. *Small Group Research, 38*(5), 615–635.

Smith, H. W. (1975). *Strategies of social research: The methodological imagination.* Englewood Cliffs, NJ.: Prentice Hall.

Smith, J. P., & Thomas, D. (2003). Remembrances of things past: Test–retest reliability of retrospective migration histories. *Journal of the Royal Statistical Society. Series A: Statistics in Society, 166*(1), 23–49.

Smith, N. W. (2001). *Current systems in psychology: History, theory, research, and applications.* Belmont, CA: Wadsworth/Thomson Learning.

Smythe, E. (2005). The thinking of research. In P. Ironside (Ed.), *Beyond method: Philosophical conversations in healthcare research and scholarship. Interpretive studies in health care and the human science*s, Vol. IV (pp. 223–258). Madison, WI: University of Wisconsin Press.

Sobell, L. C., Sobell, M. B., Leo, G. I., & Cancilla, A. (1988). Reliability of a timeline method: Assessing normal drinkers' reports of recent drinking and a comparative evaluation across several populations. *British Journal of Addiction, 83,* 393–402.

Solanke, I. (2009). Putting race and gender together: A new approach to intersectionality. *Modern Law Review, 72*(5), 723–749.

Solomon, M. J. (1981). Dimensions of interpersonal behavior: A convergent validation within a cognitive interactionist framework. *Journal of Personality, 49*(1), 15–26.

Stange, K. C., Crabtree, B. F., & Miller, W. L. (2006). Publishing multimethod research. *Annals of Family Medicine, 4*(4), 292–294.

Stangor, C. (2004). *Social groups in action and interaction.* New York: Psychology Press.

Stavrianou, A., Andritsos, P., & Nicoloyannis, N. (2007). Overview and semantic issues of text mining. *SIGMOD Record, 36*(3), 23–34.

Steinbach, M., Ertoz, L., & Kumar, V. (2003). Challenges of clustering high dimensional data. In L. T. Wille (Ed.), *New vistas in statistical physics – applications in econophysics, bioinformatics, and pattern recognition.* Springer-Verlag.

Steinbach, M., Karypis, G., & Kumara, V. (2000). A comparison of document clustering techniques. Paper presented at the meeting of the KDD Workshop on Text Mining, 2000. August 20–23, 2000, Boston, MA, USA.

Stephenson, W. (1935). Technique of factor analysis. *Nature, 136,* 297.

Stephenson, W. (1953). *The study of behavior: Q technique and its methodology*. Chicago, IL: University of Chicago Press.

Stephenson, W. (1967). *The play theory of mass communication*. Chicago, IL: University of Chicago Press.

Stephenson, W. (1977). Factors as operant subjectivity. *Operant Subjectivity, 1*(October), 3–16.

Stephenson, W. (1988). William James, Niels Bohr, and complementarity: V – phenomenology of subjectivity. *The Psychological Record, 38*, 203–219.

Stephenson, W. (2005). Theory and methodology for esthetics. *Operant Subjectivity, 28*(1/2), 13–32.

Stevens, S. S. (1946). On the theory of scales of measurement. *Science, 103*(2684), 677–680.

Stone, P., Bales, R., Namenwirth, J., & Ogilvie, D. (1962). The General Inquirer: A computer system for content analysis. *Behavioral Science, 7*(4), 484–498.

Strauss, A., & Corbin, J. (1990). *Basics of qualitative research*. London: Sage.

Strauss, A. L., Schatzman, L., Bucher, R., Ehrlich, D., & Sabshin, M. (1964). *Psychiatric ideologies and institutions*. New York: Free Press.

Suchman, L., & Jordan, B. (1990). Interactional troubles in face-to-face survey interviews. *Journal of the American Statistical Association, 85*(409), 232–253.

Sudman, S., & Bradburn, N. M. (1974). *Response effects in surveys: A review and synthesis*. Chicago, IL: Aldine.

Sudman, S., Bradburn, N. M., & Schwarz, N. (2010). *Thinking about answers: The application of cognitive processes to survey methodology*. San Francisco, CA: Wiley.

Tagg, S. K. (1985). Life story interviews and their interpretation. In M. Brenner, J. Brown & D. Canter (Eds), *The research interview* (pp. 163–199). London: Academic Press.

Tan, A. H. (1999). Text mining: The state of the art and the challenges. In *Proceedings of the Pacific Asia Conference on Knowledge Discovery and Data Mining* (pp. 65–70). Available at www.researchgate.net/publication/2471634_Text_Mining_The_state_of_the_art_and_the_challenges.

Tan, P. N., Steinbach, M., & Kumar, V. (2006). *Introduction to data mining*. Boston, MA: Pearson Addison–Wesley.

Tanur, J. M. (Ed.) (1992). *Questions about questions: Inquiries into the cognitive bases of surveys*. New York: Russell Sage Foundation.

Tashakkori, A. and Creswell, J. W. (2007). Editorial: The new era of mixed methods, *Journal of Mixed Methods Research 1*(1): 3–7.

Tashakkori, A., & Teddlie, C. (1998). *Mixed methodology: Combining qualitative and quantitative approaches*. Thousand Oaks, CA: Sage.

Tashakkori, A., & Teddlie, C. (Eds) (2003a) *The Sage handbook of mixed methods in social and behavioral research*. Thousand Oaks, CA: Sage.

Tashakkori, A., & Teddlie, C. (2003b). The past and future of mixed methods research: From data triangulation to mixed model designs. In A. Tashakkori & C. Teddlie (Eds), *The Sage handbook of mixed methods in social and behavioral research* (pp. 671–702). Thousand Oaks, CA: Sage.

Tashakkori, A., & Teddlie, C. (2010). *The Sage handbook of mixed methods in social and behavioral research* (2nd ed.). Thousand Oaks, CA: Sage.

Teddlie, C., & Tashakkori, A. (2010). Overview of contemporary issues in mixed methods research. In A. Tashakkori & C. Teddlie (Eds), *The Sage handbook of mixed methods in social and behavioral research* (2nd ed., pp. 1–41). Thousand Oaks, CA: Sage.

Teddlie, C., & Yu, F. (2007). Mixed methods sampling: A typology with examples. *Journal of Mixed Methods Research, 1*, 77–100.

Thelwall, M. (2017). Sentiment analysis for small and big data. In N. Fielding, G. Blank & R. M. Lee (Eds), *The Sage handbook of online research methods* (2nd ed.). London: Sage.

Thelwall, M., Buckley, K., Paltoglou, G., Cai, D., & Kappas, A. (2010). Sentiment strength detection in short informal text. *Journal of the American Society for Information Science and Technology, 61*(12), 2544–2558.

Thomas, D. B., & Baas, L. R. (1992). The issue of generalization in Q methodology: 'Reliable schematics' revisited. *Operant Subjectivity, 6*(1), 18–36.

Tong, R. (2001). An operational system for detecting and tracking opinions in on-line discussions. Working Notes of the ACM SIGIR 2001 Workshop on Operational Text Classification (pp. 1–6). New York: Association for Computing Machinery.

Torgerson, W. S. (1958). *Theory and methods of scaling*. New York: Wiley.

Tornberg, A., & Tornberg, P. (2016). Combining CDA and topic modelling. *Discourse & Society, 27*(4), 401–422.

Tourangeau, R., Rips, L. J., & Rasinski, K. (2000). *The psychology of survey response*. Cambridge: Cambridge University Press.

Tuhiwai Smith, L. (1999). *Decolonizing methodologies: Research and indigenous peoples*. New York: St Martin's Press.

Turoff, M. (1970). The design of a policy Delphi. *Technological Forecasting and Social Change, 2*(2), 149–171.

Uprichard, E., & Dawney, L. (2019). Data diffraction: Challenging data integration in mixed methods research. *Journal of Mixed Methods Research, 13*(1), 19–32.

Urban, J.B., Burgermaster, M., Archibald, T., & Byrne, A. (2015). Relationships between quantitative measures of evaluation plan and program model quality and a qualitative measure of participant perceptions of an evaluation capacity building approach. *Journal of Mixed Methods Research, 9*(2), 154–177.

Valenta, A. L., & Wigger, U. (1997). Q-methodology: Definition and application in health care informatics. *Journal of the American Medical Informatics Association, 4,* 501–510.

Van der Vaart, W. (1996). *Inquiring into the past. Data quality of responses to retrospective questions* (PhD thesis). Amsterdam: Vrije Universiteit.

Van der Vaart, W. (2004). The time-line as a device to enhance recall in standardized research interviews: A split ballot study. *Journal of Official Statistics, 20*(2), 301–317.

Van der Vaart, W., & Glasner, T. J. (2007). Applying a timeline as a recall aid in a telephone survey: A record check study. *Applied Cognitive Psychology, 21*(2), 217–238.

Van der Vaart, W., & Glasner, T. J. (2011). Personal landmarks as recall aids in survey, *Field Methods, 23*(1), 37–56.

van Rijsbergen, C. J. (1979) *Information Retrieval*, second edition. London: Butterworths.

van Zolingen, S., & Klaassen, C. (2003). Selection processes in a Delphi study about key qualifications in Senior Secondary Vocational Education. *Technological Forecasting and Social Change, 70*(4), 317–340.

Verd, J-M. (2013) Blending the focused ethnographic interview and case study. *Field Methods, 33* (1), 25–41.

Vidich, A. J., & Shapiro, G. (1955). A comparison of participant observation and survey data. *American Sociological Review, 20*(1), 28–33.

Vogt, P. W. (2008). Quantitative versus qualitative is a distraction: Variations on a theme by Brewer & Hunter (2006). *Methodological Innovations Online, 3*(1), 1–10.

Watts, S., & Stenner, P. (2005). Doing Q methodology: Theory, method and interpretation. *Qualitative Research in Psychology, 2*(1), 67–91.

Webb, E. J., Campbell, D. T., Schwartz, R. D., & Sechrest, L. (1966). *Unobtrusive measures. Nonreactive research in the social sciences*. Chicago, IL: Rand McNally.

Weber, M. (1922). *Gesammelte Aufsätze zur Wissenschaftslehre*. English trans. (1949) *The methodology of the social sciences*. New York: Free Press.

Webler, T., Levine, D., Rakel, H., & Renn, O. (1991). A novel approach to reducing uncertainty: The group Delphi. *Technological Forecasting and Social Change, 39*(3), 253–263.

Weick, K. E. (1985). Systematic observational methods. In G. Lindzey (Ed.), *Handbook of social psychology* (3rd ed., pp. 567–634). New York: Random House.

Weick, K. E. (1995). *Sensemaking in organizations*. London: Sage.

Wells, A.J. (2002). Gibson's affordances and turing's theory of computation. *Ecological Psychology*, 14, 141–180.

Whaley, G. L., & Ford, D. L. (2012). Examining collegiality and social justice in academia and the private sector: An exploratory SYMLOG analysis. *NMIMS Management Review*, 9–36.

Wheeldon, J. (2010). Mapping mixed methods research: Methods, measures, and meaning. *Journal of Mixed Methods Research*, 4(2), 87–102.

Wheeless, L. R., Wheeless, V. E., Dickson-Markman, F. (1982). A research note: The relations among social and task perceptions in small groups. *Small Group Behavior*, 13(3), 373–384.

Whitaker, E., & Atkinson, P. (2019). Authenticity and the interview. *Qualitative Research*, 19(6), 619–634.

Windelband, W. (1894). *Geschichte und Naturwissenschaften*. Rectorial address, University of Strasbourg.

Wish, M., D'Andrade, R. G., Goodno, J. E., II. (1980). Dimensions of interpersonal communication: Correspondences between structures for speech acts bipolar scales. *Journal of Personality and Social Psychology*, 39, 848–860.

Woudenberg, F. (1991). An evaluation of Delphi. *Technological Forecasting and Social Change*, 40(2), 131–150.

Yanchar, S. C., & Williams, D. D. (2006). Reconsidering the compatibility thesis and eclecticism: Five proposed guidelines for method use. *Educational Researcher*, 35(9), 3–12.

Yardley, A. (2014). Children describing the world: Mixed-method research by child practitioners developing an intergenerational dialogue. *Educational & Child Psychology*, 31(1), 48–62.

Yardley, A. (2019). Bricolage as method. In P. Atkinson, S. Delamont, A. Cernat, J. W. Sakshaug & R. A. Williams (Eds), *SAGE research methods foundations* (pp. xx–xx). London: Sage.

Yin, R. K. (1984). *Case study research*. Thousand Oaks, CA: Sage.

Yoshihama, M. (2009). Application of the life history calendar approach: Understanding women's experiences of intimate partner violence over the life course. In R. F. Belli, R. P. Stafford, & D. F. Alwin, (Eds), *Calendar and time diary methods in life course research* (pp. 131–156). Thousand Oaks, CA: Sage.

Yoshihama, M., Gillespie, B., Hammock, A., Belli, R. F., & Tolman, R. (2005). Does the life-history calendar method facilitate the recall of domestic violence victimization? Comparison of two methods of data collection. *Social Work Research*, *29*, 151–163.

Zelditch, M. (1962). Some methodological problems of field studies. *American Journal of Sociology*, *67*(5), 566–576.

Ziglio, E. (1995). The Delphi method and its contribution to decision-making. In M. Adler & E. Ziglio (Eds), *Gazing into the oracle: The Delphi method and its application to social policy and public health* (pp. 3–33). Bristol, PA: Jessica Kingsley.

INDEX